BENEATH THE WATERS

Guide to Civil War Shipwrecks

by
James E. Hemphill

This Burd Street Press publication
was printed by
Beidel Printing House, Inc.
63 West Burd Street
Shippensburg, PA 17257-0152 USA

In respect for the scholarship contained herein, the acid-free paper used in this book meets the guidelines for permanence and durability of the Committee on Production Guidelines for Book Longevity of the Council on Library Resources.

For a complete list of available publications
please write
Burd Street Press
Division of White Mane Publishing Company, Inc.
P.O. Box 152
Shippensburg, PA 17257-0152 USA

Library of Congress Cataloging-in-Publication Data

Hemphill, James E. 1926-
    Beneath the waters : guide to Civil War shipwrecks / by James E. Hemphill.
        p.   cm.
    Includes index.
    ISBN 1-57249-054-3 (alk. paper)
    1. United States--History--Civil War, 1861-1865--Naval operations.
2. United States--History--Civil War, 1861-1865--Antiquities.
3. Shipwrecks--United States--Registers. I. Title.
E591.H495 1998
973.7'5--dc21   98-7561
                                                                      CIP

PRINTED IN THE UNITED STATES OF AMERICA

CONTENTS

PREFACE

The artifacts should be raised, preserved, and put on exhibition to remind us of the gallant and bloody struggle these men made to establish ideals. America and her future generations will not have these valuable reminders of the struggle unless those artifacts are recovered and preserved as part of our rich American heritage.

This was my intent.

ACKNOWLEDGMENTS

Martha Cotera. As I searched the Archives of Texas, this young lady directed my research to the series *Official Records of the Union and Confederate Navies in the War of the Rebellion.*

Mrs. Virginia Cavazos, my guardian angel. Her big heart and gentle manner of prodding all contributed to getting this information into print. Without her guidance, there would be no achievement due to all.

Sandra Arrizola tackled the Herculean task of putting the card file into manuscript and literary form by typing nights, weekends, and spare time, while raising her family.

Mr. Arturo Cavazos and daughter Marcy. Besides keeping his business going, they furnished transportation for errands and encouragement to all with faith and a good smile. He shared his family time with me.

Richard Beauvais, a man of many jokes and stories, challenged my intellect with literary knowledge.

INTRODUCTION

One day after high school, I stood in front of the Capitol of Texas, where Civil War cannon with brass barrels were displayed and I asked myself, "Why was a guy like me shooting a gun like that at a guy like me?" Someday he may recognize the importance of liberty.

In this book, I have tried to bring honor and recognition to these men who fought in the navies in the war of the rebellion.

This is a significant book in Naval History. This research is the only single source of information on sunken Civil War ships available in government or private sector. The information stemmed from the thirty volumes of over twenty-eight thousand pages of "Battle Reports" in the *Official Records of the Union and Confederate Navies in the War of the Rebellion.* This category was not covered in the original printing, and the only way to obtain a listing of sunken ships and their locations was searching the "Battle Reports." Imagine, if you will, how I felt. There, within my grasp, the only narrative of the great struggle, but the topic I most wished to study was lost, buried in an encyclopedic work of over twenty-eight thousand pages—the sunken treasure of artifacts that would serve to commemorate their deeds and memorialize their gallant efforts. There was only one solution: I would make my own index, by reading the whole series and making a card index file of every destroyed or sunken ship.

This is an alphabetical listing, by name of lost, sunk in battle, or shipwrecked vessels of both navies. The battle reports of the officer involved in the action are the most authoritative source used for relative location. Other information as to size of vessels or number of cannon and shot pounds and information that might relate to location, technical information, dimensions plus cargo, and iron sheathing is given, when available.

Your research and efforts are a rewarding pastime or occupation, depending on how involved you become. You will also know more of the foundation of liberty that supports your world of today.

There are many good books on archeological preservation. The methods improve as experiences advance this underwater science, and so do the books. Ask your librarian, State Underwater Archeologist, or Officer of Corps of Army Engineers about the archives for your area of interest. Local newspapers may have a microfilm department on subjects of interest. For more exact locations contact the State Highway Department, Map Division. They may have mapped roadways along water ways, rivers, streams, and railroad bridges that give clues to a location. Your State Historical County Society may have records on changes in local landmarks.

The ships are sometimes close to adjacent towns, old forts, islands, and other landmarks.

You can go to many extremes in research and the more questions you answer the more you will ask. I could not travel to all the battle sights to trace the material or exact location of each area, but this guide will point you in the right direction.

EXPLANATION OF GUIDE ENTRIES

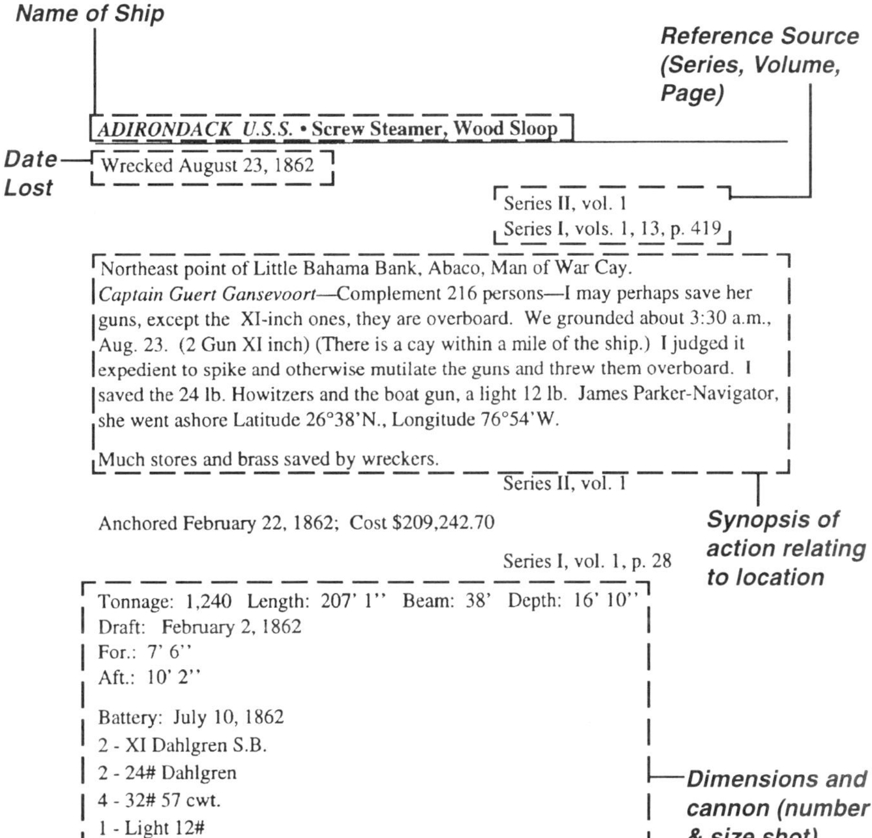

A

A.B. (Bee) • Side Wheel Steamer

August 17, 1862

Series I, vol. 9
Series I, vol. 19, p. 152

Corpus Christi, Texas,
Nueces River

Rebels burned steamer A.B. aground in narrow channel that leads to Nueces Bay. Not navigated for vessels drawing over 2'—near a point of land that runs down from Corpus. Burned to waters edge.

Series I, vol. 19, p. 302

Aground at the entrance of Nueces River.

A.C. WILLIAMS • Reb. Schooner

January 19, 1861

Series I, vol. 6, p. 787

Roanoke Island, Virginia

Sank at the barricade.

Also: *Josephine*   January 20
          Carter Schooner   January 21
          Spuiell Schooner   January 26
          Moss Schooner   January 26
          Zenith Schooner   January 27
          Rio Schooner   January 31 (?)
          Plus two unknowns

One unknown at Weir's Pt. Batt.

Anchored *Lydia* & *Martha* at 2nd barricade.

A. HOLLY U.S.S.

Series II, vol. 1, p. 29

Purchased to sink August 13, 1861

A.W. BAKER • Side Wheel Steamer

Series I, vol. 24

Red River, Louisiana

See Natchez, Mississippi

Captured.

Series I, vol. 24, p. 223

15 miles below mouth of Red River.
Just discharged cargo at Port Hudson.

Fired about 15 miles above the (near) mouth of Red River and below Warrenton by *Queen of the West*.

Series I, vol. 24, p. 224

I ascended Red River 15 miles in the hope of getting some more boats, but found nothing. Night came on as we again started on our return. I found at once that the progress of the three prizes was so slow that our short supply of coal would not permit us to wait for them. I accordingly ordered them to be set on fire; we had not time to transfer cargoes.

ABEONA U.S.S.

June 17, 1867

Series II, vol. 1, p. 27

Wrecked and recovered.

Tonnage: 206

ACADIA • Side Wheel Steamer

February 1865

Series I, vol. 22, p. 32

Velasco

Riddled by shot from *Virginia* six miles this side (S.) of Velasco, where she ran on shore after several attempts to get into Velasco.

ADA • Schooner

November 6, 1861

Series I, vol. 6, p. 407

Tonnage: 120

Rappahannock River, Corrotoman Creek

Hard and fast ashore—5 miles up creek—burned together with large quantity of firewood on shore.

Cargo: wood

ADELAIDE

October 22, 1862

Series I, vol. 8, p. 151

New Topsail Inlet, North Carolina

Fired, between less than a mile and mouth of and New Topsail Inlet.

Cargo: 600 barrels of spirits of turpentine, 36 bales of cotton and some tobacco for deck load.

ADIRONDACK U.S.S. • Screw Steamer, Wood Sloop

Wrecked August 23, 1862

Series II, vol. 1
Series I, vols. 1, 13, p. 419

Northeast point of Little Bahama Bank, Abaco, Man of War Cay.
Captain Guert Gansevoort—Complement 216 persons—I may perhaps save her guns, except the XI-inch ones, they are overboard. We grounded about 3:30 a.m., Aug. 23. (2 Gun XI inch) (There is a cay within a mile of the ship.) I judged it expedient to spike and otherwise mutilate the guns and threw them overboard. I saved the 24 lb. Howitzers and the boat gun, a light 12 lb. James Parker-Navigator, she went ashore Latitude 26°38'N., Longitude 76°54'W.

Much stores and brass saved by wreckers.

Series II, vol. 1

Anchored February 22, 1862; Cost $209,242.70

Series I, vol. 1, p. 28

Tonnage: 1,240 Length: 207' 1'' Beam: 38' Depth: 16' 10''
Draft: February 2, 1862
For.: 7' 6''
Aft.: 10' 2''

Battery: July 10, 1862
2 - XI Dahlgren S.B.
2 - 24# Dahlgren
4 - 32# 57 cwt.
1 - Light 12#

Series I, vol. 13, p. 313

September 5, 1862

The wreckers destroyed the vessel by fire—May be in employ of Rebels in Bahamas.

Captain Gansevoort destroyed all his large guns except XI inch thrown overboard and buoyed.

ADVOCATE U.S.S

Series II, vol. 1, p. 29

Purchased May 19, 1863, from Prize Court.

Sunk as obstruction in Petit Bois Channel, Alabama.

No details.

Paid for but never used for naval purposes.

AGNES C. FRY • Confederate Steamer

February 1, 1865

Cape Fear River, North Carolina

Series I, vol. 11, pp. 725, 788

Two miles to southward of Ft. Caswell (Campbell)

Built of 5/8'' iron, about 1,000 ton— is about 20 yards from low water mark in a bed formed in the quicksand.   (Worth $150,000)

AGNES LOUISA • Blockade Runner (former *GRAPE SHOT*)

September 4, 1864

Series I, vol. 10, p. 477

Put back after being out, got on reef on Hog Isl. (near Nassau New Providence Isl.), will probably be a total loss.

AID • Confederate Schooner

Series I, vol. 4

Santa Rosa Island

Series I, vol. 16, p. 644

Sunk at the east end of the isl. to obstruct pass.

Series I, vol. 16, pp. 554, 557

Men mentioned.

AID • Schooner

August 23, 1861

Series I, vol. 16, p. 644

Santa. Rosa Isl., Florida

Sunk at east end to obstruct pass.

Captured by Capt. Will H. McKean.

ALABAMA

*Military & Naval History of the
Rebellion*, p. 439

In early August 1863, accompanied by the *Tuscaloosa* (a captured merchantman transformed into an armed tender). Arrived at Capetown and captured the *Sea Bride*.

Captures 56 vessels.

ALABAMA

Fort Morgan

Series I, vol. 17, pp. 14–16

December 27, 1861

Chasing ashore of a schooner off.

Got off and brought in.

ALABAMA **(290)**

Harper's Weekly
November 1, 1862
Cover, p. 699

View.

Tonnage: 1,200   Draw: 14'   Screw, copper bottom

3 - 32# to a side and ports for two more admidships
A 100# rifled pivot gun forward of bridge and a 68# pivot on main deck and tracks laid forward and aft for bowgun and chaser.

ALABAMA **(''290'')**

Oreto - Owner John Henry Thoms
Built in Liverpool, England
Ports for 20 guns

*Military & Naval History of the
Rebellion*, p. 276

Ships captured and destroyed by:

September 6, 1862	Ship *Oemulere*	Edgartown	Burned
September 7, 1862	Schooner *Starlight*	Boston	Burned
September 9, 1862	Bark *Alert*		Burned
	Schooner *Weather Gauge*	Provincetown	Burned
	Bark *Ocean Rover*	Mattapoisett	Burned

September 13, 1862	Ship *Benjamin Tucker*	New Bedford	Burned
	Bark *Oscela*		Burned
	Bark *Virginia Tilton*	New Bedford	Burned
	Ship *Elisha Dunbar, Gifford*	New Bedford	Burned
	Brig *Allamaha*	Sippican	Burned
	Schooner *Courser*	Provincetown	Burned
October 3, 1862	Ship *Brilliant*	Hagan, New York	Burned
	Emily Farnham, Simms	Hagan, New York	Released
October 10, 1862	Ship *Tonawanda*	Philadelphia	Bonded
October 15, 1862	Ship *Lamp Lighter*	New York	Burned
	Ship *Manchester*	New York	Burned
	Brig *Dunkirk*	New York	Burned
October 23, 1862	Ship *Layfette*, small	New York	Burned
	Schooner *Ocean Cruiser*	New York	Burned
October 26, 1862	Schooner *Crenshaw*	New York	Burned
October 28, 1862	Bark *Laurietta Wells*	Boston	Burned
October 29, 1862	Brig *Baron de Castine*		
	Saunders		Bonded
November 2, 1862	Schooner *Alice*		
November 8, 1862	Ship *I.B. Wales*	Boston	Burned
November 18, 1862	Steamer *Ariel*	New York	Bonded
	Ship *Levi Starbuck*		
November 30, 1862	Bark *Parker Cook*		
	Fulton	Boston	Burned
December 5, 1862	Schooner *Union*	Baltimore	Bonded

Tilton said *Virginia* overhauled morning 17th Sept. in latitude 39°10' and longitude 34°20'.

Capt. Gifford of the *Elisha Dunbar*, 18 Sept., latitude 39°5', longitude 35°20'.

Captured the *Parke Cook* off Moro Passage Union off Cape Mais.

ALABAMA C.S.S. (Capt. Semmes)

June 19, 1864

Series II, vol. 1
Series I, vols. 2, 3, 27, 34
Series II, vols. 2, 3

Cherbourg, France
Commissioned August 24, 1862

Also known as *290* and *Enrica*—vessels captured by engagement with *Hatteras* U.S.S., January 11, 1863, *Kearsarge* U.S.S.; June 19, 1864.

Series I, vol. 1, p. 780

Vessels captured

Series I, vol. 2, p. 18

28 miles southeast of Galveston, Texas.

4 - 32#
2 - 30# Rifled Parrot
20# Rifled Gun
8 guns total

Series I, vol. 3, p. 80

Diagram of battle and sinking with U.S.S. *Kearsarge*, Capt. Winslow, Jno. A.

8 guns
68# of 9,000# (Blakely) ?
1 - 110 pd. rifle
6 - 32#

Series II, vol. 1, p. 247

Steam sloop, screw, wood copper fastened and coppered.

Tonnage: 1,050   Length: 211' 6''   Beam: 31' 8''   Depth: 17' 8''

Battery:
1 - 110#
1 - 68# Blakely
6 - 32# Blakely

ALABAMA (State)

Mobile, Alabama

Series I, vol. 20

Chasing ashore steamer near Fort Morgan

Series I, vol. 19
Series II, vol. 3, pp. 628, 698

Treasure from H.B.M.S. *Vesuvius*

Series I, vol. 22

Vessels sunk by torpedoes in and near

ALABAMA (State)

Mussel Shoals, Alabama

Series I, vol. 22

Burning of Confederate vessels

ALABAMA (State), C.S. Barges (6) and Steamers

February 7, 1862

Tennessee River (Fort of Mussel Shoals), Alabama

Series I, vol. 22, p. 570

Six burned with supplies (military).

Winter quarters of Rebel Regiment burned (Colonel James M. Crews) at Savannah, Tennessee.

Above R.R. crossing, 25 miles above Ft. Henry.

1. *Samuel Ore* cargo submarine batt. exploded.
2. Boats fired with cargo of powder, grape, cannon shot, balls, etc.

The whole river for 1/2 mile around was completely beaten up from falling by falling fragments. The *House of Union Man* was blown to pieces with design by landing boats there. Also *East Port* scuttled and suction pipes broken—repaired.

In sight of town of Florence, Alabama, three barges fired muscle loaded with lumber, sprang leak and sank above or near R.R. Bridge.

ALABAMA (State) • Ferryboats

Clifton, Alabama

Series I, vol. 22, p. 785

2 - ferryboats opposite Clifton
1 - ferryboat opposite Patriot
1 - ferryboat opposite Cull's Landing
1 - small ferryboat opposite mouth of Horse Creek
2 - small ferryboats opposite Carrollville
1 - small ferryboat opposite of Eagle Nest Island

ALABAMA • Unknown Schooner

Off Mobile Bar

January 23

Series I, vol. 17, p. 82

Aground a mile or more south of Ft. Morgan.

Heavy northern and missed eastern Swash Channel.

Inside the Swash Channel.

Loaded with cotton and naval stores.

Shots fired by U.S.S. *Huntsville*, Commander Cicero Price.

ALBEMARLE

April 5, 1862

Series I, vol. 7, p. 203

Washington, North Carolina

Ran her on the piles where she sank immediately.

Prize steamer taken at New Berne.

Pronounced a total loss and fired.

ALBEMARLE C.S. • **Ram**

October 27, 1864

Series I, vol. 10

Roanoke River
Plymouth, North Carolina

Series I, vols. 11, 12

Raising of craft.

Our Naval Heritage, p. 203

Sunk at her anchorage, Roanoke River, Albemarle Sound.

*Military & Naval History of the
Rebellion*, p. 639

The *Albemarle* was completely submerged by the explosion of the torpedo, and so remained long subsequent to the evacuation of Plymouth (N.C.), by the Rebels—by *Lt. Cushing*, (U.S. Navy)

Wreck sold at Norfolk, Virginia, October 15, 1867.

Then became the U.S.S. *Albemarle*.

ALBEMARLE C.S. • **RAM**

October 27–28, 1864

Series I, vol. 10, p. 610

Plymouth, North Carolina, Roanoke River

Picket Launch #1 (Steam torpedo launch).

Picket Launch #1 destroyed by enemy. Shot and sunk while destroying the Ram. Lt. Cushing and one other man escaped. (13 officers and men went—partly volunteers from squadron).

Distance from mouth of river to RAM about eight miles. One mile below town was the wreck of the *Southfield*.

Series I, vol. 10, p. 611

Cushing's report—*Southfield* boarded but no guns found.

Series I, vol. 10, p. 621

With Cushing aboard *Chearship*.

ALBEMARLE SOUND

May 7, 1864

Series I, vol. 10, p. 25

Offer to raise wrecks in Albemarle Sound and vicinity for 50-50 split on appraised value by Mr. George W. Lane.

Ok by Gideon Wells, Secretary of Navy.

ALBION • Norwegian Bark

May 11, 1861

Series I, vol. 4, p. 387

Cape Henry, Virginia

Steam tug and wrecking schooner sent to save Norwegian Bark *Albion* wrecked 25 miles below Cape Henry and bring cargo to Baltimore.

ALERT U.S.S.

May 31, 1863

Series I, vol. 9

Burned and sunk U.S. Tug Alert while at the wharf at the Gosport Navy Yard on Sunday, 31 May—asked to be raised and repaired if possible.

ALEXANDER COOPER • Blockade Runner Schooner

August 22, 1863 by *Shokokon* U.S.S.

Series I, vol. 9, p. 177

New Topsail Inlet

At a wharf some six miles up the Sound, fired vessel and extensive salt works.

ALEXANDRIA U.S.S.

Series II, vol. 1, p. 31

Original name: *St. Mary*

Temporarily called *Yazoo*

Sold

ALICE PRICE • U.S. Army Steamer

Series I, vols. 6, 7

ALICE PROVOST • Coal Bark

December 12, 1863

Series I, vol. 15, p. 177

Port Royal

Tonnage: 700

Went ashore coming into harbor and is a total wreck.

ALICE PROVOST • Coal Bark

December 12, 1863

Series I, vol. 15, p. 177

Port Royal Harbor, Carolina

700 tons coal went ashore while coming into the Harbor and is a total wreck.

ALICE WIEBB • Schooner

November 13, 1863

Series I, vol. 9, p. 780

New York

Discharged, scuttled and abandoned in three feet of water in the breakers—10:35.

Latitude and meridian 34° 37' N., U.S.S. *Mount Vernon.*

ALLEGHANIAN • Ship

October 28–29, 1862

Series I, vols. 5, 8

Yorktown, Virginia

Series I, vol. 5, pp. 137–41

Anchored five miles outside York River mouth.

Cargo: Guano

ALLEN COLLIER • Steamer

November 7, 1863

Series I, vol. 25

Mississippi River, Whitworth's Landing

Opposite and one mile above Lanconia.

Later U.S.S. *A. Collier.*

Sold.

$20,000 Rebel stores on board. They did not know.

$10,000 mostly cotton.

ALLIANCE • Schooner

September 23, 1863

Series I, vol. 9, p. 203

Milford Haven, Virginia (?)

Captured and aground on the bar at Milford Haven when discovered and fired upon.
Confederates fired her. Suttlers stores.

Some cargo saved (2%).

ALTHEA U.S.S.

March 12, 1865

Series II, vol. 1, p. 33

Blakely River, Alabama

Torpedo—Blakely River, Alabama

Raised and sold.

ALVARADO

August 5, 1861

Series I, vol. 6, p. 56

Fernandina, Florida

Chased ashore near mouth of St. Mary's River.

Cargo—sheep skins, goat skins, buckskin hides, and 70 tons iron; also, wool.

Southeast side of shoal making out from Lighthouse Point—distance 5/8 mile.

Destroyed by fire—nothing in sight but sternpost by morning.

Series I, vol. 6, p. 59

C. S. Rept. 1 1/2 miles from shore—skins, old copper and iron.

ALVARADO • Bark

August 5, 1861

Series I, vol. 6

ALVARADO U.S.S. • Schooner Sail

Series II, vol. 1, p. 33

Hatteras Inlet, North Carolina

Purchased to sink in Hatteras Inlet. One of the Stone Fleet.

AMANDA U.S. • Bark

May 29, 1863

Series I, vol. 17

Wrecked, West Coast, Florida
St. George's Sound, Florida

Examination of wreck by *Somerset* U.S.S.

Series II, vol. 1, p. 33

4th Bark
Tonnage: 368 Length: 177' 6'' Beam: 27' 9'' Depth: 12' 6''

Battery:
6 - 32# (42 cwt)
1 - 12# Howitzer
1 - 20# Parrott

Series I, vol. 17, pp. 453, 464,
467

May 29, 1863

Acting Lieut. George E. Welch

Carried 6 - 32# and 1 - 20# Parrott rifle and 12# Howitzer near east pass in St. George's Sound, Florida. Shoal flats of the mainland 200 or 300 yards from beach—country adjacent low and mars by intersected by crooked rivers and bayous—Topsail Bluff distant 1 mile—(wreck examined 150 yards from shore, 18'' water—Topsail Bluff on port quarter)—last half of gale from S.W.—ungrounded from Dog Isl—should be S.W. of there—Crosman landed on Dog Isl. opposite steepest port of bank. Six wrecked barks near.

Recovered: 6 - 32#, quantity of kentledges, 253 solid shot 30 shells, some spars and iron work, 100 fathom chain cable, 1 kedge, a barrel & loose grape and canister and some water casks by *Commander A.F. Crosman* of the *Steamer Somerset.*

AMAZON U.S.S. • Bark

Sunk December 20, 1861

> Series II, vol. 1, p. 34

Charleston, South Carolina

Sunk at entrance to Charleston Harbor.

Tonnage: 318

AMELIA • Confederate Schooner

Captured May 9, 1863, leaving Charleston, South Carolina
Sank June 15, 1863

> Series I, vol. 14, p. 182

Off Cape Hatteras, North Carolina

Prize schooner with cargo of cotton—seams opened and pumps gave out—abandoned and fired.

AMERICA • Blockade Schooner

August 29, 1863

> Series I, vol. 20, p. 488

Texas

Turtled while in tow of U.S. Bark *W.G. Anderson.*

Cargo: Cotton

About 50 miles north of Rio Grande.

From Caney Creek, Texas, to Rio Grande.

AMERICA U.S.S. • 4th Schooner

> Series II, vol. 1, p. 34

Dunn's Lake, Florida

147 miles from mouth of St. John's River, Florida.

> Series I, vol. 13, p. 495

Where we raised the Yacht America, January 1, 1863.

Series I, vol. 13, p. 496

Blockading of Charleston, January 3, 1863.

Raised and sold, June 20, 1873.

Tonnage: 100 Length: 111' Beam: 25' Depth: 11' Draft For.: 7' 6'' Aft.: 12'

AMERICA U.S.S. • Ship Rig

Series II, vol. 1, p. 34

Sunk Stone Fleet.

Tonnage: 418

Purchased November 8, 1861

AMERICA • Yacht

Military & Naval History of the Rebellion, p. 805

St. Augustine, Florida

Which had been sunk was raised.

March 1862 by Samuel Francis DuPont, Rear Admiral.

Raised.

AMERICAN U.S.S.

December 20, 1861

Series II, vol. 1, p. 34

Charleston, South Carolina
Sunk at entrance to Charleston Harbor.

Tonnage: 329

ANGLO-AMERICAN and One Unknown Steamer

June 18, 1863

Series I, vol. 20, p. 235

Plaquemine, Louisiana

Burned along with the *Sykes*. Trying to get the *Sykes* off being stuck on the head of a pile in trying to get out of Bayou Plaquemine. Also, a little boat that ran down the bayou for cotton.

Unknown—see *Belfast*

ANGLO-NORMAN • Rebel Ram

Harper's Weekly
May 24, 1862, p. 327

New Orleans, Louisiana

At the levee, just by the Customs House, lay a burning ram.

Another ram was sunk on the Algiers side.

ANN MARIA • Schooner (English)

November 18, 1862

Series I, vol. 8, p. 218

West of Shallotte Inlet

Ran ashore—hauled off, bilged and sank in four (4) fathoms.

Cargo: salt, flour, lard and sugar

Tonnage: 80

ANNA DALE • Schooner, Armed Rebel

February 18, 1865

Series I, vol. 22, p. 42

Pass Cavello, Texas

Tonnage: 70

Grounded in close proximity to the batt. at entrance to Bayou.

Tied up 1/2 mile up the Bayou—cut loose.

Series I, vol. 22, p. 45

12# Dahlgren Howitzer brought off and 10 rifles and shotguns captured by boarding party from *Panola*.

Govt. Records Ex. Doc. 253–295
40th Cong., 2nd Sess.

February 18, 1865
Pass Cavallo by *Panola*.
Destroyed.

ANNA ELIZA • Sloop

May 14, 1864

Series I, vol. 17, p. 704

Rescue of crew, May 14, 1864, by U.S. Mortar Brig *Sea Foam*—The crew (7) rescued.

34° 35' N. Long. 74° 55 Min. W.—Waterlogged and dismasted out of Nassau, New Providence from Santee River, S.E. to Nassau. $10,000 gallons of spirits of turpentine—nothing saved from wreck.

ANNA TAYLOR

Series I, vol. 17, pp. 42, 86

Louisiana

On the coast of Louisiana prior to January 1, 1862.

6 ton burden tender to Santee left ship 18th Nov.

ANNA U.S.S. • 4th Schooner

Wrecked January 1865

Series II, vol. 1, p. 35

On coast of Florida.

Cost: $1,575—sails wood 4th Schooner

Tonnage: 27 Length: 46'2'' Beam: 14'9'' Depth: 4'6'' D. Laden: 5'

Battery.: February 11, 1864
1 - 12# Rifle pivot

Name changed from *La Criolla* to *Anna*, April 3, 1863.

Tender to ordnance *Ship Dale* at Key West, Florida.

ANNE S. DAVENPORT • Schooner

Series I, vol. 10, p. 115

Order to be towed June 2, 1864

Roanoke River, North Carolina
Albemarle Sound

For sinking in the cut-off between Middle and Roanoke River—so we have perfect command of Middle River.

ANNIE • Steamer

Series I, vol. 3, p. 711

Ft. Fisher, North Carolina

The Steamer *Annie* got aground outside Ft. Fisher last night while running in.

Cruise of C.S.S. *Chickamauga*.

ANNIE U.S. • Schooner

Series I, vol. 17, pp. 800–801, 807-8

Captured under name *Anna*.

Sank in six fathoms—Cape Roman bearing N.E. by N. distant about 10 miles.

Her gun could not be discovered—anchors and chain procured.

She was so thoroughly wrecked she must have been blown up.

Investigated by Act. Vol. Lieut. C.H. Rockwell aboard U.S.S. *Hendrick Hudson*, February 7, 1865.

ANTELOPE U.S.S. • Tinclad Side Wheel Steamer

Sunk September 23, 1864

Series II, vol. 1
Series I, vol. 21

Mississippi River

Sunk in Mississippi River September 23, 1864, in New Orleans.

Tonnage: 173

Battery: May 30, 1864.
2 - 30# Parrott rifles on Bow
4 - 24# broadside

Series I, vol. 21, pp. 658, 660

Leaky condition—hit snag—sank some seven miles below New Orleans

Proceeding to New Orleans Helm hard sport (beached).

All small arms and equipment saved—battery saved.

ANTOINETTE • British Schooner

December 8, 1863

Series I, vol. 15, pp. 173, 174

St. Andrew's Sound, Georgia, on Cumberland Beach
About halfway down Cumberland Isl.

Total loss—anchors, chain and sails saved by U.S. Bark *Braziliera*.

ANTOINETTE • British Schooner

December 8, 1863

Series I, vol. 15, pp. 173–74

Cumberland Isl., Georgia
About halfway down Cumberland Island, becoming a total loss - anchors, chains, sails, saved by U.S. Bark *Braziliers.*

ANTONICA • Blockade Runner, Confederate Steamer

December 20, 1863

Series I, vol. 9
Series II, vol. 3

Frying Pan Shoals

Formerly *Herald.*

11 1/2 knot screw

Tonnage: 563

Ashore on Frying Pan Shoals. Unsuccessful efforts made to get her afloat. Will prove a total loss and little of her cargo saved.

Large quantities of liquor. No arms or ammunition. Dry good provisions and clothing.

Side wheel steamer (563 ton) from Nassau.

Three miles south of south point of Smith's Isl.

APHRODITE • Chartered Transport Steamer

October 7, 1864

Series I, vol. 10, p. 523

Cape Lookout, North Carolina

12 or 15 miles N. or Lookout Light. Bilged—with 400 Navy recruits. Has 9' water in her and cannot be got off.

12 miles N. N. E. of Cape Lookout—2 recruits drowned swimming in surf after landing.

U.S. *Keystone State* and *Shokokon* commenced getting out government stores.

Series I, vol. 10, p. 531

Some stores saved—broken in two and a total wreck. Will require organized wrecking party to save anchors and cable.

APPELTON BELLE • Steamer

February 7, 1862

Series I, vol. 22

APPELTON BELLE C.S.

February 8, 1862

Series I, vol. 22, p. 821

Near Paris-Tenn. River
Mouth of Duck River

Burned to prevent capture.

ARABIAN

Series I, vol. 10, p. 125

New Inlet (on bar), North Carolina (?)

Sketch of position.

ARABIAN • Blockade Runner

September 18, 1863

Series I, vol. 9, p. 211

New Inlet, Wilmington, North Carolina

Pick up nine bales of cotton, 15 miles E.N.E. from Ft. Fisher supposed to have come from wreck of *Arabian* driven on shore by Blockade Fleet and destroyed in a gale of wind.

Between Ft. Fisher and wreck of *Hebe*.
Was going out last night and was chased by blockaders. Mistook entrance over bar and ran ashore.

Series I, vol. 9, p. 214

Near New Topsail Inlet.

ARCADIA • Steamer

Series I, vol. 25, p. 133

Yazoo River, Mississippi

Between Mississippi and Ft. Pemberton.

Series I, vol. 25, p. 756

About one mile below the Edd. Gay. Sunk at the mouth of the Yalobusha.

Upper works out of water and nearly filling river at this stage of water.

ARCHER U.S.S.

December 20, 1861

Series II, vol. 1, p. 36

Charleston, South Carolina

Sunk at entrance to Charleston Harbor as part of Stone Fleet.

Tonnage: 322

ARGO • Steamer

May 24, 1863

Series I, vol. 25, p. 134

Sunflower River, Mississippi

In a small bayou about 75 miles up the Sunflower.

ARGOSY • Steamer

Series I, vol. 25

Sold.

ARGUS • Steamer

October 27, 1863

Series I, vol. 25

Red River, Louisiana

ARGUS C.S. • Steamer

October 7, 1863

Series I, vol. 25, p. 450

Red River, Louisiana

Finding he could not get them over the bar and out of Red River, burned them (&
Robt. Fulton).

No cargo.

Series I, vol. 25, p. 456

Map

Inline from Mississippi—started for Red River this morning from U.S.S. *Osage* off
Mr. Jontee's (Gentil's)—came out bend below within half mile saw chimneys of
steamer —steamer on opposite side of river—approach on spit opposite her. I knew
I could not get them out of the river and ordered the first one destroyed and
embarked on second and steamed down to the landing where I first struck river—
where I ordered her set on fire.

ARIEL • British Schooner

Series I, vol. 8

Purchased by Navy Department from Prize Court and became U.S.S. *Ariel*—sold after war.

ARIEL • Schooner (English)

November 18, 1862

Series I, vol. 8, p. 218

West of Shallotte Inlet

Ran ashore, 80 ton—ovt. of Halifax.

Cargo: salt, lard, sugar and flour.

Further west ran ashore Ann Maria (much same cargo).

Hauled off but bilged and sank in four fathoms.

ARIZONA U.S.S.

February 27, 1865

Series II, vol. 1, p. 38

38 miles below New Orleans, Louisiana

Battery: June 15, 1864
1 - 30# Parrott Rifle
1 - 12# Rifle
3 - 32# 42 cwt.
1 - 32# 33 cwt.

Former *Caroline*

ARIZONA U.S.S.

Destroyed by fire February 27, 1865

Series II, vol. 1
Series I, vol. 22

Mississippi River, Louisiana
38 miles below New Orleans

Former *Caroline* built in 1858.

Sidewheel Steamer Iron, 3rd.

Tonnage: 959 Length: 200' Beam: 34'   Depth: 17' 6''

Battery:
1 - 30# Parrott Rifle
1 - 12# Rifle

3 - 32# 42 cwt.
1 - 32# 33 cwt.

Series I, vol. 22, p. 58

Drifted to west bank and lodged and burned. Nothing recovered.

ARKANSAS • Confederate Ram

Military & Naval History of the Rebellion, p. 200

Baton Rouge, Louisiana

5th August 1862

The *Arkansas* dropped down the river to help vigorous land attack which was repulsed after a severe contest. Was not brought into action as one of her engines had broken down. The next morn porter was then at Baton Rouge with the *Essex*, moved up to attack her, but before the fight had fully begun her other engine gave way and she was run ashore, abandoned and set on fire by crew. One hour later she blew up.

Series I, vol. 19, p. 135

Headed toward river bank when starboard engine gave away and drifted toward enemy—finally she grounded near river bank, stern downstream. In present condition ship immovable.

Engine broken up with axes, bedding fired, magazine opened, cartridges scattered about and loaded shell placed on the gun deck between guns.

Her batt. being loaded and guns run out, she gradually drifted down toward Fed. Fleet.

Harper's Weekly
August 23, 1862, p. 531

Lt. Stephens commanding.

She left Vicksburg on Monday to cooperate in the attack on Baton Rouge. After passing Bayou Sara, her machinery became disabled, and while attempting to adjust it, several of the enemy's gun boats attacked her. After a gallant resistance, she was abandoned and blown up. Her officers and men reached the shore in safety.
—dispatch from General Van Dorn to Sec. Mallory
Richmond, August 8, 1862

Series I, vol. 19, p. 131

On rounding the point the starboard engine broke down and the ship drifted ashore in sight of Baton Rouge, on Arkansas side—it was determined to make another trial trip—proceeded some 500 yards up the river when engines again broke—engaged all night in repairs.

At 9, the *Essex* came around the point and opened fire.

Lines were cut and started for *Essex* with intention of running her down—proceeded 300 yards in her direction—larboard engine stopped made for bank stern down—*Essex* continued to advance and when within 400 yards, crew ordered ashore and vessel fired.

Series I, vol. 19, p. 135

Officers and crew sent ashore with small arms and ammo.

Series II, vol. 1
Series I, vols. 19, 23

Twin screw, iron clad, wood, covered with railroad iron.

Length: 165'   Beam: 35'   Draft: 11' 6''

Battery:
2 - 8'' 64#
2 - rifled 32#
2 - 100# Columbiads
6'' naval gun on each broadside

Series I, vol. 19, p. 124

Several wounded were conveyed four miles inland by planter named Bird who also supplied her with coal the day previous.

She had 6 - 8'' guns and 4 - 50#s and 18,000# powder

Received extra layer of rail iron.

Series I, vol. 19, pp. 125, 130

Did not approach more than 1/4 mile on the morning of 5th. *Arkansas* made appearance in the bend about eight miles above Baton Rouge—she remained there, steam up moving about a little.

The crew and officers got ashore on the right bank of the river opposite Baton Rouge where they blew their vessel to pieces.

Harper's Weekly
August 30, 1862, p. 547

6th August 1862

About four miles above Anchorage of *Essex* (W.D. Porter) on river—engaged at 10:00 a.m. for 20 minutes. Set on fire and blew up at noon.

Crew; 180 men, mounting ten guns, 6 - 8'' and 4 - 50# rifled cannon, plated with railroad iron.

Harper's Weekly
August 30, 1862, p. 556

View of Baton Rouge

Harper's Weekly
September 6, 1862, p. 565

View of battle

Harper's Weekly
September 6, 1862, p. 571

Detail of battle
Union boats; *Essex, Sumter, Kineo, Katahdin*

Series I, vol. 19, p. 120

August 6, 1862

Around the point about five miles above the city. The *Essex* engaged her and was shortly reported on fire and at 1:00 p.m. exploded.

Engines became disabled and they ran her ashore. Saw gunboats coming up and the Capt. (Lieut. H.K. Stevens-Brown took sick at Vicksburg) set the Ram on fire and told crew to go ashore.

On our turning the point, four miles above Baton Rouge, she (*Arkansas*) immediately opened fire on this ship (*Essex*) at about the distance of one mile—continued on—and the action for nearly half an hour—He (*Arkansas*) had coaled up a mile above the attack. Counted 14 shell holes on starboard side when within 300 yards—*W.D. Porter.*

ARKANSAS • **Post of**

Series I, vol. 24, p. 124

Arkansas River

A small village—capital of Arkansas County—on elevated ground above reach of floods and defining for some miles the left bank of the river—settled by French in 1685—50 miles above the mouth of the river—117 miles below Little Rock and surrounded by fruitful country.

Fort Hindman—a square full bastioned fort was erected within this village upon the bank of the river at the head of bend resembling a horseshoe.

ARLETTA • **B.R. Schooner**

March 3, 1864

Series I, vol. 15, pp. 354–55

Savannah, Georgia

Tonnage: 50

Cargo: Alcohol, whiskey, coffee, pepper.

All saved.

Ran on shore (high & dry) south end of Tybee Isl.

Capt. John Wicks

ARLETTA • Schooner Mortar, 2 Masted

March 3, 1864

Series I, vol. 15, pp. 354–55

Cargo: Alcohol, whiskey, coffee, pepper.

On south end of Tybee Island.

Near picket station of 3rd Regiment, Rhode Isl.
Heavy artillery—Capt. D.B. Churchill
Nearly day at high water.
Cargo transported to Martello Tower.

Sold, November 30, 1865

ARTHUR U.S. • Bark

Series I, vol. 9, p. 703

Aransas Pass, Texas

6 - 32#
1 - 30# Parrott

Draw: 14'
74 men well equipped with small arms.

ARTIC • Schooner

September 15, 1862

Series I, vol. 5, p. 85

Great Wicomico River, Virginia (?)

Burned

(*Artic* and *Sarah*)

Series I, vol. 5, p. 277

Captured and burned—up eastern branch.

May 28, 1863

ARTIC C.S. • Floating Batt., Iron Plated

Series II, vol. 1, p. 248

Wilmington, Delaware

Three gun—burned by Confederates at fall of Wilmington, Delaware, in 1865.

ASHUELOT U.S.S. • Sidewheel Steamer

February 17, 1883

Series II, vol. 1, p. 40

Near Amoy, China

Battery: April 1866
On Spar Deck:
4 - Dahlgren SB VIII
2 - 60# Parrott rifle
On Hurricane Deck:
2 - 24# Howitzers
2 - 20# Dahlgren rifles

Tonnage: 1030   Draft For.: 8'   Aft.: 9'

Double Ender Schooner, iron.

ASPINWALL, New Grenada

Treasure Ships

*Military & Naval History of the
Rebellion*, p. 439

The vigilance of the flying squadron under Acting Rear Admiral Wilkes was organized to protect American interests in that quarter (west India water), and especially to guard the treasure ships in their transit to and from Aspinwall.

Series I, vol. 27, p. 473

December 29, 1862

Let the *Connecticut* be prepared to leave Hampton Roads on the 1st of January to take all the treasure from Aspinwall to New York—*G.Wells, Sect. of Navy*

December 31, 1862

The Department has promised the *Connecticut* will meet the California Steamer off the west end of Mariguana Isl. and accompany her to Aspinwall, after which she (*Connecticut*) will carry out written instructions of yesterday—G.W.

Series I, vol. 27, pp. 704, 705

October 24, 1862

At 8:00 a.m., made town of Aspinwall bearing S. 1/2. W. at 9:00 a..m. entered Lemon Bay Harbor. S.W. of St. Domingo.

Series I, vol. 27, p. 484

Bay of Aspinwall, New Grenada

Harbour Master haul the vessel falmasted into the stream.

Series I, vol. 16, p. 601

Homeward bound steams is through the Crooked Island Passage.

ASTER

Series I, vol. 11, p. 30

New Inlet, North Carolina

Near Caroline Shoal in 6'.

ASTER U.S.S.

Wrecked October 8, 1864

Series II, vol. 1, p. 40

Carolina Shoals

Purchased under "Alice" for $75,000.

Tonnage: 285   Length: 122'6''   Beam: 23'   Depth: 10'

Battery: August 13, 1864
1 - 30# Parrott rifle
2 - 12# Heavy SB

Sheathed in yellow metal (brass)?

ASTER U.S. • Tug

October 8, 1864

Series I, vol. 10, p. 541

New Inlet, North Carolina on Caroline Shoals

At the entrance of New Inlet (Drew 12').

Arrived #1 Night Station on bar five fathoms at 10:40. Mound light bearing W. at 11:00 p.m., cruising S.W. by S., saw blockade runner to westward of us heading for inlet. Helm hard at port, head to northward—ranged ahead of him—hauled up more to westward to cut him off, lead at the time showing 1/4 less, 5 fathoms—before sounding could be taken again, the Aster struck on eastern extremity of Caroline Shoals. Mound light bore W. 1/2 N.—24# Howitzer moved aft. Strange steamer ashore and about 250 yards to southward and westward of us. (Annie B.R.), 15 crew and boat captured. Ft. Fisher fired at flames.

ATLANTA (former *FINGAL*)

June 17, 1863

Captured *Warsaw Sound* near Mouth of Wilmington River in Georgia by *Weellawken* U.S.S. and *Nahant*.

Tonnage: 1000 Length: 191' Beam: 40'

2 - 6'' rifles
2 - 7'' rifles

Repaired and joined the U.S. Fleet

ATLANTA C.S. • Ram

Series I, vol. 9, p. 83

Her commander said his ironclad was lost by getting aground.

Brooke rifles.

ATLANTA C.S.S. & *GEORGIA* C.S.S.

Series I, vol. 13, p. 819

Charleston

As of February 16, 1863, at anchor in Savannah River, between Ft. Jackson and first obstructions only a few hundred yards from the Georgia.

Causton's Bluff eight miles below.

2 - 7''
2 - 6.4'' rifles

100 wrought and cast iron bolts for each gun.

ATLANTIC • Steamer

Series I, vol. 14, p. 187

Lake Erie

Diver E.P. Harrington—I raised the *American Express* safe from the wreck of the steamer—in Lake Erie at a depth of 170'—claims 12 years experience, May 11, 1863.

B

B.M. RUNYAN • Steamer

Mississippi River

> Series I, vol. 26, p. 485

Ran into a snag and sunk at the foot of Island #84 with 500 passengers. The *Prairie Bird* saved about 350—I will send all government stores to Quartermaster at Memphis or Vicksburg and all private trunks and boxes to Capt. Pennock.

With some 500 passengers, ran on a snag and sunk at the foot of Island #84. The *Prairie Bird* happened to be near and saved about 350.

Assistance rendered by *Prairie Bird* U.S.S. (#11), former *Mary Miller*.

B.T. MARTIN • American Brig

> Series I, vols. 1, 6
> Series II, vols. 1, 3

By *Union* U.S.S.

> Series II, vol. 3, p. 509

Captured by *Privateer York*. Run on shore and burnt.

North Carolina Coast.

> Series I, vol. 6, p. 40

August 24, 1861

American Brig in possession of Rebels run on shore a few miles north of Cape Hatteras—well upon shore—fired—from Phili. to Cardenas.

Cargo: one cylinder boiler, a large iron refinery, cast iron framing and 3 large iron tanks, stoves and 40 barrels of potatoes.

BAINBRIDGE U.S. • Brig

Foundered August 21, 1863

> Series II, vol. 1
> Series I, vol. 14

Hatteras, North Carolina, off Cape Hatteras

Tonnage: 259

Length: 100' Beam: 25' Depth: 11' 6'' Draft: For.: 10' Aft.: 13' 6''

Battery:
6 - 32# (27 cwt.)
1 - 12# rifle

Series I, vol. 14, p. 514

One survivor.

BANSHEE • Steamer

June 21, 1863

Series I, vol. 9, p. 77

Wilmington, North Carolina

Burned at the wharf at Wilmington.

Reported, not confirmed.

BARON DE KALB U.S.S. • Gunboat

July 13, 1863

Series I, vol. 16, p. 432

Yazoo River, Mississippi
Yazoo City or Manchester, Mississippi

Formerly the *St. Louis*

Sunk one mile below Yazoo City by torpedo.

Series II, vol. 1, p. 42

Guns and valuables all recovered and vessel blown up underwater.

Series II, vol. 1, pp. 283, 285

Abreast the navy yard—lower end of town.

Before sinking the vessel, was made fast to the bank and small arms and much movable property saved. Battery completely saved.
20' water.

Military & Naval History of the Rebellion, p. 363

The enemy burned three steamboats on the approach of the gunboats. The *DeKalb* was blown up and sunk in 15' of water by the explosion of a shell.

Series II, vol. 2, p. 530

About July 15th, 1863 (approximately)

July 13, gun was sunk by torpedoes.

BARRATARIA (291) U.S.S. • Ironclad Gunboat

April 7, 1863

Series II, vol. 1, p. 43

Lake Maurepas, Louisiana

Struck a snag in Lake Maurepas at the mouth of Amite and was fired and abandoned.

Ironclad gunboat.

Transferred from Army January 1, 1863.

Series I, vol. 20, p. 123

April 7, 1863

At the mouth of the Amite River in Lake Maurepas our draft 3' 6''—Just as we were entering the mouth struck snag in 8' of water—spiked and threw overboard forward gun—set on fire—magazine exploded—had left south pass Manchac Bridge 50–75 yards from shore, hard and fast on east bank of river—one brass rifled gun still above water—boat 125' long covered.

Series I, vol. 20, p. 125

April 7, 1863

Amite River, Louisiana

Destruction of U.S.S. *Barrataria* at the mouth of

Boat 125' long covered with 1'' iron.

BAZELY U.S.S. • Tug

Series I, vol. 11, pp. 141, 162, 169, 174, 176, 192, 398

Off Jamesville, Roanoke River, North Carolina

Known also as *J.E. Bazely, Tug No. 2,* and U.S.S. *Beta*

See Rainbow Bluff, North Carolina, expedition against December 9–28, 1864

Sank beside the U.S.S. *Ostego*—by mine 2 1/2 fathoms

Sharp bend just below Jamesville coming to anchor

Off Jamesville Bluff

The guns and all articles of value that could be reached was saved (no arm)

Sunk December 10, 1864 (sunk by torpedo in Roanoke River, North Carolina, near Jamesville)

Tonnage: 50

Length: 70' Beam: 16' Depth: 6'6'' Draft: 7' Light: 6

BEATRICE • British Steamer

November 27, 1864

Series I, vol. 16, pp. 112–14, 354

Off Charleston, South Carolina
Drunken Dick Shoal, South Carolina
Sullivan's Isl. Channel

Tonnage: 200

All valuables removed.

BEAUFORT C.S.S. • Screw Steamer, Iron Tug

April 14, 1865

Series II, vol. 1, p. 249

Richmond, Virginia

Burned by Confederates at evacuation of Richmond, Virginia

Length: 85'   Beam: 17' 5''   Depth: 6' 11''

Battery:
1 - 32# rifle in pivot forward

BEAUREGARD C.S. • Schooner

May 4, 1862

Series I, vol. 7, p. 785

Norfolk, Virginia
James River

Bound from City Point to Norfolk with a cargo of coal for the *Virginia*. Was
burned by the enemy off Ragged Isl. this morn at 2 a.m.

BEAUREGARD U.S.S. • Schooner

Series I, vol. 7

Sold at auction.

Was Confederate Privateer.

Captured 1861.

Tonnage: 101

Battery:
1 - 24#

BELFAST • Steamer

June 17, 1863

Series I, vol. 20, p. 306

Plaquemine, Louisiana

Down Bayou Plaquemine about four miles to get a load of molasses.

BELLE ALGERINE • Confederate Steamer Tug

Ft. Jackson, Louisiana

Series I, vol. 18, p. 297

Series I, vol. 18, pp. 249, 250,
252, 268, 270, 291, 305, 844

Destroyed in action, defense of Ft. St. Phillip and Fort Jackson. Capt. (Jackson)

BELVEDERE • Steamer

November 5, 1861

Series I, vol. 6, p. 416

At sea

Brought to off Cape Lookout Shoals in leaky state and making for Hatteras Inlet.

Possible.

BEN BOLT • Barge

February 24, 1863

Series I, vol. 8

Back Creek, Virginia
Near Puquosin River from York River

Also several skiffs and canoes.

BENDIGO • Steamer, Blockade Runner

January 3, 1864

Series I, vol. 9, p. 385

Lockwood's Folly Inlet, North Carolina

Formerly *Milly*

Iron paddle Wheel.

Aground at the entrance and a fire. No cargo and woodwork mostly consumed. Close to beach aground. Entire length destroyed.

Tried to run between land and wreck of the *Elizabeth.*

Tonnage: 178

Series I, vol. 9, p. 396

1/2 mile west of Lockwood's Folly Inlet.

BEROSA • Reb. Steamer

April 8, 1863

Series I, vol. 14, p. 161

At sea

Abandoned in sinking condition.
Sailed from St. Mary's River

Lat. 29° 50'
Long. 79° 50'

BERWICK BAY

Series I, vol. 24, p. 224

Red River, Louisiana

Came out of Red River and immediately seized.

200 barrels of molasses
10 Hogsheads of sugar
30,000# flour
40 bales of cotton

Set on fire about 15 miles above the mouth of Red River by *Queen of the West.*

BIBB U.S. • Coast Survey Steamer

Explosion of torpedo under March 17, 1865

Series I, vol. 16, pp. 295, 296,
385

Charleston, South Carolina

Not sunk.

BIENVILLE C.S.S.

1862

Series II, vol. 1, p. 249

Lake Ponchartrain, Louisiana

Light draft side wheel steamer of yellow pine and white oak.

Battery:
5 - 42#
1 - small rifle

BLACK HAWK U.S.S.

April 22, 1865

Series I, vol. 27, p. 54

Former Steamer *New Uncle Sam.*

Burned and sunk in Ohio River, three miles above Cairo; magazine exploded—14 guns.

Raised and sold at St. Louis, April 1867.

Series I, vol. 27, p. 154

Took fire from coal oil, 10:30 a.m.

Divisional reports on sunken vessels asked to make out duplicates (some records saved from *Flagship B.H.*).

BLACK JOKER • Steamer - *BLACK HAWK*

March 15, 1862

Series I, vol. 18

Known also as *Vanderbilt*, which, also *Black Hawk*.

Foundered at sea with a load of coffee, zinc, sheet copper, oil and paper—left Havana on 12th and heavy head sea produced leak.

BLACK WARRIOR C.S. • Schooner

February 10, 1862

Series II, vol. 1, p. 249

Two guns burned and abandoned by crew during fight of Elizabeth City, North Carolina.

BLANCHE • Steamer

October 8, 1862

Series I, vol. 19

Marianao Harbor, Cuba

Mentioned also as *Gen. Rusk.*

Fired on and boarded when aground and burned by Fed. Gunboat *Montgomery.*

Gen. Rusk valued at $150,000.

BLOCKADE RUNNER

December 16, 1863

Series I, vol. 9, p. 354

New Inlet, North Carolina

Northward of New Inlet—put vessel on beach with heavy sea running—Union's ships fired upon by batteries to the north and south of wreck.

BLOOMER U.S.S. • Sidewheel Steamer

Series II, vol. 1, p. 46

Sunk in East Pass, Santa Rosa Island, Florida.

Tender to Frigate *Potomac*.

Tonnage: 130

Battery: March 1, 1864
1 - 32# 57 cwt.
1 - 12#

Wreck sold to S.P. Griffin & Co., Woolsey, Florida, September 22, 1865.

BOMBSHELL U.S. • Army Steamer

April 18, 1864

Series I, vol. 9, p. 653

Plymouth, North Carolina

Sunk by Confederate batteries.

Raised and put in service and recaptured May 5, 1864, by U.S.S. *Mattabisett*.

Sank at the wharf from several shots below the waterline.

BOSTON U.S. • Army Steamer

May 26, 1864

Series I, vol. 15, pp. 400, 459–62

Chapman's Fort, Ashepoo River, South Carolina

When arrived at Chapman's Fort, I found a lance Yankee steamer aground 300 yards below the piling in the Ashepoo River accompanying gunboats after she was shelled. Took off her crew and troops, finding her very disabled they set her on fire and retired down the river.

One battery at the fort and 2nd at Mr. William Means' Causeway.

Some lives lost and about 60 horses burned. Destroyed to prevent falling into hands of Rebels.

BOSTON U.S.A. • Transport

May 25, 1864

Series I, vol. 15, p. 459

Ashepoo River, South Carolina

Grounded under fire and destroyed to prevent falling into Rebel hands.

Got on shore under Ft. Chapman's Battery above Mosquito Creek.

Below small island and opposite shore of Ft.—nothing removed at of September 27, 1864.

BRANDYWINE U.S.S. • Frigate

September 3, 1864 Burned

Series II, vol. 1, p. 47

Tonnage: 1,708

Length: 175' Beam: 45' Depth: 14' 5'' Draft: 22'

Battery: 50 gun

Raised and sold.

BREAKER C.S.

August 12, 1862

Series I, vol. 19, p. 151

Corpus Christi, Texas

Armed vessel—after rounding McGloin's Bluff, opened with Parrott and she was beached and fired. Put out fire and hove her off.

Former pilot boat at Pass Cavallo.

BREWSTER U.S.A. • Gunboat

May 9, 1864

Series I, vol. 10, p. 46

Appomatox River, Virginia

About 30 minutes above Gilliam's Bar.

Gilliam's Bar above Point of Rocks.

BROCKENBOROUGH • Sloop

Series I, vol. 17

Captured under name *G. L. Brockenborough*, also known as U.S. Sloop *Brockenborough*.

Abandoned beached.

BUCKSKIN • Sloop

November 9, 1864

Series I, vol. 5, p. 492

Chopawamsic Creek, Virginia

Burned in the creek.

BUFFALO • Prize Sloop

March 22, 1864

Series I, vol. 15, pp. 372–74

Ossabaw Isl., Georgia

Wind from N.E., drove ashore. High and dry at low tide. Hauled up for Ossabaw (Sound). Fell of (S.W.) with breakers all along to leeward—wind N.E.

BUFFALO • Sloop (Prize)

March 22, 1864

Series I, vol. 15, p. 373

Ossabaw Isl., Georgia

Ran ashore.

BURNSIDE • Propeller

February 21, 1864

Series I, vol. 15, p. 282

Off Mayport Mills, Florida

Is a wreck having struck on the bar coming in and dragged down the coast and last night slipped her cables and came on to the beach.

BURNSIDE • Propeller

February 20, 1864

Series , vol. 15, p. 282

Mayport Mills, Florida

Is a wreck struck on the bar coming in and dragged down the coast—slipped her cables and came onto the beach.

C

C.A. NICHOLS • Canal Boat

February 11, 1862

Series I, vol. 6, p. 571

Croatan Sound
Battle of Roanoke Isl, Virginia
Redstone Point

Fort was two canal boats filled with sod and mud, braced on outside with timbers—one was fired and magazine blown up—will destroy other.

Fort 220' long, mounted 9 cannon (another fort 3 miles above this).

CAIRO U.S.S.

December 12, 1862

Series I, vol. 24

Yazoo River, Mississippi

Blown up by torpedo.

Series I, vol. 23, p. 575

Sketch of Yazoo River

Blown up by torpedo.

Series I, vol. 24, p. 203

January 27, 1863

Between Chickasaw Bayou and Benson Blakes House—no recovery evidenced—pickets headed toward Vicksburg. Pickets were at the mouth of the Yazoo where it connected with the old bed of Mississippi River—no part of wreck visible.

Series I, vol. 25, p. 499

In 20' of water—3' water on wheel house—chains hung over bow taken off by Rebels—nothing else taken—lies near right hand bank going up river about 1 1/4 miles from Blakes lower plantation—14 gun carriages rammers, sponges, sights, mostly lost.

Series II, vol. 1, p. 49

December 12, 1862

Sunk 4 or 5 miles below Hayne's Bluff. Sunk in less than 5 minutes. Struck by torpedo 18 miles up the Yazoo River.

Battery:
6 - 32# 43 cwt.
3 - army rifles 80 cwt.
3 - 8 in VIII 63 cwt.
1 - 30# Parrott rifle

Tonnage: 512

Series I, vol. 25, pp. 141, 282

In 5 fathoms of water
10-20' under water.

Sent from Helena—in advance of rest of fleet to clear torpedoes. Got to within 3 miles of forts (Snyders Bluff—generally called Haynes Bluff)—moving up to protect small boat dragging ran on torpedo and sank in 11 minutes. Sank out of sight in deep water and has never been found; drifting away with current.

Series I, vol. 23, p. 545

Nothing could be seen but the top of her pipes which the (*Queen of the West*) *Lioness* hauled out and sunk to prevent Rebels from finding the spot—nothing saved but a few hammocks and bags belonging to the men, which floated off. December 17, 1862

Series I, vol. 23, pp. 547, 548

Recently plated with railroad iron—hole blown through forecaster near port bow gun—run on shore. Hawser got out to bank but she slid off. Some 16 miles from mouth in 6 fathoms in 12 minutes in sight of enemy's fort (varied 12 to 18 miles up).

Series I, vol. 23, p. 554

Haynes Bluff, 23 miles up Yazoo

CALEB CUSHING C.S.S.

April 18, 1863

Series II, vol. 1, p. 249

Portland Harbor

Set on fire and abandoned to avoid recapture.

Captured by *Archer*.

Battery:
2 gun

CALHOUN C.S.S. • Privateer, Sidewheel Steamer

1862

Series II, vol. 1, p. 250

Tonnage: 500

Battery:
1 - 18#
2 - 12#
2 - 6#

Burned by Confederates after fall of New Orleans.

CAMBRIA U.S.S. • Schooner

Series II, vol. 1

Purchased to sink.

Purchased August 13, 1861, at Baltimore, Maryland, for $1,500.

CAROLINE ANDERSON • Schooner

May 23, 1863

Series I, vol. 5, p. 273

Found on fire, saved captain and crew. Fired into her to scuttle her—Act. Master
Morris Coeur de Lion

CAROLINE GERTRUDE • Confederate Schooner

December 28-29, 1863

Series I, vol. 17, pp. 617, 629

Off OK Lockover River (near St. Marks), Florida

Inside the bar at the mouth of the river. Aground 100 yards from beach on Oyster
Bank. Fired.

Cargo of cotton taken off and vessel fired.

CARONDELER C.S.S. • Sidewheel Steamer

1862

Series II, vol. 1, p. 250

Lake Pontchartrain, Louisiana

Light draft sidewheel steamer

Destroyed by Confederates.

Battery: April 27, 1862
5 - 42#
1 - 32# rifle

CASSIE HOLT • Sloop

February 29, 1864

Ex. Doc. 279 40th Cong.
2nd Session

San Louis Pass, Texas

Destroyed.

Series I, vol. 21, p. 119

Anchored inside of Galveston Island. Grounded hard in 16' of water—burned, deck

Load: Cotton.

CASWELL C.S.S. • Wooden Side Wheel Steamer

1865

Series II, vol. 1, p. 250

Wilmington.

Burned by Confederates at Fall of.

CATHARINE • British Schooner

August 14, 1863

Series I, vol. 19, p. 480

Sabine Pass, Texas

Running in—stranded by crew—set fire and escaped.

CATSKILL U.S.S.

August 9, 1864

Series I, vol. 15, p. 624

Off Ft. Moultrie, South Carolina

Destruction of Blockade Runner.

CEARS • British Steamer, Blockade Runner

December 6, 1863

Series I, vol. 9, p. 336

Wilmington, North Carolina
Smith's Island

Aground and on fire.

Off Bald Head Lighthouse, western bar.

Bald Head about 1 1/4 mile from Ft. Caswell.
Main Channel of river between them.

On western bar on shoal, near Smith's Isl., North Carolina.
Ft. Caswell bearing N. 1/2 E. and Bald Head Lighthouse bearing N.E. 1/2 N.

Fired on boarding from batt. to left and west of it and Ft. Caswell.

Iron prop 300 ton from Bermuda, misc. cargo.

Floated off and towed to Beaufort.

Series I, vol. 9, p. 583

Anchor and chain recovered.

CECILIA • British Schooner

December 5, 1863

Series I, vol. 15, p. 159

Murrell's Inlet, South Carolina

1 1/2 miles from mouth.

Landed on Magnolia Beach.

Not reported sunk.

Party from U.S. Brig *Perry* landed on Magnolia Beach near Murrell's Inlet, South Carolina.

November 5, 1863

Cecilia was lying about 1 1/2 miles from mouth.

No record of being destroyed except index.

CELT (*SYLPH*) • British Steamer, Blockade Runner

February 15, 1865

Series I, vol. 16, p. 369

Charleston, South Carolina

Got ashore coming out and was destroyed.

Cargo: Cotton—salvaged

Near the breakwater off Sullivan's Isl.

Machinery not worth recovery.

Ran ashore abreast of Moultrie.

CELT (believed same as *SYLPH*) • Blockade Runner

February 14, 1865

Series I, vol. 16, pp. 246, 256, 258

Sullivan's Isl.
Charleston, South Carolina

Run ashore near the breakwater on—abreast of Moultrie-Sullivan's Isl.—going out.

Cargo: cotton

CHAMPION *#3* and
U.S. PUMPBOAT #3

April 26 and 27, 1864

Series I, vol. 26, pp. 75, 81, 87

Red River
Cane River, mouth—a point above

Disabled, set fire to and burned up.

Five miles above the mouth of Cane river.

New Champion captured, disabled and floated ashore on river bank under batt.

Champion #5 disabled, ran ashore opposite where crew escaped and it burned.

New Champion repaired by Rebels and running.

CHARITY • Schooner,

GAZELLE • Schooner, and

FLIGHT • Schooner

May 27, 1863

Series I, vol. 5, p. 581

Yeocomico River

Burned by cutter crew of U.S.S. *Anacostia*. Left mouth under tow at 1:00 p.m. and returned at 7:00 p.m.

CHARLESTON C.S. • Ironclad Sloop

1865

Series I, vol. 16, p. 459

Charleston Harbor, South Carolina

Commander I.N. Brown

6 guns as of November 5, 1864
2 - 8'' rifles
4 - rifled 42#
Crew - 140

Speed 6 or 7 knots

Series II, vol. 1, p. 250

Destroyed by Confederates at the evacuation of Charleston, 1865. November 5, 1864. 4 Guns.

At anchorage opposite Mt. Pleasant Ferry Wharf in the Cooper K.   Possible the one 350 yards S by E from wharf—mach. under 2' at low tide. Listed S.C. Charleston.

CHATTAHOOCHEE C.S. • Gunboat

Series I, vol. 22, p. 258

Columbus, Georgia

Twelve miles below Columbus

At the race pass—machinery under water and burned as far as possible.

CHATTAHOOCHEE C.S.S. • Wooden Steam Gunboat

Series II, vol. 1, p. 250

Chattahoochee River, Georgia

Burned by Confederates on the Chattahoochee River at close of war.

Battery:
1 - IX Gun
1 - rifle 32#
4 - 32#

CHICKAMAUGA • Reb Gunboat and
TALLAHASSEE

*Military & Naval History of the
Rebellion*, p. 645

Cape Fear, North Carolina
(Ft. Fisher Campers) (Wilmington)

The remaining works covering the mouth of the river, including Ft. Caswell and the forts at Smith's Island, Smithville, and Reeves Point, together with the gunboats *Chickamauga* and *Tallahassee* were destroyed or evacuated.

Burned at the fall of Wilmington, 1865.

Screw steamer cruiser.

Battery:
3 gun

Series I, vol. 12, pp. 17, 57, 63,
71

N.W. Branch Cape Fear River, below Indian Wells.
Sunk across stream at Indian Wells with a chain just below—her two gun on bluff on west bank of river.

Sunk across the narrow part of channel but current swept her alongside bank.

CHICORA C.S. • Ironclad Sloop Steamer

1865

Series I, vol. 16, p. 459

Charleston Harbor, South Carolina

Commander T.T. Hunter

4 guns as of November 5, 1864

1 - 8'' rifle forward and 1 aft., 9'' Dahlgren on each side and crew of 60 men.

Burned by Confederates at the evacuation of Charleston in 1865.

Length: 150'   Beam: 35'   Depth or Hold: 12'

Battery: April 30, 1864
2 - IX S.B. Shell Guns
2 - VI Brooke Rifles

CHRISTIANA KEENE • Schooner

Series I, vol. 4, pp. 516–17

Potomac River

Off Virginia shore on flats, wreck now lies opposite Cedar Pt. Schooner first grounded fast in 4 1/2' only 1/2 mile from Virginia shore on the weather side of river where it is 2 1/2 miles wide and channel near Maryland shore.

Boarded and burned by 30 or 40 Rebels in rowboats.

Series I, vol. 4, pp. 533, 553, 565

Within 1/4 mile of Dr. Hooe Place on or near Mathias Point opposite Port or Point Tobacco.

20 miles from Fredericksburg, Virginia

Lower Cedar Point Shoals.

CINCINNATI

May 10, 1862

Military & Naval History of the Rebellion, p. 167

Plum Point, Arkansas
At the bend above Ft. Pillow on Tennessee bank.

Run on shoal at foot of Plum Isl. and sunk due to condition received in battle.

Series I, vol. 23, p. 55

Plum Point—4 miles above Ft. Pillow

Series I, vol. 23, pp. 19, 20

The *Cincinnati* ran into the bank below where we land when you left and sunk in 11' of water. Will be raised in 24 hours.

On the bar immediately below where the *Benton* formerly lay in 12'.

Left from Cairo last evening (May 15).

Ft. Pillow 80 or 90 miles above Memphis, 3 to 5 miles of Breastworks.

Series I, vol. 23, pp. 4, 5

50 miles S. of New Madrid and 30 miles to Ft. Pillow.

Anchored 2 1/4 miles above Ft. Pillow.

Mound City—Holed—sunk and recovered.

Ft. Randolph—12 miles below Ft. Pillow.

Series I, vol. 23, p. 30

Chickasaw Bluff—6 miles from fort.

CINCINNATI U.S.S.

May 27, 1863

Series I, vol. 22

Mobile Bay

Destruction of launch of, by torpedo.

Series I, vol. 25

Sinking, Vicksburg batteries.

Harper's Weekly
February 22, 1862, cover

Length: 175' Width: 51 1/2' Draws loaded: 5'

Bow and bulwark 3' oak timber and sheathed 2 1/2'' wrought iron plate side same sheathing but less timber.

Pierced for 13 guns. Bow guns are 84# rifled cannon and the other are 8'' Columbiads.

5 boilers.

Ex. Doc. 279, 40th Congress,
2nd Session

#82 sold at New Orleans, March 28, 1866.

Tonnage: 512

Series I, vol. 25, pp. 37–38

Went down in shoal water. She disappeared in a bayou and I supposed she was taking a short cut through Old River—ran upstream near R. hand shore—sank in 3 fathoms—can be raised.

Attacked upper water battery, pulled ashore, 1 1/2 up in the bend. Lt. Commanding George Bache, steered her out of action himself.

Series I, vol. 25, pp. 96, 112–13, 116

Guns being removed, June 26, 1863.

A turreted iron clad of largest class.

Run aground on Mississippi shore.

Carried 14 guns.

Series I, vol. 25, p. 141

Lies in 3 fathoms water, sets up straight and spar deck even with water—there is no current and she is about 20 yards from shore.

Series I, vol. 25, p. 366

She is afloat and on her way to Cairo. Everything saved.

CITY BELL • Transport Steamer

May 4, 1864

Series I, vol. 26, pp. 107–8

Captured and burned 30 miles above Fort DeRussy.

At Wilson's Plantation 15 miles below Alexandria, Louisiana.

CITY BELLE U.S. • Transport

May 1, 1864

Series I, vol. 26, pp. 105, 107, 117, 123, 782

David's Ferry, Louisiana
Near Marksville

Captured about 30 miles above Ft. DeRussy. Fired upon at Wilson's Plantation, 15 miles below Alexandria, Louisiana, about 4 miles below Wilson's, came up with *Covington* and *John Warner* upon rounding the point opposite Dunn's Bayou, enemy engaged.

Covington on fire and abandoned—magazine exploded. *Warner* surrendered. *Signal* surrendered.

Dunn's Bayou on right, going down river.

Wrecks of U.S.S. *Covington*, U.S.S. *Signal*, Transport *John Warner, City Belle*

CLARA AMES or EAMES • Steamer

May 30, 1864

Series I, vol. 26, pp. 339, 406, 804, 806

Gaines Landing, Arkansas

Cotton boats and Lebanon

Everything of value removed.

Smith's Plantation 4 1/2 miles above Sunnyside

Columbia, 3 1/2 miles above.

By Colton Green, Col. Commanding Brigade

CLARENCE C.S.S. • Brig

June 12, 1863

Series II, vol. 1, p. 250

Captured by C.S.S. *Florida*, May 6, 1863

Battery:
1 - 12# Howitzer

Burned June 12, 1863

CLEOPATRA • French Frigate

November 11, 1861

Series I, vol. 12, p. 292

Burned to water's edge off Hatteras; all saved.

CLIFTON • Confederate Steamer, Sidewheeled

March 24, 1864

Series I, vol. 21, p. 159

Sabine Pass, Texas

Former U.S.S. *Clifton*

Tonnage: 892

Length: 210' Beam: 40' Depth: 13' 6''

Surrendered at Sabine Pass—September 8, 1863.

Sidewheeled steamer—diagonally iron strapped.

Cotton laden, grounded on bar going out and to prevent recapture burned by crew.
March 21, 1864—outside and hard aground on west side of channel.

COFFEE • Side Wheel Steamer

Military & Naval History of the Rebellion, p. 63

Hatteras Inslet, North Carolina

2 gun

The *Coffee*, Steamer *Marion* and Schooner *York*, were consorts of the Gordon in Hatteras Inlet. The *Coffee* was wrecked—a total loss—1861.

COLOMBIA • Schooner, Blockade Runner

April 5, 1862

Series I, vol. 18, pp. 104–8, 828

San Luis Pass, Texas

Of Galveston, Capt. Davidson

Cargo: Cotton

Burned

Govt. Records
Ex. Doc. 253-(279)-295
40th Cong. 2nd Sess.

April 5, 1864, Coast of Texas by the *Montgomery.*

Destroyed.

Series I, vol. 9, p. 546

Loaded with cotton in channel back of the pass, captured and consumed in flames April 5, 1862, by U.S. *Screw* prop. Montgomery (Capt. Hunter).

COLONEL KINSMAN U.S.S. • Gunboat

February 23, 1863

Series I, vol. 19, pp. 623, 624

Berwick Bay, Louisiana

Snagged and went down in the Atchafalaya.

Struck a snag in Berwick Bay and although run ashore, slid off and sank in 50' water at or near Brashear City—Boilers and mach. protected by iron—heavy guns on board.

Struck snag (floating) 100 yards from Fort. Steered down the bay for the flat below the wharf—when opposite the wharf, water reported rising fast. Headed in shore, ran aground with full head of steam raising bows 2 feet out of water—let go anchors a few minutes afterwards her stern began to settle, causing her to slide down the steep bank and sank.

Series I, vol. 19, p. 625

Nearly to our station 1 1/2 miles from Berwick Bay just below fort and 20 yards from shore. 15 minutes after vessel struck, turned and headed down river when we passed the wharves, reported vessel sinking—ran ashore with bow grounded in 3' and no bottom under stern with 15' pole—sank in 18 fathoms.

COLONEL LAMB • Blockade Runner, Steel Plated, Steamer

Series I, vol. 10, pp. 602, 606

November 21, 1864, is reported as having 16 guns, many heavy caliber in her hold.

Report from U.S. *Consul* at Nassau.

Reported by C.S. *Consul* at Halifax, Nova Scotia, as draws too much water to enter any inlets and will be able to enter only main channel at Wilmington—October 25, 1864.

COLONEL LONG • Schooner

Series I, vol. 6, p. 166

At Sea
South of Savannah

Tonnage: 14

Scuttled by U.S. Sloop of War, *Jamestown*.

COLONEL LONG • Steamer

Series I, vol. 6

COLONEL LOVELL C.S. • Ram, Steamer

June 6, 1862

Series II, vol. 1, p. 251

Off Memphis, Tennessee
In Mississippi River

Mississippi River, Defense Fleet

COLUMBIA C.S.S. • Screw Steamer, Ironclad Ram

Series II, vol. 1, p. 251

Charleston, South Carolina

Length: 216' Beam: 51' 2'' Depth: 13'

Caught on sunken wreck at Charleston and broke in two by falling tide.

COLUMBIA U.S. • Frigate

Series I, vol. 4

Scuttling and abandonment

Tonnage: 1,708

Length: 175' Beam: 45' Depth: 14' 4'' Draft: 22'

Burned at Norfolk, Virginia, April 20, 1861.

Raised and sold, October 10, 1867.

COLUMBUS U.S. • Ship

Series I, vol. 4

Scuttling and abandonment

Tonnage: 2,480

Length: 191' 10'' Beam: 52' Depth: 21' 10'' Draft: 25' 8''⁁

To prevent Confederates from getting it, burned, Norfolk Navy Yard, April 20, 1861.

Class: Ship of the Line

COMMODORE JONES U.S.S. • Sidewheeled Steamer

Torpedoed May 6, 1864

Series I, vol. 10

City Point
James River

Military & Naval History of the Rebellion, p. 639

The land forces were safely convoyed up the river to their landing places at City Point and Bermuda Hundred with no disaster to the fleet beyond the destruction by torpedoes of 2 small paddle-wheel gunboats—Commodore Jones and Shawsheen (Sheshonee)

Torpedoes in the channel

> Ex. Doc. 253-(279)-295
> 40th Cong. 2nd Sess.

Tonnage: 542

Length: 144' Beam: 32' 6'' Depth: 11' 8''

> *Secret Missions of the Civil War*
> p. 213

The lowest torpedo station was a place called Deep Bottom, about 5 miles above City Point by land but more by water. Locate Galvanic Batt. and 200 men on R. bank of the river—as soon as the fleet rounded the point below Presque Isl., they began shelling our tow 50.

> Series II, vol. 1, p. 61

Battery:
1 - IX Dahlgren S.B.
1 - 15# Dahlgren rifle
2 - 30# Parrott rifles
3 - 24# Smooth Bore

> Series I, vol. 10, pp. 3, 10, 12, 13

Near 4 mile creek, opposite Jones Neck.

At Jones Point.

Deep bottom—opposite Jones Point.

Deep Bottom opposite Sturgeon Town, James River, Virginia.

COMMODORE McDONOUGH U.S.S. • Sidewheel, 4th Rate Ferry Boat

August 23, 1865

> Series II, vol. 1, p. 63

At sea

Tonnage: 532

Draft: 8' 6''

While being towed from Port Royal, South Carolina, to New York.

Battery: June 2, 1863
1 - 100# rifle
1 - IX Dahlgren S.B.
2 - 50# Dahlgren Rifles
2 - 24# Howitzer

CONCHITA • **Confederate Schooner**

October 1862

Series I, vol. 19, p. 227

Lake Calcasieu, Louisiana

Burned

CONCHITA • **Schooner**

Govt. Records
Ex. Doc. 253-(279)-291
40th Cong. 2nd Sess.

Series 1, vol. 19

Burned in October 1862, coast of Texas by Crocker's Expedition.

CONCORDIA • **Schooner**

October 6, 1863

Series I, vol. 20

Calcasieu Pass, Louisiana

At daylight anchored off the pass and discovered the schooner in the Bayou, some 5 miles distance—*Cutter* discovered *Calvary* on bank near her anchorage. Schooner to be on fire.

CONDOR • **Blockade Runner**

October 1, 1864

Series I, vol. 10, p. 531

New Inlet, North Carolina

Bound in

On Swash Channel bar near the *Night Hawk* and under Ft. Fisher. Along, low, 3 pipe side wheel steamer. The two wrecked Blockade Runner partially obstruct the channel.

Lies on the North Reef with very valuable stores on board.

CONDOR • British Steamer

October 1, 1864

> Series I, vols. 10, 11
> Series II, vols. 2, 3

Lost aboard: Mrs. Rose Greenhow, Confederate Spy, drowned at Cape Fear.

CONESTOGA U.S.S.

March 8, 1864

> Series I, vol. 27, p. 289

Bondurant Point, Mississippi River

Sunk by collision.

Reported September 27, 1865—wreck near Bruinsburg, Mississippi on Mississippi River with all armament, machinery and stores on board.

July 11, 1865—Considerable sum of money taken from 2 individuals (Graveline) trading illegally and put in charge of Paymaster Ilsley—on trip from Vicksburg to Red River was run into and sunk immediately.

> Series I, vol. 26, pp. 18, 19

Below Grand Gulf, Mississippi, about 10 miles below—sank in 4 minutes—March 9, 1864.

Total loss—nothing but tops of wheel house showing and water is very low. Near the mouth of Bayou Pierre.

CONGRESS U.S. • Frigate

March 8, 1862

> Series I, vol. 7
> Series II, vol. 3

50 guns (10 - 8'' S.B.) (40 - 32#s)

> *Harper's Weekly*
> February 15, 1862
>
> Ex. Doc. 253-(279)-295
> 40th Cong., 2nd Session

50 guns

Tonnage: 1,867

Built in Kittery 1841.

Length: 179'　Beam: 47' 10''　Depth: 22' 10''

Series II, vol. 3, p. 363

At Newport News under the guns of enemy battery.

Driven ashore and burned.

Raised and sold March 8, 1862.

CONGRESS U.S.S.

March 8, 1862

Series I, vol. 7, pp. 4, 8, 33, 35, 36

Aground on Signal Point.
Aground on Newport News Point.
Aground just above Signal Point.

Cumberland lying 800 yards above us. C.S. *Merrimack* passed up James River.

Grounded immediately on the sand banks south of the entrance to the river.

Minnesota draws left Ft. Monroe when C.S. *Merrimack* passing out by Sewell's Point and attacked *Congress* and *Cumberland*. Latter hid from us by land.   When 7 or 8 miles from Ft. Minn., grounded but stood on.   *Minnesota* grounded 1 1/2 miles from Newport News and draws 23 feet.

CONQUEROR H.M.S.

Series I, vol. 8, p. 219

Rum Cay Bahama

Wrecked here.

CONSTANCE • Blockade Runner

October 6, 1864

Series I, vol. 16, pp. 8–9, 34, 37
Series I, vol. 10
Series II, vol. 3

Charleston, South Carolina
Off Long Island

Sunk near the wreck of the *Georgiana* off Long Island—bowd in.

Bound in with cargo.

While at a station (2 1/2 fathoms, inner buoy on Rattlesnake Shoals, bearing S. 1/2 west distant about 1/2 mile), I discovered a steamer sunk near the wrecks of the *Georgiana* and *Mary Bowers*. She has 2 masts, 2 smokestacks, and sidewheels.

Completely submerged in 3 fathoms. Opinion she struck wreck of *Georgiana* and put wheel hard astarboard to clear it, thus bringing her head off shore and sinking about 250 yards from and outside the *Georgiana* and *Mary Bowers*—Act. Mast. Chas. W. Lee

About Latitude: 32° 46' N Longitude: 79° 46' 10'' W   U.S.S. *Wamsutta*

CONSTITUTION U.S. • Frigate

Series I, vol. 6, p. 13

Annapolis, Maryland

Launch used by Prof. Hopkins, of the Naval School in recovering the anchors and chains of the Frigate *Constitution*—July 18, 1861.

CONTINENTAL • Steamer

Series I, vol. 25

Off Bayou Goula, Louisiana

Grounding of

COQUETTE • Schooner

September 25, 1863

Series I, vol. 5, p. 345

Port Royal, Virginia

Tonnage: 50

Stripped and scuttled.

COREA U.S.S. • Stone Fleet

Series II, vol. 1, p. 66

Tonnage: 356

COSSACK U.S.S. • Bark, Stone Fleet

Series II, vol. 1, p. 67

Tonnage: 254

COTTON PLANK

May 24, 1863

Series I, vol. 25, p. 154

Yazoo and Sunflower River Area

Sunk in Lake George—nothing out of the water but the tops of her smokestacks.

1 gun (?)

COTTON • Rebel Gunboat, Side Wheel River Steamer

January 1863

Military & Naval History of the Rebellion, p. 366

River Teche, Louisiana

The river was obstructed a few miles above its mouth. To prevent the obstructions being removed, the enemy had thrown up earthwork, extending from the bank back to an impassable swamp, and planted a battery. Gen. Moulton and 1500 men and Gunboat *Cotton* resisted Gen. Weitzel successfully.

The enemy, supposing the object to be the gunboat, removed her stores and ammunition immediately after and burned her. Subsequently the water washed a channel aground the obstruction.

Burned in Bayou Teche, Louisiana, by crew to avoid capture.

Battery:
1 - 32# S.B.
2 - 24# S.B.
1 - 9#

COUNTESS • Confederate Steamer

Series I, vol. 26, pp. 31, 164

Red River, Louisiana

Burned by the Rebs after grounding on the falls.

Off Alexandria, Louisiana

Marksville, March 12

I shall retain the Steamboat *Countess* here to carry off whatever may be necessary and send her off the last moment it will be safe for her to remain—J.C. Walker, Maj. Gen.

COUNTESS • River Steamer

March 15, 1864

Series I, vol. 26, p. 31

Alexandria, Louisiana

Burned by Rebels—to escape capture on the Falls.

COURIER • Steamer

August 22, 1864

Series I, vol. 26, p. 516

Mississippi River
Mound City, Illinois

While putting stores on board the *Volunteer* took fire accidentally and was destroyed with a great part of her cargo.

COURIER U.S. • Store Ship

June 14, 1864

Series I, vols. 17, 27

Abaco Isl., Bahamas

Ashore about 10 miles south of Elbow Cay Light-house

Ship total loss, store and cargo saved but damaged, includes 3 brass cannon saved—complement 75 MEU

Act. Master S.C. Gray

4th class ship

Tonnage: 556

Length: 135' Beam: 30' Depth: 15'

Battery:
2 - 32# (33 cwt.)
2 - 24# S.B.
1 - 12# rifle

COURIER U.S.S. • Ship, Stone Fleet

Series II, vol. 1, p. 67

Tonnage: 381

COVINGTON U.S.S. • Side Wheel Steamer

Sunk May 5, 1864

Series I, vol. 26, pp. 113–14

Red River, Louisiana

Acting Vol. Lieut. Lord U.S.N. Commanding

Magazine exploded

Sunk about 20 miles below Alexandria

Tonnage: 224

Length: 126' Beam: 37' Depth: 6' 6''

Battery:
4 - 24# S.B.
2 - 32 Parrott rifles
2 - 50# Dahlgren rifles
1 - heavy 12#

At Dunn's Bayou (R. Going down) continued downstream until she came to Short Point Point.

Started upstream with U.S.S. *Signal* in tow but got adrift.

Spiked guns and burned—tied to bank, U.S.S. *Signal*, also, May 5, 1864

COWSLIP U.S.S. • Paddle Wheel

Series I, vol. 22, p. 253

Mississippi Sound

Sunk and raised

2 guns

CROCUS U.S.S.

Run aground August 17, 1863

Series II, vol. 1
Series I, vols. 9, 14

Bodies Island, North Carolina

Loss of the U.S. Tug *Crocus* off of Bodies Island.

Tonnage: 122

Length: 79' Beam: 18' 6'' Depth: 9' 3'' Draft: 7' 6''

Commanded by Act. Ens. J.L. Winton when wrecked.

Series I, vol. 9, p. 162

U.S. Steam Tug *Crocus*, 2 guns

Vessel stranded—bilged and sea making a clean breach over her

CUBA • Confederate Steamer

May 17, 1863

Series I, vol. 17, pp. 402, 444

Gulf of Mexico

Ex. Doc. 253-(279)-295
40th Cong., 2nd Session

Burned May 17, 1863, Latitude: 28° Longitude: 87° by *DeSoto*

Latitude: 28° 47'   Longitude: 87° 58'

Cargo worth in Cuba $400,000 in specie and if landed in Mobile, Alabama, would have been worth one million to million and a quarter. Chased by U.S. *DeSoto*— Capt. W.M. Walker.

Contraband cargo out of Havana.

McConnel l—cotton cargo out of U.S. Suwanee River at capture—T. Ducey Capt. Supercargo Patrick H. Pepper.

Series I, vol. 19, p. 105

August 25—Cuba brought full cargo of arms, ammunition, medicines and blankets.

CUMBERLAND U.S. • Ship, Sloop of War

Sunk March 8, 1862

Series I, vol. 7, pp. 21, 65, 155, 186, 403

Harper's Weekly
February 15, 1862, p. 100

Tonnage: 1,726

24 Guns

Built in Charleston 1842

Ex. Doc. 253-(279)-295
40th Cong., 2nd Session

Anchored under the guns of enemy battery at Newport News by *Merrimack* (Confederate Ironclad).

Tonnage: 1,708

Draft: 19' 2''   Aft.: 21' 2''

Battery:
22 - 9'' S.B.
1 - 10'' S.B.
1 - 70# rifle

March 21, 1862

Office of Johnson & Higgins
Average Anusters & Ins. Brokers
89 Wall Street, New York

Applied to by government to make proposition for raising and requesting information as to exact location and extent of injury and depth of water.

April 1, 1862—The Dept. (Navy) desire you (Flag—Off Goldsborough) to secure anything above water worth saving. *Sgn. Gid Wells*

Series I, vol. 7, p. 403

You are directed to allow Mr. Loring Bates, of Mass., to examine with his submarine apparatus the sunken Frigate *Cumberland* in view of ascertaining her exact condition and reporting the same to the Department—Rept. May 20, 1862

May 23, 186—Party engaged in examining

May 24, 1862—The Dept. proposes to contract with responsible parties for the raising of the vessels in the waters about Norfolk and Hampton Roads.

Rept. dated March 18, 1862, Camp Butler

Series I, vol. 7, p. 140

Cumberland—sunk deck underwater perpendicular to shore 800 yards from my battery of 4 Columbiads and 1 James gun, bows out with 3 masts 45° pointing to south guns and every article in her just as she went down prow foremost. This ship can be raised whole and taken into Ft. Monroe and her guns landed. Before long, she will fill up with mud and be more difficult to handle.

Congress—Keel is square off the shore 500 yards—blew up after burning to water's edge and guns must now be accessible. *Brig. General Jos. K.F. Mansfield*

Series I, vol. 7, p. 21

We discovered two steamers at anchor (*Patrick Henry & Jamestown*) off Smithfield Point on left hand or western side of River (James ?), distant about 12 miles. 12 miles, discovered three vessels standing down Elizabeth River, toward Sewell's Point.

Series I, vol. 7, p. 65

Moored at the entrance of James River.

CUMBERLAND • Frigate and

CONGRESS • Frigate

Military & Naval History of the Rebellion, p. 223

Newport News, Virginia

Cumberland—24 guns

Congress—50 guns

Merrimac, 10 guns, 1/2 past 11, Sat., March 8th, 1862, accompanied by *Patrick Henry*, Com Tucker (6), *Jamestown*, Lt. Barney (21), *Raleigh,* Lt. Alexander, *Beaufort*, Lt. Parker, *Teazer*, Lt. Webb, each 1 gun.

Sprung across Channel eleven 9 & 10'' Dahlgren guns and two pivot guns of same pattern. *Merrimac* crushed in just forward of main chains near W.L. Backed off and most firing 300 yards. Finally after 3/4 hour, the Frigate sank and after the hull grounded on sand 54'' below.

Then captured and fired the *Congress.*

CUMBERLAND and CONGRESS

December 9, 1861

Series I, vol. 6, p. 748

Hampton Roads

Both ships, two cable lengths apart, under the battery less than 1/2 mile distant.

CURLEW C.S.S. • Sidewheel River Steamer

February 7, 1862

Series I, vol. 6, pp. 553–54, 571, 574, 594, 712

Roanoke Island, North Carolina
Croatan Sound

Sunk in Battle of Roanoke Isl.

2 guns

Took refuge under the battery at Redstone Point in disabled condition. Fired and blown up, February 8, 1862.

February 11, 1862—trust to have the 32# on the *Curlew* on board by night.

Disabled by U.S.S. *Morse*—abandoned and ashore

2:30 p.m., C.S. Rpt.,—Heavy shell perforated deck—passed through magazine and driving out one of iron plates of which her bottom consists caused her to fill so rapidly as to make it necessary to run towards shore, near which she sank while recovering the rifled gun and other articles of value from the wreck of Curlew.

Tonnage: 260

Length: 150' Draft: 4 1/2'

Speed 12 or 13 m.p.h.
Carries 8 to 10 days fuel.

CYGNET • Pilot Boat

March 30, 1862

Series I, vol. 17, pp. 202, 204

Apalachicola River, Florida

Grounded in 7' water inside the bar

By eight armed boats from U.S.S. *Mercedita* and (H.S. Stellwagon) U.S. Gunboat *Sagamore*

Also, burned Pilot Boat *Mary Olivia* and Schooner *New Isl.*

D

D.C. PEARCE • Bark

May 15, 1861

Series I, vol. 5, p. 632

Norfolk, Virginia

Sunk in channel at Norfolk as obstruction.

D.H. BILLS • Schooner

Series I, vol. 7

Grounding of *D.H.Bills.*

DAI CHING U.S.S.

Abandoned onshore January 26, 1865

Series I, vol. 16, pp. 190, 192

Port Royal, South Carolina
Combahee River

Ran into bank on starboard side. Headed downstream while making sharp bend at one mile below Tar Bluff.

Fought seven hours and then fired to prevent capture.

Battery: Must be "Head on'' at 2,100 yards

Court of inquiry.

Only heavy gun; a 100#.

Only her pipe above water—grounded under the fire of enemy. Batt. and fought seven hours.

Run into bank on starboard while trying to position in reach below battery on Tar Bluff (3 Gun) 2-7'' rifles and smooth bore. Six fathoms at stern. Burned to water's edge.

Sharp turn forces ship to go head on to batt., 2,100 yards.

Tar Bluff batt. —about 17 miles from mouth of river.

All of *Dai Ching* that was above water was her pipe.

Tonnage: 520

Length: 170' 6''   Beam: 29' 4'' Depth: 11'   Draft: 9' 6''

Battery:
4 - 24 # SB
2 - 20# Parrott Rifles
1 - 100# Parrott Rifle

DAN U.S.S.

February 1863

Series II, vol. 1, p. 71

Mississippi River

Battery:
1 - 20# Parrott Rifle
1 - 12#   Boat Howitzer

DARIE • Blockade Runner, Confederate Steamer

January 7, 1864

Series I, vol. 9, p. 388

Lockwood's Folly Inlet, North Carolina

Ran on the beach a little to the north of north inlet in the neighborhood of Georgetown, South Carolina.

Aground broadside on the beach and fired.

Georgetown light S.S.W. 10 miles distant.

179.46 ton

DAVE HUGHES • Steamer Barge

Series I, vol. 26, pp. 604–5

Tennessee River

Steamer *Dave Hughes* with barge loaded with government stores was burned yesterday (October 31) afternoon, 15 miles above this post by guerrillas—L.P. Williams, Capt. and Assnt. Quartermaster, Clarksville

A light draft boat valued at $5-7000 and chartered by me sometime since— Lieutenant S.H. Stevens.

DAYLIGHT U.S.S.

Series II, vol. 1, p. 72

Petit Bois Channel, Alabama (?)

Purchased May 19, 1863 from New York Prize Court by Navy.

DEE • Confederate Steamer Twin Propeller

February 6, 1864

Series I, vol. 9, p. 467

Near one mile to south of Masonboro Inlet.

Ran ashore—fired—170 pigs of lead.

Hove overboard—it being too rough to bring it away.

Cargo: 200 pigs of lead, bacon and spirits

DEFIANCE C.S.S.

April 28, 1862

Series I, vol. 18
Series II, vol. 1, p. 251

Mississippi River
New Orleans, Louisiana

Capt. McCoy

Smooth bore 32# on army carriage

Pivoted Aft.

Battery:
1 - 32# SB

DELAWARE U.S. • Ship

Series I, vol. 4
Series II, vol. 2

Scuttling and abandonment of vessel.

Old line of the battleship *Delaware* and *Columbus* were scuttled and sunk at the moorings.

Tonnage: 2,633

Length: 196' 4'' Beam: 53' Depth: 22' Draft: 26' 2''

Battery: 84 guns

Burned April 20, 1861, at Norfolk, Virginia

DELAWARE FARMER U.S.S. • Schooner, Stone Fleet

Series II, vol. 1, p. 73

Purchased at Baltimore

DELPHINA • 3 Masted Schooner

January 22, 1865
Cut out and destroyed

Series I, vol. 22, p. 17

Calcacieu Pass, Louisiana

Hard ashore on the flats close to the beach—was proceeding down river—norther drove water out till she was in 1'.

Destruction of vessels.

By boat expedition from U.S.S. *Chocura*.

DENBIGN • Blockade Runner, Side Wheel Steamer

May 24, 1865

Series I, vol. 22, p. 197

Galveston, Texas

Iron 162 ton

Discovered aground on Bird Key Spit near Bolivar Point—burned and now a complete wreck.

DeSOTO U.S. • Army Steamer

Series I, vol. 24

DEW DROP • Steamer

Series I, vol. 25, p. 134
Series I, vol. 18

Sun Flower River, Mississippi

Ten miles up Bayou Quiver (Quiver River).

Burned *Dew Drop*.

Possible near 150 miles up Yazoo.

DIANA C.S.

April 14, 1863

Series I, vol. 20, p. 823

Franklin, Louisiana

Fell back through Franklin to the cut-off road and set fire to the bridge. Capt. Semmes (of the Artillery) holding the *Diana* in position and set her on fire when Gen. Moulton had fallen back.

Above Franklin and take position on the right of our line.

From Franklin to New Iberia.

Series I, vol. 20, p. 830

June 24, 1863

2 - 24# Brass Howitzers

Series I, vol. 20, p. 847

October 27, 1863

2 - 12# Howitzers

DIANA C.S.

April 10–18, 1863

Series I, vol. 20, p. 818

Camp Bisland, Louisiana

Line of battle described.

DIANA C.S.S.

April 12, 1863

Series I, vol. 20

Bayou Teche, Louisiana

Formerly U.S.S. *Diana*, March 23, 1863

Series II, vol. 1, p. 74

Wood Steamer

Series II, vol. 1, p. 251

Five gun.

Series I, vol. 20, p. 106

April 11, sail through Berwick Bay into Grand Lake and land on southwestern shore at Madam Portor's Plantation—sailed around the point about six miles farther, came to anchor at McWilliams Plantation—the Gunboat *Diana* dropped down the stream a short distance was blown up and fired.

DIURNAL • Transport

September 17, 1863

Series I, vol. 25, p. 417

White River, Arkansas

Snagged in going out and is a total wreck.

DOLLY • Steamer

Series I, vol. 12, p. 165

Virginia

Lighter containing iron plating sunk in canal.

DOLPHIN U.S. • Brig

Series I, vol. 4

Scuttling and abandonment of

Tonnage: 224

Length: 88' Beam: 25' Depth: 11' Draft Forward: 10' 6'' Draft Aft.: 13'

Scuttled and burned April 20, 1861, at Norfolk Navy Yard.

DOURO • Blockade Runner, Steamer Prop.

October 11, 1863

Series I, vol. 9, p. 233

New Inlet, North Carolina

Lies a perfect wreck just above the Hebe (eight or nine miles north of Ft. Fisher).

Out of Wilmington with cargo: Cotton, tobacco and turpentine and rosin.

Ran ashore at full speed and falling tide.

Burned.

Series I, vol. 27, p. 698

Near New Inlet

DOURO • British Steamer

Series I, vol. 9

Captured March 9, 1863
Destroyed October 11, 1863.

DOVE U.S.S. • Bark, Stone Fleet

Series II, vol. 1, p. 75

Purchased at New London.

Tonnage: 151

DRAGON U.S.S.

March 9, 1862

Series I, vol. 7, p. 72

Newport News, Virginia

Moored along side U.S.S. *Minnesota.*

Aground.

Sank with exploding boiler.

Series I, vol. 7, p. 91

March 11, 1862, to be towed to Baltimore.

DREWRY • (Wood) Reb

January 23, 1865

*Military & Naval History of the
Rebellion*, p. 670

Richmond, James River (Trents Reach), Virginia

Tempted the enemy at Richmond to make a demonstration for the purpose of
breaking the pontoon bridges over the James and cutting the communication
between the Federal Forces on the two banks—a fleet consisting of the *Virginia,*

Fredericksburg and *Richmond* iron-clads carrying four guns each and the wooden vessels *Drewry, Nansemond* and *Hampton* with two guns each, the *Buford*, 1 gun, the Steamer *Torpedo* and three torpedo boats left Richmond on January 23. About midnight the fleet passed Ft. Brady—the chain in front of the obstructions beyond the lower end of Dutch Gap Canal was cut and the *Fredericksburg* passed through. The *Drewry* grounded and could not be got off and was abandoned as daylight appeared and was blown up by a shell from the battery.

Series I, vol. 11, p. 659

Aground near left bank some 1,500 yards above Battery (below Ft. Brady) Parsons—batteries consist of Parsons, Wilcox and Sawyer (on south side of Trents Reach).

DRIVER H.B.M. • Steam Sloop

August 3, 1861

Series I, vol. 16, p. 643

Jamaica, Mariguana Passage, Caribbean

Commander: Horatio Nelson

A wreck was discovered on the reef.

DRY DOCK, Floating

Around September 2, 1863

Series I, vol. 25, p. 397

Walnut Bend, Arkansas

She was run up into the mouth of the bayou at high water and at low water she was so far from the main channel that she was out of reach of observation.

Burned by unknown parties.

DUNBAR Reb.

Series I, vol. 23, p. 77

Tennessee River
Florence, Alabama

Found the *Dunbar* some distance up Cypress Creek, which is two miles below Florence, Alabama. Sunk the water being above her gard. Impossible for me to raise her.

April 21, 1862

Had been used a gunboat previous to fall of Ft. Henry.

DUNBAR C.S. • Transport Steamer

Series I, vol. 22, p. 671

Near Florence, Alabama

Cypress Creek, heard they were sunk and had been raised but had seen no trace and doubt report—March 24, 1862—Lt. Command Wm. Gwin, U.S. Gunboat *Tyler*

Series I, vol. 24, p. 6

January 7, 1863

It's reported that Roddey has raised the Steam Gunboat *Dunbar* sunk by our gunboats last winter and is trying to fix up her engines.

Series I, vol. 24, p. 44

February 24, 1863

Caught a rise in the Tennessee River and got six miles above Florence, Alabama. Chased *Dunbar* above Great Mussel Shoal.

E

EAGER • Schooner

May 30, 1863

Series I, vol. 20, p. 281

Point Isabel, Texas

Lying at the wharf loaded with merchandise (burned to prevent falling into Union hands).

Also, small schooner, in charge of custom house officials. Captured, ran aground and fired.

Near point Isabel Lighthouse.

EAST PORT C.S.

Series I, vol. 22, pp. 572, 822

Tennessee River

280' long

Sunk.

EASTPORT U.S.S. • Gunboat

Sinking April 15th
Destroyed April 26, 1864

Series I, vol. 26, pp. 63, 68, 69, 73, 74, 79, 110

Red River, Louisiana
Grand Encore, Louisiana

Former C.S. Gunboat.

Raised

Finding her immovably fixed on a bed of logs. She was blown up on 26th, 60 miles above Alexandria. Guns and stores saved.

About 6 miles below Grand Encore.

Most formidable iron clad of Mississippi Squadron.

Sunk 1 1/2 to 3 miles below Montgomery, Louisiana, by torpedo above mouth of Cane River. Blown up by Adm. D.D. Porter.

Class ironclad steam gunboat.

Blown up 60 miles above Alexandria.

Tonnage: 700

Battery:
2 - 100# Parrot rifles
2 - 50# Dahlgren rifles
4 - 9'' IX Dahlgren S.B.

Gun being removed.

About eight miles below Grand Encore.

April 23, 1864, made 20 miles down river under own steam with pump alongside of her when she got out of channel and it seems impossible to move her ahead.

The vessel had already been brought 60 miles on her way.

20 miles above a point five miles above Cane River.

Blown up across channel.

ED J. GAY

February 15, 1864

Series I, vol. 25, p. 756

Yalohusha River

At the mouth of the Yalohusha—her decks being just above water near Greenwood, Mississippi.

EDISTO • Sloop

February 14, 1862

Series I, vol. 12, pp. 547–50

Bull's Bay, South Carolina

1600 bushels rice—sunk

Inside the shoals—N. N. W. part of bay.

EDWARD U.S.S.

Series II, vol. 1, p. 77

Stone Fleet

Purchased at New Bedford, Massachusetts, November 15, 1861, to sink.

EDWARD BARNARD

October 19, 1861

Series I, vol. 16, p. 732

Mississippi River

Run on shore upon one of the mud banks of South West Pass.

Prize—leaked hopelessly in gale.

ELFIN U.S. • Steamer

Sunk November 4, 1864

Series I, vol. 27, pp. 284, 335,
604–7, 683, 687

Former *W.C. Mann*—order raising of vessel.

Tonnage: 192

Length: 155' Beam: 31' Depth: 4' 4''

Battery:
8 - 24# Howitzer

Recovered as of June 29, 1865, by A.U.L. Rogers of U.S.S. *Kate.*

2 - 24# Howitzers

August 8, 1865—Kate sent to Mound City to discharge ordinance of
decommissioned ships (Steam Capstan).

ELIZA • Confederate Sloop

October 1862

Series I, vol. 19, p. 227

Lake Calcasieu

Burned.

ELIZA G. • Steamer

June 16, 1862

Series I, vol. 23

White River, Arkansas

ELIZABETH

Series I, vol. 9, p. 386

Lockwood's Folly Inlet

Off entrance.

ELIZABETH • Blockade Runner

September 24, 1863

Series I, vol. 9, p. 234

Lockwood's Folly, North Carolina

Former *Atlantic*—bound in with cargo steel and salt peter—ashore 12 miles from Ft. Caswell.

ELIZABETH • Schooner

February 14, 1862

Series I, vol. 12, pp. 547–50

Bull's Bay, South Carolina

1,800 bushels rice—sunk.

Inside the shoals in N.N.W. part of bay.

ELLA • Blockade Runner

Ashore December 3, 1864, Destroyed December 5, 1864

Series I, vol. 11, pp. 126, 134

1,000 ton burden.

Draw: 6'

Cape Fear River, South Carolina

Off western bar, ashore 1 1/2 miles S. by W. of Bald Head Point.

South end of Marshall Shoal (Smith's Island).

Long low sidewheel steamer schooner rigged with two smoke intakes.

S.E. end of Reeper Shoal—60 yards in from 2 1/4 fathoms—250 yards from beach (near Battery Holmes) off Hill Battery.

Cargo—arms and ammunition—Enfields.

The *Ella* is ashore 1 1/2 miles from shore opposite Hill Battery of left of land fronts.

ELLA & ANNIE

November 9, 1863

Series I, vol. 9, pp. 283, 291

Masonboro, North Carolina

North of New Inlet.

First seen near Masonboro Inlet.

Captured off Masonboro Inlet in four fathoms, 18 miles north of Ft. Fisher.

Captured.

Left Hamilton Bermuda with 10,400 disbursement money.

ELLEN

June 18, 1862

Series I, vol. 13, p. 106

Stono River

2 Parrotts

ELLEN U.S.S.

October 10, 1862

Series I, vol. 13, p. 377

Port Royal Harbor

Vessel past repair—directed to be beached.

Machinery removed.

ELLEN U.S.S. • Goldsboro Schooner, Stone Fleet

Series II, vol. 1, p. 78

Purchased at Baltimore, August 13, 1861.

ELLIS C.S.S.

Series I, vol. 8

Captured February 10, 1862.

Abandoned and fired in New River, North Carolina, November 25, 1862.

Sidewheel steamer

Two guns

Tug boat

ELLIS U.S.S.

November 23, 1862

Series I, vol. 8, p. 230

New River Inlet, North Carolina

Passed the narrow and shallow place called "The Rocks" and started up river—five miles from mouth came upon vessel loaded with turpentine and cotton bound out. Enemy fired her—on return, I came to anchor five miles from outer bar to await high water and daylight. At daylight, got under way and almost reached worst place in channel about 500 yards from Bluff's, pilot ran hard and fast aground— headway had forced her over a shoal—fought, abandoned and fired ship having transferred most gun and cannon to prize—left pivot gun, 2 ton coal—ammo— some small arms. Pulled 1 1/2 miles in small boat down river, reached schooner and made sail for sea. *Ellis* mag exploded—C.S.—November 28, 1862.

Enemy attempted to fire her but being of iron, little damage was done—armament, small arms and ammo will be saved.

ELMA

February 20, 1863

Series I, vol. 8, p. 566

Mobjack Bay, Virginia

Up the East River (above the mouth) in Mobjack Bay.

Burned to water's edge.

Evidently unloaded and burned.

ELMA C.S. or *MAJOR MINTER*

August 12, 1862

Series I, vol. 19, pp. 151, 783

Corpus Christi, Texas
Nueces Reef

Armed schooner fired and abandoned in the channel to Nueces Bay, at the same time—run into channel and grounded.

Also known as *Major Minter*.

EMERALD U.S.S. • Ship, Stone Fleet

Series II, vol. 1, p. 78

Tonnage: 518

Purchased at Sag Harbor, New York, November 21, 1861.

EMILIE • B.R. Side Wheel (former *WILL SEABROOK* of Charleston)

July 7, 1862

Series I, vol. 13, p. 177

Bull's Bay, South Carolina (60 miles above Beaufort, South Carolina) inside the isl.

Draft: 6'

Aground in the channel leading to Charleston some five miles from the bar—the river here makes a bend—boarded on port gangway and starboard.

Threw overboard iron cans of some kind of acid, 700 or 800 lbs. each (10 or 12).

About 15 miles from city of Charleston.

Floated and hauled out.

EMILY

Series I, vol. 21, p. 883

Velasco, Texas

March 22—Blockaders fired at *Emily*.

Wrecked below here—all rigging is removed and she fast filling with sand and water and will prove a wreck—C.S. report.

EMILY

June 26, 1862

Series I, vol. 7, p. 589

Ft. Casewell

Burned on the bar.

EMILY • Schooner

June 26, 1862

Series I, vol. 21, p. 153

Wrecked near Velasco, Texas.

March 22, 1864

Still on the beach—all cargo safe.

EMILY • Schooner, Blockade Runner, [*Nassau*]

June 26, 1862

Series I, vol. 7, p. 504

Off Wilmington, North Carolina

Cargo: Salt

Grounded—towed out.

Burning and sank her in deep water.

EMILY • Screw Steamer, Blockade Runner

February 10, 1864

Series I, vol. 9

Cargo: Salt and a few barrels

Brig rigged but dismantled for run. block.

Set on fire and destroyed.

Burned some time when exploded and stern settled.

Cargo of salt—possibly something under it.

EMMA

May 3, 1864

Series I, vol. 26, p. 102

Alexandria, Louisiana
Red River

Burned 50 miles below at the bank.

EMMA • Confederate Steamer

Series I, vol. 13

Grounding.

EMMA • Steamer

January 10, 1863

Series I, vol. 13, p. 508

Charleston, South Carolina
Savannah River

Now ashore near Ft. Pulaski.

Order requesting salvage of cargo of cotton and turpentine and machinery.

EMMA • Steamer, U.S. Transp.

Series I, vol. 26, pp. 102, 123

Red River, Louisiana

Burned 50 miles below Alexandria, Louisiana.

EMMA BETT

May 30, 1863

Series I, vol. 25, p. 134

Quiver River (Bayou Quiver), Mississippi

Up Big sunflower?

At the mouth of Bayou Quiver—heard of steamers expedition, went 10 miles up and burned the *Dew Drop* and *Emma Bett*.

Captured 14 miles up Bayou and brought back.

Possible near 150 miles up Yazoo.

EQUATOR C.S.S.

1865

Series II, vol. 1, p. 252

Wilmington

Burned at the fall of.

Steam gunboat, wood.

One gun.

EREBUS U.S. • Tug

April 15, 1862

Series I, vol. 23, p. 676

Plum Point, Arkansas
Mississippi River

Accidentally burned today.

Possibly reported mortar boat destroyed.

ETIWAN

May or June 1863

Series I, vol. 16, pp. 386, 412

Was run on shore near Ft. Johnson, one torpedo having exploded under her and she being in a sinking condition.

Batteries on Morris Isl. opened on her next morning.

Another steamer plying from Sumpter up the harbor was struck by one (torpedo) and beached on the shoal near Johnson.

ETIWAN • Reb. Steamer

Series I, vol. 16, p. 388

Charleston, South Carolina

Probably sunk on evacuation.

On chart pub in report of Secretary of Navy 1865.

ETTA • Schooner

Series I, vol. 17, p. 676

Off Cedar Keys, Florida

EWING C.S.

Series I, vol. 22, p. 257

Near Pensacola

Abandoned.

Boiler raised from wreck November 1865.

EXPERIMENT • Reb Schooner

May 3, 1864

Series I, vol. 21, p. 238

Texas

Run out of Galveston last night for Tampico. Boarded 11:30, May 3—removed cargo (31 bales) and destroyed her.

EXPERIMENT • Schooner Cotton

Ex. Doc. 253-(279)-295
40th Cong. 2nd Session

May 3, 1863, Coast of Texas by *Virginia*.

Destroyed.

F

FAITH • Union Bark Coal

August 8, 1863

Series I, vol. 27, p. 566

Martin's Industry Shoals, South Carolina
Near Port Royal Harbor
Aground inside of—bilged

500 Ton coal

Series I, vol. 14, p. 431

Come in without a pilot.

Bilged of Port Royal.

FARRAGUT, Admiral (not a vessel)

Series I, vol. 19, p. 778

Extract from Diary of Lt. Roe F.A., U.S.N., on U.S.S. *Pensacola*.

Comment on exposure of U.S. *Winona*, Port Hudson, Mississippi River.

The ship is cut up, crippled and valuable. life lost without object or result. It is strange that Admiral does insist upon such reckless and useless exposure of his officers, men and ships. But nearly or quite every officer I know does not give him credit for judgment or prudence or even a proper regard for the lives or reputation of his people. Nearly every commanding officer of the River Squadron remonstrated on this foolish exposure. We are losing confidence in Admiral Farragut, for he displays no judgment or prudence. He is wasteful of life and blood to a criminal degree.

FAVORITE • Schooner (Small)

July 18, 1861

Series I, vol. 4, p. 577

Yecomico, Virginia
Anchored off Piney Point.

Sunk by collision or neglect to pump out.

FAWN U.S. • Mail Boat

September 9, 1864

Series I, vol. 10, p. 457

Albemarle and Chesapeake Canal
Near Norfolk, North Carolina

Burned by twenty men led by Hopkins.
Sold at auction.

Series I, vol. 1, p. 83

Name changed from *Fanny Barker*.

FERRY

November 15, 1863

Series I, vol. 25, p. 569

Mississippi River, off Natchez

Destroyed Ferry at Simmes'.

FINGAL

Harper's Weekly
August 23, 1862, p. 531

2 - 100# rifle guns
6 - 10'' Columbiads
4 - 50# rifle guns

2 - 24# for grape and canister

With a massive beak at either end.

Said to resemble the *Merrimack* in shape and form.

Converted British Blockade Runner Steamer *Fingal*.

FINLAND • Ship

August 26 and burning August 28, 1861

Series I, vol. 16, pp. 646, 647

Apalachicola, Florida

About 4 miles from outer buoy while trying to beat out.

Burned to water's edge. Off N.E. entrance to Apalachicola.

Been waiting to receive cargo of cotton.

FIREFLY C.S. • Steam Tender

December 21, 1864

Series 1, vol. 16, p. 484

Savannah, Georgia

Upon landing at Sereven's Ferry, the wharf there was fired, and the *Firefly* which was alongside of it.

FIREFLY C.S.S. • Side Wheel Steamer

December 21, 1865

Series I, vol. 16, pp. 461, 469, 484, 493, 499

Savannah, Georgia
Savannah River

Burned at Wharf of Sereven's Ferry.

FLAMINGO • Steamer

Series I, vol. 35, p. 316

Charleston, Virginia

On the morning of 23 October 1864, a sidewheel steamer was seen ashore almost opposite Battery Rutledge, Sullivan's Isl—she was running into Charleston when headed off by some of our picket boats and run aground.

She now lies a total wreck.

FLIGHT • Schooner

Series I, vol. 5, p. 581

Yeocomico River

See *Charity* Schooner

FLORA • B. R., British (700 Ton)

October 22, 1864

Series I, vol. 16, pp. 29, 32

Ft. Moultrie, Charleston, South Carolina

South Bank of Maffit's Channel.

Large side wheel iron steamer.

Ashore opposite Batt. *Rutledge*, Sullivan's Isl.

Distant from Ft. Putnam—2,700 yards, Batt. *Chatfield*—2,600 yards, Ft. Strong—3,500 yards.

Run in.

FLORA • Steamer, Blockade Runner

October 22, 1864

Series I, vol. 16, pp. 29–37, 357

Charleston, South Carolina
Off Ft. Moultrie

Tonnage: 437

Another wreck added to the ornaments of the channel said to be the *Flora* on the shoal side of the channel, southern bank of Maffit's Channel. Large side wheel steamer with two smokestacks was discovered ashore opposite Bat. *Rutledge*, Sullivan's Isl, on a shoal. About 700 ton burden—running into Charleston now lies a complete wreck.

Distant from Ft. Putnam—2,700 yards, Batt. *Chatfield*—2,600 yards, Ft. Strong—3,500 yards.

98 shells struck vessel.

FLORENCE NIGHTINGALE • Schooner

March 2, 1863

Series I, vol. 17, pp. 369–72, 375

Later captured by the *Octorana* and sent to Key West.

FLORIDA C.S.S. • Cruiser

Series I, vols. 1, 2, 3

Series II, vols. 1, 2, 3

Also known as *Manassas* and *Oreto* (lapwing bark tender).

Lt. Maffitt, C.S.N.

Cost: $75,000

4 guns.

Length: 191' Beam: 27' 2'' Depth: 14' Draft: 13'

Battery:
6 - 6'' rifles
2 - 7'' rifles
1 - 12#

Captured 72 vessels.

Military & Naval History
of the Rebellion, p. 439

Series I, vol. 3, pp. 271-74

Anchor the *Florida* in a safe place above Newport News. 1 pivot, 1 broadside, and 1 brass Howitzer landed Fort Norfolk. Proceed with the *Florida* to Newport News and anchor under the guns of the *Atlanta*, taking care to be sufficiently far from shoals that in the event of dragging you will not go onshore.

Jonathan Baker—Acting Master USN of captured C.S.S. *Florida* when sunk.

Run into by Army Transport Alliance.

Sunk in 9 fathoms with 45 fathoms on each chain with open Hawser to N.W.—moored within range of guns of U.S.S. Ironclad *Atlanta*—lies with list to port and her tops even with water.

She filled so rapidly that only a few articles of the little property left on board could be saved—Log of U.S.S. *Malvern*, November 28, 1864

Series I, vol. 12, p. 736

Down James River, 3 p.m., passed Gen. Putnam aground, at 3:20 passed Ram *Atlanta*, also Rebel Privateer *Florida* sunk near the *Atlanta*, at 3:30 passed Newport News, and at 4:00 came to anchor of Ft. Monroe, November 29, lying at anchor in Hampton Roads.

FLORIDA • Reb Cruiser

Military & Naval History
of the Rebellion, p. 649

Hampton Roads, Virginia

In November (1864?) the *Florida* was brought into Hampton Roads and while lying there to await the decision of the delicate international questions which her capture involved, was accidentally run into by a steam transport and sunk.

By Army Transport *Alliance*

Hit November 19, 1864—sunk November 28, 1864, off Newport News, Virginia, in 9 fathoms.

FLYCATCHER and unknown Schooner loaded with brick

October 1862

Series I, vol. 19, p. 328

Atchafalaya River, Louisiana
Near Brashear City.

Obstructions about 5 miles above Pattersonville and 3 miles from mouth of Teche (Bayou?) sun in channel—they retreated above a bridge called Cornay Bridge. Centerville—three miles above obstructions.

November 9, 1862

January 14, 1863, trying to pull up obstruction and follow *Cotton* up River Teche.

FLYING CLOUD C.S. • Sloop

June 2, 1863

Series I, vol. 5, p. 282

Tapp's Creek, Virginia

No cargo.

FLYING CLOUD • Sloop

May 10, 1863

Series I, vol. 5, p. 606

Tapp's Creek

Left ship 12 p.m., returned 4 p.m.

June 4, 1863 - raised.

FORREST C.S.S. • Wood Steamer, Tugboat

February 10, 1862

Series I, vol. 6

Elizabeth City

Burned on the ways.

Battery:
1 gun

Disabled at Battle of Roanoke Isl., February 7, 1862.

FORT U.S.S. • Canal Boat, Stone Fleet

Series II, vol. 1, p. 85

Tonnage: 112

Purchased July 16, 1864, at Philadelphia, Pennsylvania.

FORTUNATE • Reb Sloop

Series I, vol. 27, p. 678

Florida

Out of Indian River Inlet.

Transferred cargo to U.S.S. *Bermuda* and proceeded north. Prize filled with water and sank. 3:30 min after start.

FOX • Blockade Runner

Series I, vol. 17, p. 552

Run into shore and fired soon after making East Pass of Horn Isl.

Was able to enter the Sound and met the *Jackson* and *Calhoun* near Round Isl.

FOX • Confederate Steamer

September 12, 1863

Series I, vol. 17, pp. 550–53

Captured mouth of Mississippi—brought to Mobile by Act. Master George Andrews, CSN.

Tonnage: 432

FRANCES ELMOR

October 8, 1862

Series I, vol. 5, p. 118

Potomac River

Two hours drifting down stream from Bluff Point (about White Point ?).

Burned loaded with hay.

FRANKLIN • **Bark and 5 Schooners**

June 1864

> Series I, vol. 10, pp. 130, 148,
> 150, 194

James River, Virginia
Trent's Reach

For sinking

June 15, 1864—Five vessels sunk off Trent's Reach bar.

Sunk in deepest water.

Can be pumped out.

Four vessels in main channel

> Series I, vol. 10, p. 211

Bark *Franklin* near left bank.
Schooner *Haxall*
Schooner *Mist*
Schooner *E.W. Benton*
Schooner *Julia A. Whitford*
Schooner *Colonel Satterly* is sunk in South Channel

In the Artificia Channel, on the left bank are sunk one bark and 4 schooners and in the small channel on the river bank another schooner is sunk.

FREDERICKSBURG **C.S.S. • Ironclad Steam Ram**

April 4, 1865

> Series II, vol. 1, p. 253

Draft about 11'

Burned by Confederates below Richmond, Virginia.

FREDONIA **U.S.S. • Ship**

August 23, 1868

> Series II, vol. 1, p. 88

Arica, Peru

Tonnage: 800

4th class receiving ship.

Battery:
4 guns carronades

Destroyed by earthquake.

FRIENDSHIP U.S.S. • Schooner, Stone Fleet

Series II, vol. 1, p. 88

Purchased August 13, 1861, at Baltimore, Maryland.

FROLIC

Series II, vol. 17, p. 410

Bayport, Florida

Large schooner on inside Bayport. Fired by Rebels. Containing 300 bales of cotton by expedition of armed launches from U.S. *Flagship*, *St. Lawrence* and *Sagamore*—clearing coast from Suwanee River to Anclote Keys—the masts fell and the vessel disappeared entirely.

(South of Cedar Keys below with Lacuoctler River, Crystal River, Homosaassa River, Chassahowitzkaa River.)

Series II, vol. 17, pp. 179, 827

Map of Florida.

Coast Florida, Alabama and Mississippi from St. Georges Sound to Ship Isl.

FROLIC • Prize Schooner

October 18, 1861

Series I, vol. 16, pp. 690, 704, 714–15, 725, 733

Mississippi River

Pilot boat, S.W. Pass.

Sold—notorious blockade runner.

Driven high up into West Bay in three feet of water. Wrecked, stripped and burned. Could get no more than 6' of water a mile out.

FROLIC • Tender

October 18, 1861

Series I, vol. 16, p. 733

Mississippi River.

Drive up West Bay in 3' water.

Wrecked by gale—stripped and burned.

FULTON U.S.S. • Side Wheel Steamer

May 10, 1862

Series II, vol. 1, p. 89

Pensacola Navy Yard, Florida

Destroyed on Navy Yard Way S.

Tonnage: 698

Draft: Frwd: 9' 6'' Aft.: 10' 2''

Series II, vol. 1, p. 253

Battery:
3 guns

Series I, vol. 25, p. 456

Map

G

G.O. BIGELOW • British Schooner

December 9-16, 1863

Series I, vol. 9, p. 344

Bear Inlet, North Carolina

December 16, 1863—Scuttled and set fire, her crew having run her aground and abandoned her a few minutes before they got on board—was without cargo.

Series I, vol. 9, p. 377

Near the mouth.

GAINS • Reb Steam Sloop, Side Wheel Steamer (Wood)

Series I, vol. 20
Series II, vol. 2

Mobile, Alabama

6 guns

Run ashore in a sinking condition and abandoned.

Designed for 8 guns.

1st Lieut. J.W. Bennett

Sunk August 5, 1864, Battle Mobile Bay

Draft about 6'

Battery:
6 - VIII in broad side

Series I, vol. 21, pp. 441, 589

Beached near the hospital at Ft. Morgan.

Within 500 yards of Ft. Morgan.

Small arms & ammo landed—guns not spiked.

October 23, 1864—guns and machinery removed.

GALENA

Harper's Weekly
April 5, 1862, p. 220

Excellent full page view overall, gun deck and cross sectional mounting of guns with rope border for all.

Wrecked on Gay Head—Martha's Vineyard. Went out of commission July 23, 1890.

Tonnage: 738

Length: 210' Beam: 36' Depth: 12' 8'' Draft: 13'

Battery:
8 - IX 9'' Dahlgren
1 - 60# Parrott rifle
1 - 30# Parrott rifle
1 - light 12#

GALVESTON

January 1, 1863

Series I, vol. 21, p. 176

Captured.

Harriet Lane and Barks *Cavallo* and *Elias Pike* laden with coal.

Westfield—blown up.

Captured by *Bayou City*.

64# on lower deck and 32# on upper.
High pressure river boat and cotton piled as high as hurricane deck.

GARLAND U.S.S. • Bark, Stone Fleet

Series II, vol. 1, p. 90

Tonnage: 243

Length: 92' 5''   Beam: 24' 4''   Depth: 16' 6''   Draft: 12' 2''

Built at Quincy, Massachussetts, as privateer 1815. Rebuilt at New Bedford, Massachusetts, 1845.

GARONNE U.S.S. • Stone Fleet

Series II, vol. 1, p. 90

Petite Bois Channel

Paid for but never used for naval purposes.

GAZELLE • Schooner

Series I, vol. 5, p. 581

Yeocomico River

See *Charity*

GEN. BEAUREGARD • Blockade Runner

December 11, 1863

Series I, vol. 27, p. 554

Ft. Fisher, Virginia

A side wheel steamer, supposed to be the *Beauregard*, in attempting to run in was run on shore between the wrecks and Ft. Fisher by the U.S.S. *Howquah*.

GEN. BEAUREGARD C.S. • Ram, Steam

June 6, 1862

Series I, vol. 23

Off Memphis, Tennessee
Mississippi River, Defense Fleet

GEN. BEAUREGARD • Steam

December 12, 1863

Series I, vol. 9, pp. 355, 370

New Inlet

Charged ashore by blockaders above Ft. Fisher, near Batter (Gatlin) Gadin and set on fire.

Batteries about 5 miles and 10 miles above Fisher.

GEN. EARL VAN DORN C.S. • Ram

Series II, vol. 1, p. 253

Yazoo River, Mississippi

Burned by Confederates.

GENERAL FINEGAN • Sloop

May 28, 1864

Series I, vol. 17, pp. 709–12

Cargo removed and sunk.

GENERAL HUNTER U.S.A. • Trans.

April 16, 1864

Series I, vol. 15, p. 314

St. John's River, Florida

On way from Picolata (45 miles above) to this place (Jacksonville).

Sunk in 5 minutes—making a turn in channel.

Took place near wreck of *Maple Leaf.*

GEN. HUNTER U.S. • Army Steamer

April 16, 1864

Series I, vol. 15, p. 314

St. John's River, Florida

At a turn in the channel, blown off to leeward.

Near the wreck of the *Maple Leaf.*

Series I, vol. 35, pp. 1, 115, 387

In evacuating *Palatka*, transferred to *Picolata.* The Steamer *Hunter*, on a return trip from *Picolata*, having on board Quartermasters property, was destroyed by a torpedo near the wreck of the *Maple Leaf—Brig. Gen. John P. Hatch* to Gen. J.W. Turner, Jacksonville, Florida.

A large double stack side wheel steamer is sunk in St. John's River opposite mouth of Doctor's Lake, 15 miles above Jacksonville, Florida, supposed to be *Maple Leaf.*

GEN. LOVEL • Gunboat

Military & Naval History of the Rebellion, p. 168

In front of the City of Memphis, Tennessee

Sunk with 50# ball from rifled Parrot from Flagship *Benton.* Hit aft. above W.L., tearing great hole and sinking in 4 minutes in 75 ft. water.

GEN. M. JEFF THOMPSON C.S.S.

June 6, 1862

Series I, vol. 23
Series II, vol. 1, p. 253

Memphis, Tennessee

GENERAL MEIGS • Transport

Military & Naval History of the Rebellion, p. 443

Cape Fear

On the morn of June 24, 1862, the Blockader *Sumpter*, while cruising off Smith's Isl., in a dense fog, came into collision with the Transport *General Meigs*, from the effects of which she soon after sunk, being very rotten. The officers and crew got off in boats and were taken on board the Schooner *Jamestown*, but everything else in the ship went down with her.

GEN. POLK C.S.S. • Steamer, Man of War

June 26, 1862

Series II, vol. 1, p. 253

Yazoo River, Mississippi

Destroyed by Off.

Battery: 6

GEN. PRICE

Series I, vols. 23, 25

Former C.S. Ram *Sterling Price*.

General Sterling Price, Memphis, Tennessee

June 6, 1862.

Sold.

Series I, vol. 27, p. 54

February 21, 1865

4 guns.

GEN. QUITMAN C.S.S. • Steamer

Series I, vol. 18, p. 296

New Orleans, Louisiana

Known also as *Orizaba* and *Galveston*

Louisiana gunboat, destroyed April 24, 1862, below New Orleans.

Battery:
2 - 32#

GEN. RUSK • Foreign Name

October 7, 1862

Series I, vol. 19, p. 270

Marianao Creek, Cuba

Real name *Blanche* (417 ton) British Steamship.

Cargo: cotton; out of Texas, Pt. Lavaca

About 9 miles from Havana—near of opposite the village of Mariel, about 7 or 8 miles from; forced on shore (aground) within a marine league of beach—30 yards from beach. Capt. considered prudent to run in Marianao Creek.

GEN. SCOTT C.S. • Guard Boat

Series I, vol. 7

GENERAL WHITING • Small Steamer

April 15, 1865

Series I, vol. 12, p. 118

Raised.

GEORGE P. UPSHUN U.S.S. • Schooner, Stone Fleet

Series II, vol. 1, p. 94

Purchased at Baltimore, August 13, 1861.

GEORGE PAGE C.S. • Steamboat

March 9, 1862

Series I, vol. 5, pp. 23–25

Quantico Creek, off Potomac

Blown up and entirely destroyed when C.S.A. abandoned battery at cockpit and shipping points.

Series I, vol. 4, p. 725

See Potomac map.

March 17, 1862

To *George Page* to proceed to Quantico Creek and bring away what machinery left of *George Page*.

GEORGE PAGE C.S.S.

Series II, vol. 1
Series I, vol. 5

Burned at Quantico, Virginia

Sidewheeled steamer with 2 guns.

Name changed to *City of Richmond*.

GEORGE WASHINGTON • Army Steamer

April 19, 1863

Series I, vol. 14, p. 115

Coosaw River
Vic. Port Royal Ferry
Beaufort

U.S.S. *E.B. Hale* from Beaufort to four miles below Port Royal Ferry. Grounded on a shoal—*Washington* preceded Port Royal Ferry and returned.

When three miles below the ferry, sighted wreck of Washington abandoned, burned and sunk some 500 yards from shore at the edge of a marsh.

Series I, vol. 14, p. 127

Above brickyard and four miles below Port Royal Ferry shoal at brick yard.

May have been towed into Beaufort?

GEORGE WASHINGTON • Schooner

March 27, 1862

Series I, vol. 12, pp. 660–68

Santee River, South Carolina

3,200 bushels rice, 50 bushels corn, 20 bushels rice meal

Fired.

Inner channel communication between Santee and Charleston.

Proceed to Cape Roman Lighthouse—two schooners coming down Santee—boarded close to old sawmill.

Julia Worden got out but this one I couldn't on drawing too much water. Scuttled in two places and set on fire.

GEORGIA C.S. • Ironclad S. Floating Battery

Series I, vol. 16, p. 459

Savannah River

1st Lieutenant W. Gwathmey

Four guns as of November 5, 1864.

Series II, vol. 1, p. 254

Battery:
2 - 9'' Dahlgren S.B.
2 - 32# Rifles on broadside
1 - 32# Rifle

November 5, 1864, four guns

Destroyed by Confederates at fall of Savannah.

GEORGIA C.S.S. • Floating Battery

Series I, vol. 15, pp. 702–3

Savannah, Georgia

Description

Armed with five guns; four on broadside bearing on Ft. Jackson and one gun on extremity which is 32# rifled of 5,700#.

Broadside guns are two IX Dahlgren Smooth bore and two 32# rifled

Series I, vol. 16, pp. 482–94

December 1864

Crew left ship for Screven's Ferry at same time scuttling ship.

GEORGIANA

Series I, vol. 15, p. 659

Off Charleston, South Carolina

Mary Bowers, Blockade Runner, struck the wreck of the Steamer *Georgiana* off Long Island, about four miles east of Breack Inlet and one mile from the beach.

GEORGIANA • Blockade Runner

Series I, vol. 16, p. 37

Charleston, South Carolina

Off Long Island

GEORGIANA • British Steamer, Blockade Runner

March 19, 1863

Series I, vol. 13, pp. 754, 769,
771–72, 774–75
Series II, vol. 3, p. 740

Charleston, South Carolina

Chasing ashore.

Attempted to run in through Maffitt's Channel. Grounded her in 14' of water.

Filled with valuable cargo—rifled guns.

Fired.

Cargo saved: 8 enfields, 9 bayonets, 8 battle axes, 1 patent lead and line, 10# glue, 5 jars of preserves, 1 dozen guilt buttons, 1 table cover and 19 sabers.

Being within 3/4 miles from shore with an armament of guns and carriages in her hold.

2 miles to eastward of Breach Inlet.

Powerful screw steamer.

Tonnage: 407

150 horsepower

1 mile off and 2 miles up Long Isl. Beach.

GEORGIANA McCAW • Steamer

June 2, 1864

Series I, vol. 10, p. 114

Off Western Bar, Cape Fear River
Wilmington, North Carolina

Driven ashore by *Victoria*, U.S.S.

Of Liverpool, from Nassau

60 tons of cargo.

Lies in 10' of water, within easy range of Fort Caswell, Western Batt. and Ft. Campbell.

Saved 2 chronometers, 1 barometer, 1 sextant, 1 marine clock

Series I, vol. 11, p. 51

Under fire of Ft. Caswell and Bug Light batteries.

Probably 1/4 mile east of Batteries.

GERMANTOWN U.S. • Sloop

Series I, vols. 4, 5
Series II, vols. 1, 2
Series II, vol. 2, p. 78

Norfolk, Virginia

Scuttling and abandonment of raising wreck by Confederate.

April 20, 1861, at Norfolk Navy Yard

Battery:
20 guns

Tonnage: 939

Raised April 22, 1863.

Series II, vol. 1, p. 257

C.S.S. burned at evacuation of Navy Yard.

Norfolk, Virginia

Series I, vol. 5, p. 806

Arrangements being made to raise.

GILLUM

Series I, vol. 27, p. 683

Sabine Pass, Texas

September 3, 1864; at 7 p.m., picked up boat containing 9 men from wrecked steamer from New Orleans to Matamoros.

GLASCOW U.S.S. • Sidewheel Steamer

Series I, vol. 22, p. 188

Mobile, Alabama

2 guns

Sunk off Mobile on the Obstructions

Raised July 15, 1865

GLAUCUS U.S.

Series I, vol. 3, p. 394

Bahamas

Struck upon Molasses Reef near S.W. point of Great Inagua Isl. at 4 o'clock, December 8, 1864. Her gun deck battery was thrown overboard to lighten ship forward.

Sold.

Battery: October 28, 1863
1 - 100 Parrott rifle
2 - 30# rifle
8 - VIII 55 cwt.

GLEN COVE • Rebel Steamer

June 26, 1861

Series I, vol. 5, p. 748

James River

Running up James River—destroyed by fire.

GLIDE U.S.S.

February 7, 1863
Recovery of Battery

Series I, vol. 24, pp. 305–7, 354

Cairo, Illinois

Burned and sunk.

One mile below Cairo, Illinois, on Kentucky Show, was tin clad, stern wheeled steamer.

Battery:
6 - 24# Howitzers

The light draft gunboat glide was totally consumed by fire this morning at 1/2 past 5, expect to recover guns and machinery.

After burning sometime, she grounded about 2 miles below.

She drifted ashore at Ft. Holtz and burned to waters edge. Magazine did not explode but fixed ammunition seemed to fire slowly as shell and shrapnel continued to burst in the air for an hour after she grounded.

Lies in 5' of water on Kentucky shore.

February 12, 1863

All recovered.

GOLDEN AGE • Steamer

Series I, vol. 25

Yazoo River, Mississippi
(Greenwood)

15 miles out of Ft. Pemberton from mouth.

Sunk on bar.

GOLDEN GATE

Harper's Weekly
August 23, 1862, pp. 540–41

Mexico

Pacific Mail Co. Sidewheel Steamer, built 1850.

Burned at sea, July 27, 1862

Length: 285' Width: 38' Draft: 16'

Manzanilla—The steamers from S.F. call there to ship treasure from the mines of Columbia. About 300 miles south of Acapulco—on 27 at a 1/4 of S, 15 miles North of Manzanilla—the Steamer was headed for shore 3 1/2 miles distant. Struck the beach soon after 5:15. The ship burned to the waters edge and disappeared.

GOLDEN LINER • British Schooner

April 27, 1863

Series I, vol. 8, p. 828

Murrell's Inlet, South Carolina

Cargo: flour, brandy, sugar, coffee

Via entrance, a long pull close to heavily wooded land.

Landed on beach abreast ship—crossing narrow sand spit and wading marsh.

Boarded and destroyed.

Schooner lying in the inlet near the shore of this island.

GOLDEN ROCKET • Clipper

Series I, vol. 16, p. 599

Isle of Pines

Capt. Baily

Tonnage: 1,100

Taken and burned by Semmes of the Sumter

GOLDEN ROD

August 24, 1863

Series I, vol. 5, p. 345

Rappahannock River, Virginia

Stripped and burned near mouth of river because site drew too much to go up and cargo of coal.

GOOD HOPE • Schooner

April 18, 1864

Series I, vol. 17, pp. 607–9, 616, 683, 825

St. Martin's Reef, Florida

By *Fox* U.S. Schooner—   March 2, 1865, the Rob Roy
                            December 20, 1863, Powerful

Crossed St. Martin's Reef and stood to northward.

Run ashore and abandoned near the mouth of the Homosassa River.

150 Ton burden with cargo of salt and few dry goods.

Fired and consumed.

GOVERNOR

Series I, vol. 27, p. 382

The *Rhode Island* touched at Port Royal to communicate with Flag Off. Dupont—received from Frigate Wabash officer and crew off wrecked Steam. Gov.—November 19, 1861.

GOVERNOR • Transport

November 2, 1861

Series I, vol. 12, p. 233

Off Port Royal, South Carolina

Reports of Maj. Reynolds, U.S. Marine Corps (Aboard, Capt. Ringgold, U.S.S. *Sabine* Rescue Ship, Act. Master, Weidman, Off Gov.)

Saved nearly all arms, ammunition and clothing.

GOVERNOR MOORE C.S.S.

April 24, 1862

Series I, vol. 18, pp. 201, 208, 215, 296, 304-9, 315-17, 359, 723, 779

New Orleans, Louisiana
(below New Orleans)

Formerly *Charles Morgan.*
2 - 32# rifled guns

Tonnage: 1200

93 men

GOV. MOREHEAD

July 20, 1863

Series I, vol. 9, p. 164

Tarboro, North Carolina

Gen. Potter destroyed this and two unarmed River Steamboats; one of iron, sternwheel, drawing 20 inches and the *Gen. Hill,* drawing 6' and sternwheel, along with gunboat building on stocks.

There was then a high flood in the river.

GRAMPUS C.S.S.

January 11, 1863

Series I, vol. 22

GRAMPUS #2

January 11, 1863

Series I, vol. 24, p. 136

Memphis, Tennessee

Ran her to Reg Ferry Landing at Mound City, 5 miles above Memphis—there were with the *Grampus* 5 goal boats which were turned loose and sank.

Fired, floated to the foot of the Isl. that is opposite Mound City.

Stripped.

GRAMPUS, NO. 2 • **Steamer**

January 11, 1863

Series I, vol. 22, p. 721

Mississippi River

Sunk on abandoning island No. 10.

Mississippi River —4 steamers afloat have fallen into our hands and 2 others with the Rebel Gunboat *Grampus*, are sunk, but will be easily raised.

Mounted 2 or 3 brass field pieces.

Series I, vol. 23, p. 107

Steamboat with powerful pump with which I designed to raise the Rebel boat, the *Grampus*—Rept.—May 25, 1862

GRAND DUKE

December 1863

Series I, vol. 25, p. 685

Shreveport, Louisiana

Burned.

GRANITE CITY • **Confederate Steamer**

January 21, 1865

Series I, vol. 22, p. 17

Former U.S.S. *Granite City* .

Chased ashore near Velasco, Texas.

Sidewheeled steamer—iron hull

Tonnage: 450

Length: 160' Beam: 23' Depth: 9' 2'' Draft fwd.: 4'
Draft aft.: 5' 6''

Battery:

6 - 24# Howitzers

1 - 12'' rifle pivot gun

1 - 20'' Parrott rifle

No cargo.

Ran ashore 1/2 mile N.E. of entrance to Velasco under the enemy's batt.

About 25 persons aboard.

GRATITUDE • Schooner and
CHARLES HENRY • Schooner

February 24, 1864

Series I, vol. 5, p. 592

Wicomico River

Near head.

GREENLAND • Bark

July 1864

Series I, vol. 10, p. 429

At sea of Cape Henry, Virginia

Position nearly corresponds with that given by Capt. Ridgely of the *Shenandoah*.

GREENWOOD

Series I, vol. 25

Yazoo River

15 miles below, in Yazoo, 4 boats sunk across channel—burned to water's edge.

Scotland, R.J. Lockland, John Walsh and *Golden Age*.

GYPSY • Confederate Trade Boat

July 19, 1863

Series I, vol. 24, p. 268

Bayou Larto, off Red River

2 miles up and burned the trading boat.

H

HAMPTON C.S.S. • Screw Steamer, Wood

April 4, 1865

Series II, vol. 1, p. 255

Burned at Richmond, Virginia

Tonnage: 80

Burned by Confederates.

Battery:
1 - 8'' pivot forward
1 - 8'' pivot aft.

HANNAH

August 12, 1862

Series I, vol. 19, p. 151

Corpus Christi, Texas

Ran across the bay to Corpus Christi when the Sloop *Hannah* was also run ashore and burned.

Series I, vol. 19, p. 783

Did not pass—stood back for town intending to run on flats—was run on shore above the town on a bold bank at least 4' high.

HANNAH • Armed Sloop

August 12, 1862

Ex. Doc. 253-(279)-295
40th Congress, 2nd Session

Corpus Christi, Texas, by Arthur

Burned by Rebels.

HANNAH • Rebel

Series I, vol. 9, p. 618

Corpus Christi, Texas

Jack Sands, Capt., in trying to get over Nueces Reef Channel, was blocked by the *Elma* or *Major Minter,* which was grounded and on fire—fearing the explosion of powder on board, came around and stood for the town. The boat was run on shore above the town on a bold bank at least 4' high. The enemy came to anchor 400 yards. Fearing they would cut her out and immediately fired her and she was consumed.

HANNIBAL • Steamer

About October 2, 1863

Series I, vol. 25, p. 443

Donaldsonville, Louisiana

She is sunk to her guards near the left bank, just around the first point above Donaldsonville—she is within easy range (3,100 yards) of our 100# rifle.

Cargo being removed.

HANOVER • Schooner

May 10, 1863

Series I, vol. 20, p. 177

Galveston, Texas

Off Galveston, 11:15 a.m., received orders to chase strange vessel. Steamed southward and westward. At 12:30 p.m., sail in sight from deck. Made all sail and steam in chase. At 1:30 p.m., fired a shell from XI inch and rifle guns. Schooner heading in toward beach flying English flag. At 2:15, schooner ran ashore. At 3:15, cutter crew boarded and set on fire—horsemen advancing from direction of Galveston. Shelled beach. At 4:00 p.m., schooner in full blaze.

HARRIET A. WEED U.S. • Army Steamer

May 10, 1864

Series I, vol. 15, pp. 426–30

St. John's River, Florida

Torpedoed.

Between Trout Creek to Daniels (Dame's) Point.

On her way to the bar and following the Boston exterior side of channel in from 10' to 12' of water.

HARRIET DeFORD • 1 Mast Propeller, Steamer, U.S. Transport

April 7, 1865

Series I, vol. 5, pp. 545, 551, 552

By *Commodore Read*, U.S.S.

Was in Indian Creek (off Potomac River?) Rappahannock River

Burned to waters' edge in Dimer's Creek, Virginia—fired into to destroy machinery.

Got aground several times and threw some of the cargo overboard.

April 22, 1865

Gun whereabouts not known.

April 29, 1865

Gun recovered (Brass 6# Trunnion piece).

HART • Confederate Ironclad Steamer

Series I, vol. 20, p. 380

Bayou Teche, Louisiana

Nearly raised when heard of the arrival of our gunboats. It was immediately sunk and now lies under water—July 28, 1863—U.S.S. *Clifton.*

HARVEST U.S.S. • Bark, Stone Fleet

Series II, vol. 1, p. 99

Tonnage: 314

Purchased October 21, 1861

At New Bedford, Massachusetts

HARVEST MOON U.S.S.

March 1, 1865

Series I, vol. 16, p. 282

Winyah Bay, South Carolina
Georgetown

Proceeded down river by Marsh Channel, when about 3 miles from Batt. *White.*

Sank in 2 1/2 fathoms.

Ship sank in Swash Channel, Winyah Bay, 3 miles S.E. by E. from Batt. *White* in 2 1/2 fathoms.

Flagship for Rear-Admiral Dahlgren.

Sank in 5 minutes.

HARVEST MOON U.S.S.

Sunk March 1, 1865, by torpedo

Series I, vol. 16, p. 371

Winyah Bay, South Carolina
Georgetown, South Carolina

Below Battery *White* (Mount 15 gun) which is about 8 1/2 miles up from entrance—from entrance to Georgetown is 11 1/2 sea miles.

Series I, vol. 16, pp. 282–86

Dropped down to Battery *White* 2 or 3 miles below Georgetown—this morning early, weighed anchor and steamed down the bay. She had not proceeded far when explosion took place.

At 7:15, got under way and proceeded down the river through Marsh Channel, tug "*Clover*" in company.

At 7:45, when about 3 miles from Battery *White*—sank in 5 minutes in 2 1/2 fathoms.

Sank in Swash Channel, Winyah Bay, 3 miles S.E. by E. from Battery *White* in 2 1/2 fathoms.

Sidewheeled steamer
Tonnage: 546

Length: 193' Beam: 29' Depth: 10' Draft: 8'

Maximum speed 15 mph—average speed 9 mph

Battery:
4 - 24# Howitzers
1 - 20# Parrott rifle
1 - 12# rifle

Wreck abandoned after taking out machinery, etc.

HATTERAS

*Military & Naval History
of the Rebellion*, p. 280

Off Galveston, Texas

On 11 Jan. 1863, about 3 p.m., as the Federal Squadron, consisting of the steamers *Brooklyn*, *Hatteras* and five others were cruising off Galveston, a vessel hove in sight at the southeast, which the *Hatteras* was ordered to proceed to and learn her character. As she came in sight she appeared to be trying to escape. Just after dark, the officers of the *Hatteras* perceived she was bark rigged and set a top gallant sail; as they approached found her lying to under steam. Both started ahead under full steam exchanging broadsides as fast as they load and fire. The heavy guns of the *Alabama* soon disabled the *Hatteras* and 2 guns fired to leeward. She soon sank. Officers and crew paroled in Kingston, Jamaica.

Debris washed ashore on Mustang, Isl.

Series I, vol. 2, p. 18

28 miles S.E. of Galveston (4 - 32#, 2 - 30# Parrott Rifle, 20# Rifled Gun).

Series I, vol. 19, pp. 507–8

The wreck lies 9 1/2 fathoms, about 20 miles, south true from Galveston Light House.

Mastheads standing upright and out of water. Tops and gaffs awash.

Series I, vol. 19, p. 837

February 10, 1863

Mounting 3 rifled guns and 4 32#.

HATTERAS U.S.S.

Sunk January 11, 1863

Series I, vol. 2, p. 18
Series I, vol. 19

Off Galveston, Texas

Lt. Commander Blake, U.S. Navy

28 miles S.E. of Galveston

8 guns

4 - 32# Short
2 - 30# Parrot Rifled
1 - 20# rifled gun

Sunk in 10 minutes—battle; 13 minutes

By C.S.S. *Alabama*—Capt. Semmes, C.S.N.

Sidewheeled iron steamer
3 masted schooner

Tonnage: 1,136

Length: 210' Beam: 34' Depth: 18'

Battery: October 31, 1861
4 - 32# 27 cwt.
1 - 20# rifle

HATTERAS INSLET • Chart and Channel

Harper's Weekly
February 15, 1862, p. 103

Anchorage of Burnside Exp.

Ships sunk by bad weather.

HAVANAH

June 5, 1862

Series I, vol. 17, p. 262

Dead Man's Bay, Florida

Destruction of Steamer *Havana* (*Hanna*); June 5, 1862

Series I, vol. 17, p. 664

Destruction of Schooner, March 2, 1864

Series I, vol. 17, p. 825

Destruction of Schooner *Rob Roy,* March 2, 1865.

Havanah fired by crew when almost finished unloading cargo of lead by Tender *Ezilda* (U.S.S. *Somerset*). At time boarded, had on deck 10 tons lead which melted and sank with vessel.

Rob Roy, at Belize Honduras, anchored S. side of bay near shore—tried to run but could not make it and ran ashore and fired—cargo: cavalry sabers and farming and mechanical implements; 60 ton.

HAVELOCK • Blockade Runner

June 10, 1863

Series I, vol. 14, p. 252

Charleston, South Carolina

On shore north end Folly Isl. on fire—which did not destroy vessel.

Large sidewheel steamer

Within 800 yards of lowest rebel batt. on Morris Ils., nearly high and day at low water.

200 yards off shore.

HAVELOCK • Steamer

June 5, 1863

Series I, vol. 14

Known also as *Beauregard.*

HEBE

Military & Naval History
of the Rebellion, p. 443

Wilmington, North Carolina

August 18, 1863—the Steamer attempted to run into Wilmington by the New Inlet entrance; but being intercepted by the *Niphon*, she headed for shore a few miles above Ft. Fisher. Hard aground in 7' water.

HEBE • Sidewheel Steamer

August 18, 1863
Destroyed August 23, 1863

Series I, vol. 9, pp. 158, 165–67

Driving ashore.

Run ashore and destroyed.

Attempting to run into Wilmington by New Inlet entrance. Ran ashore in 7' water a few miles above Ft. Fisher (on Federal Point). Shore within 10 rods.

Set on fire by boats from *Niphon.*

Is an iron prop. like *Kate.*

2 guns (one Whitworth) captured and brought off from beach.

About 9 miles from Fisher on narrow and low beach between sounds and ocean. About same distance from city.

August 24, 1863

Hebe 8 miles north of Ft. Fisher.

Cargo: drugs, coffee, clothing.

HELEN • Sloop

Series I, vol. 17, pp. 406, 409

Bayport, Florida

Burned off Crystal River, Florida.

Loaded with corn shelled.

Lying in shore south of the harbor.

HELEN • Steamer

Series I, vol. 9, p. 802

At sea

HELENA • Barge

December 11, 1863

Series I, vol. 20

HENRY ANDREW • U.S.S.

August 24, 1862

Series I, vol. 7, p. 674

Cape Henry

Went on shore and bilged—15 miles south of Cape Henry—have sent tug for men and her guns. Powder and rifle shells lost. 20# Parrott, paymaster's stores saved.

15 miles south of Cape Henry in a gale.

Propeller steamer.

Tonnage: 177

Length: 150' Beam: 26' Depth: 7' 6''

Battery:
2 - 32# 33 cwt.
1 - 20# Parrott rifle

HENRY CLAY • Steamer Transport

April 16, 1863

Series I, vol. 23, p. 409

Mississippi River
Vicksburg, Mississippi
Vicksburg Batteries

Through carelessness of her fireman, caught fire in passing and was soon ablaze all over.

Military & Naval History
of the Rebellion, p. 346

April 16, 1862—The *Clay* became a great blazing mass that floated down the river until it disappeared below Warrenton. The fact of her floating so far shows that her hull was uninjured.

These boats took a quantity of supplies for the Army cargo—50,000 rations.

HENRY W. JOHNSON • Wrecking Schooner

Series I, vol. 11, p. 207

Belonging Johnson & Higgins, New York.

Issac Walling, Mate Commencement of War.

HENRY NUTT • Schooner

September 28, 1861

Series I, vol. 6, pp. 263, 273

Hatteras Inlet

Cargo: Mahogany

Found hard aground near upper bulkhead, when I entered the inlet and forced her down to lower bulkhead, where she now is hard aground.

September 30, 1861

Afloat and ready for sea.

HERALD U.S.S. • Ship, Stone Fleet

Series II, vol. 1, p. 101

Purchased New Bedford, October 24, 1861.

Tonnage: 274

HERCULES • Steamer

February 17, 1863

Series I, vol. 24, pp. 136, 423

Memphis, Tennessee

Captured opposite Memphis on Ark side and burned on spot with seven coal boats while under fire of gunboats. Lying at Memphis Wharf.

Landed at a point on the Ark shore. Set on fire by Rebels and burned to water. One coal barge sunk with her.

HERO U.S.S. • Stone Fleet

Series II, vol. 1, p. 102

Purchased August 13, 1861, at Baltimore, Maryland.

HINES and Unknown Gunboat

Prior to March 4, 1864

Series I, vol. 26, pp. 10, 17

Mouth of Arkansas River and Devall's Bluff
Believed on White River

I regret the loss of the gunboat and the *Hines*.

Your communication of February 23, 1864—
The foolish move up the Ark has sunk one gunboat and shot up another—*Porter*.

HOPE • Steamer

Series I, vol. 26, p. 452

She was lost by one of our vessels being driven into her during a gale—owners
justified at $7,500—July 1, 1864.

HOPE • Steamer

February 17, 1864

Series I, vol. 25, p. 767

Collision with U.S.S. *St. Clair*

Pay owners $7,500—one of our vessels being driven into her in a gale of wind.

Sold at public auction.

Wind strong, a little up the river and on the city shore.

HORIZON • Steamer

Series I, vol. 25, p. 45

Near Port Gibson
Below Grand Gulf, Mississippi.

I was down to the *Horizon* yesterday and succeeded in getting out 3 gun cartridges
and guns if still aboard—May 27, 1863.

The boat has not moved any.

June 5, 1863

Careened with falling water and only 2 caissons found—others may have slipped
overboard in 5 fathoms.

Believe between Pt. of Rocks (Rock Hill Point) at mouth of Big Black and Grand
Gulf.

HORNET • Steam Torpedo Boat

February 19, 1865

Series I, vol. 12, p. 185
Series I, vol. 11, p. 810

James River, Virginia

Sunk above the graveyard by collision with the *Allison*.

HOUSATONIC U.S.S. • Screw Steamer

Sunk February 17, 1864
Off Charleston, South Carolina

Series I, vol. 15, pp. 328–29, 331,
333–34, 336, 338

About 9 p.m., while lying at anchor in 27' of water off Charleston, South Carolina, bearing E. S.E. and distant from Ft. Sumter about 5 1/2 miles—wind moderate from N.W. and tide half ebb, ships head about W.N.W.

12 guns

Nine months later, sitting in upright position and settled in sand about 5', much worm eaten. Coal is scattered about her lower decks as well as muskets, small arms and rubbish.

Propeller is in upright position.

Area dragged for 500 yards around wreck for torpedo boat—nothing.

Sank stern first and healed to port. Span deck 15' below water.

U.S.S. *Canandaigua* steamed by *Housatonic* and took up near old Anchorage in 5 fathoms—*Sumter* bearing N.W. 1/2 W. and Breach inlet N.N.W.

February 17—bearing of vessels at sundown was *Wabash* S. 1/4 E.—*Mary Sanford* N.N.E., *Houstonic* N.N.E. 3/4 E., *Paul Jones* N.N.E.

Tonnage: 1,240

Length: 207' Beam: 38' Depth: 16' 10'' Draft Fwd.: 7' 7'' Draft Aft.: 9' 7''

Battery:
1 - 100# Parrott rifle
3 - 30# Parrott rifle
1 - XI 11'' Dahlgren S.B.
2 - 32# 33 cwt.
1 - 12'' rifle
2 - 32# cwt.

Series I, vol. 16, p. 427

Gunboat sunk off Battery Marshall.

Our Naval Heritage, p. 264

The submarine *Hundley* out from Charleston to attack U.S.S. *Housatonic*. Corvette of 1264 tons. Her torpedo sank both.

*Military & Naval History
of the Rebellion*, p. 645

On February 17, the Gunboat *Housatonic* was destroyed by a torpedo off Charleston.

HUNLEY C.S. • Torpedo Boat

October 15, 1863

Series I, vol. 15, p. 692

Charleston, South Carolina

Sank today while going under receiving ship.

Capt. H.L. Hunley

October 18, boat located preparing to recover.

HUNLEY C.S.S. • Sub Torpedo Boat

February 17, 1864

Series II, vol. 1, pp. 255–56

Off Charleston, South Carolina

Sunk with U.S.S. *Housatonic*, which she torpedoed.

Internal height 5', breadth 4'.

HUNTRESS • Blockade Runner

Series I, vol. 8, p. 458

Charleston, South Carolina

Huntress destroyed while running blockade into Charleston.

HUNTSVILLE C.S.S. • Ironclad Steamer, Floating Battery

Series II, vol. 1, p. 256

Mobile, Alabama
Spanish River

4 guns

Sunk 12 miles above Mobile at evacuation of city.

I

IBERVILLE • Steamer

Series I, vol. 1, pp. 18–20, 22, 25–26

Red River, Louisiana

Grounding of vessel.

Got off

IDA U.S.S. • Steam Tug

Series I, vol. 22, p. 131

Mobile Bay, Alabama

Blown by torpedo in main ship channel near Choctaw Pass, April 13, 1865, near Mobile Bay.

Wreck was sold.

Tonnage: 124

1 gun

Guns taken off, April 15, 1865

INDIA U.S.S. • Ship, Stone Fleet

Series II, vol. 1, p. 107

Purchased November 14, 1861, at New Bedford.

Tonnage: 366

INDIAN #2

July 19, 1862

Series I, vol. 19, p. 76

Sabine to Beawick Bay

Capt. E.H. Skaggs professed gambler and speculator as well as planter in Louisiana—lives in New Orleans.

Account of confiscation of part of cargo and ensuing receipt for goods from Geo. F. Emmons, Commander, U.S.S. *Hatteras* and subsequent presentation for payment $5,000.00 from D.G. Farragut.

Commanding West Gulf Block, Sq.

INDIAN CHIEF C.S.S.

Series II, vol. 1, p. 257

Charleston, South Carolina

Burned at Charleston, South Carolina.

Receiving ship at Charleston, South Carolina.

INDIANOLA U.S.S. • Ironclad Gunboat

Military & Naval History
of the Rebellion, p. 341

Louisiana

174' long, 50' beam, 10' from top deck to keel—8' 4'' clear, her side for five feet down were 32'' thick, having beveled stick of oak laid outside the hull proper. Outside of this was 3'' thick plate iron. Her deck as 8'' solid with 1'' iron plate. Her casemate stood at an angle of 26 1/2° and was covered with 3'' iron, as was her ports and heavy grating on top of casemates. Coal bunkers 7' thick alongside her boilers. She had seven engines, 2 for sidewheels, 2 for propellers and 2 for capstans and one for supplying water and working bilge and fire pumps. Forward casemate 2 11'' Dahlgren and after casemate, two 9'' and one gun on each side (8?)

Queen of the West and the *Webb*

Captured, run ashore in danger of sinking. Blown up by Confederates near where she was taken. February 24. Mouth of the Big Black. Not a gun was saved.

Series I, vols. 23, 24

February 13–24, 1863
Examination of wreck.

Sunk by the C.S. *Queen of the West* and *Will H. Webb*.

Raising of.

Series I, vol. 24, pp. 403, 405,
411, 446, 543, 552, 572, 738

Vicksburg, 30 miles off

2 - 6# field pieces thrown overboard by wrecking party on approach of false mortar boat.

April 11, 1863

Drew 6 1/2'

Immediately opposite Jo Davis's Plantation.

Sand bar dry 6 mos. of year beinning June.

(1 - 1X ing gun lost overboard and believed sunk deep in sand.)

April 17, 1863

Much shattered—Reb got two 9 inch guns, one 11' hurst and the other fell overboard and lying alongside in 9' of water.

April 20, 1863

1 - 9'' gun fell overboard and cannot be found. 25 miles below Vicksburg.

> Series I, vol. 24, p. 403

Just above New Carthage, near the foot of Palmyra Isl.

> Series I, vol. 25, p. 738

Palmyra Isl. called Hurricane Isl.

> Series I, vol. 24, pp. 381, 391–92, 394

February 24, 1863

Below Vicksburg, Mississippi River

The IX inch guns were thrown overboard and the others disabled.   XI placed muzzle to muzzle.

Below Warrenton

I knew it was as much as I could do to get by the *Warrenton* batteries before daylight the next morning (9:30 p.m.)

Towing two coal barges at sides.

Bow run ashore.

He was about 13 miles below our batt. at Vicksburg when he first saw the enemy and it was 1/2 hour after *Queen of the West* hove in sight before he was struck by her. Engaged nearly 2 hours (1' 27'')

> Series I, vol. 24, pp. 391–93

Just passed Grand Gulf and on evening of same day were just above the head of Upper Palmyra Isl. when at 9:30 discovered lights of vessels in pursuit 4 miles astern—

At 20'' before 10, she was turned about and headed downstream, when fight immediately commenced.

Grounded and sunk on sand bar in 10' water opposite head of lower Palmyra Isl.— opposite side of river from Louisiana.

Ships involved:
  C.S.S. *Webb*

C.S.S. *Dr. Beaty*
C.S.S. *Grand Era*
C.S.S. *Queen of the West*

Nothing saved before being blown up by fake mortar boat.

Series I, vol. 24, p. 397

Shows bow and upper works out near Mr. Joe Davis's Plantation (President).

Series I, vol. 20, p. 4

Sold.

March 19, 1863

About 10 miles above Grand Gulf on right bank of river, saw wreck of *Indianola*.

Series I, vol. 25. pp. 172, 182,
218

Regarding inspection of *Indianola*, as to raising and deliver to St. Louis for 20,000 from Bureau of Construction.

9'' gun exhumed and ready for transport.

Letter reporting agent's findings and the *Indianola* already caulked and lying on sand bar, Palmyra Isl, waiting for a rise in water and with certainty can raise *Cincinnati* and recover a great deal of property there.

INDUSTRY • Schooner

February 2, 1863

Series I, vol. 8, p. 499

New Topsail Inlet, North Carolina

Tonnage: 200

About 5 miles north headed south 160 yards from beach—sunk in 3 fathoms.

Cargo: salt.

IONA • Blockade Runner

Series I, vol. 9, p. 539

Consul at Queenstown reports she foundered 24 hours after leaving Queenstown.

IRON AGE U.S.S. • Screw Steamer

January 10, 1864

Series I, vol. 9, p. 396

Grounded January 11, 1864

Lockwood's Folly Inlet, North Carolina

Tonnage: 424

Length: 144'   Beam: 25'   Depth: 12' 6''
Battery:
3 - 30# Dahlgren rifles
6 - VIII 8'' Dahlgren S.B.

In attempting to tow off the *Bendigo*, beached 1/2 mile west of Lockwood's Folly Inlet.

Series I, vol. 9, p. 399

Drawing 9' 6' aft. and 8' forward, 5' on starboard side, 4' on port.

Grounded by slight current to east. May have grounded 2 1/4 fathoms.

Threw over gun deck battery 1 and 4 at 8' 5 on port side at 4:00, fired and, 5:40, she blew up—morning of 11th, at high water p.m. had only 7' alongside.

Series I, vol. 9, p. 437

Parrott rifle from *Iron Age* recovered by C.S.A.

IRONSIDES • Iron Clad Frigate

Harper's Weekly
August 23, 1862, p. 535

240' Long   Berth
58' 6'' wide   Gun and
25' Deep   Spar Deck
Draws 16'

Tonnage: 3,250

Frames white oak and average thickness of sides, 20'' iron plating 4' below W.L. Brass. 4 Blade Propeller, 13' diameter.

16 - 11'' Dahlgren on gun deck
2 - 200# Parrott gun on spar deck

3 masts bark rigged

Built Philadelphia, Pennsylvania, Cramp & Son & Merrick & Son at foot of Reed Street.

IROQUOIS

Harper's Weekly
August 16, 1862, p. 526

Bark rigged.

6 heavy guns.

2nd class steam sloop screw

Tonnage: 1,016

6 guns

Built New York 1858

ISAAC N. SEYMOUR • Steamer

February 20, 1862

> Series I, vol. 6, p. 591

Total loss—run on anchor—machinery and ordnance saved.

> Series I, vol. 6, p. 657

Stove hole in bottom with an anchor which had been left in the channel of the bulkhead by an army vessel and sank immediately in 9 1/2'—everything taken from her including most of machinery.

Anchor in the center and near the entrance to the Swash Channel in 7 1/2'.

> Series I, vol. 7, p. 415

May 22, 1862

Is again in commission and as good as new.

> Series I, vol. 7, p. 671

August 24, 1862

About 3 miles above New Berne, struck edge of a bank projecting nearly midway across river, 5' forward, 19' aft., grounded. Got off and started to fill—ran her on bank. Trying to raise her. All ammo saved.

> Series I, vol. 8, pp. 3, 82

Neuse River, North Carolina

Reported August 27, as sunk up Neuse River.

Investigation ordered.

Raised.

> Series I, vol. 6, p. 452

Raising of vessel.
Sinking of, February 20, 1862
Sinking of, August 24, 1862

2 - 32# of different weight

ISAAC SMITH U.S.S.

January 30, 1863

Series I, vol. 13, p. 557

Stono River

About 1 miles above Legareville and in a bend of the river.

Aground about 1/4 mile above the bend in river.

Steam escaping.

Has been towed up the Stono and under the guns of Ft. Pemberton.

ISABEL • Schooner

May 18, 1863

Series I, vol. 20

Mobile Entrance, Alabama

Station—close to Swash Channel—saw vessel close under Ft. Morgan—aground within 200 yards.

Cargo: 200 bales cotton

Fired.

ISABEL (ISABELLA) • British Steamer, Blockade Runner

Captured May 28, 1864
Loss June 2, 1864

Series I, vol. 21, p. 305

Seized trying to run into Galveston, Texas. Prize sank near Quarantine Station either injured by fire of U.S.S. *Admiral* or crew before surrender.

Cargo: Powder, arm percussion caps, hardware and medicines.

On 2nd June, we hauled her alongside the bank of river and made her fast with hawsers and lines to the trees. During the night, she parted her fastenings, slid off the bank into deep water and sank.

ISLAND BELLE • Tug, Side Wheel Steamer

June 29–30, 1862

Series I, vol. 7, pp. 524, 724–25

Appomattox River
Gilliam's Bar

June 28, 1862

Tonnage: 123

Aground—burned to prevent capture

2 guns

Enemy felling trees on a bluff abreast of them.

Not being able to start her––stripped her and set her on fire.

ISLAND BELLE U.S.S. • Side Wheel Steamer

June 28, 1862

Series II, vol. 1, p. 110

Appomattox River

Tonnage: 123

Length: 100'   Beam: 20' 4''   Depth: 6' 7''

Battery:
1 - 32# 27 cwt.
1 - 12# rifle

ISONDIGA C.S.S. • Wood Steamer, Steam Gunboat

December 21, 1864

Series I, vol. 16, pp. 484, 489, 496–97

Savannah River, Georgia

Ashore above Pontoon Bridge in Black River.

Fired and abandoned.

Draft: 6' 6''

In attempting to come down to Screvens Ferry, grounded and was destroyed.

Series II, vol. 1, p. 256

3 Battery:
1 - 6.4 Brooke Rifle
1 - 9'' Dahlgren S.B.
?

IVANHOE • Blockade Runner, Steamer

June 30, 1864
Destroyed July 6, 1864

> Series I, vol. 21, pp. 797, 817

Chased ashore by U.S.S. *Glasgow*, former U.S.S. *Eugenie*.

Run on shore under the forts—under the fire of its guns—trying to get in.

Fire by boat party.

1 3/4 miles east of Ft. Morgan.

In 6' water—everything removed to beach.

IVY C.S.S. • Side Wheel River Steamer

1863

> Series II, vol. 1, p. 256

Yazoo River
Mouth Yazoo River

Tonnage: 454

Length: 191'   Beam: 28'   Depth of Hold: 9'

Battery:
1 - VIII 132'' rifle
2 - 24# brass Howitzers

April 1862—2 gun

Burned to avoid capture.

> Series I, vol. 24, p. 133

June 1, 1863

Found sunk near Liverpool Landing.

> Series I, vol. 25, p. 764

Directly opposite Liverpool and in the narrowest part of the river—to the right of her there is plenty of water.

J

J. APPLETON • Schooner (Revenue Cutter)

August 15, 1861

Series I, vol. 16, pp. 667–68

Edgemont Key, Florida

Directed to put her in blockade.

Tender to *Coyler*, U.S.N.

Parted the cables and went ashore near the lighthouse—driven on the beach 30'
above low water mark—stripped and burned.

J.A. BELL

Series I, vol. 20, p. 830

June 24, 1863

1 - 24# iron gun
1 - 12# Mountain Howitzer

October 27, 1863
1 - 32#

J.A. COTTON C.S. • Gunboat

January 13, 1863

Series I, vol. 19, pp. 519, 521

Teche River, Louisiana

Reported destroyed.

Swung across bayou and burned below Franklin, Louisiana.

Troops encamped 12 miles below Franklin on plantation of J.M. Carpenter.

Iron over her machinery.

J.C. DAVIS • Barge

Series I, vol. 5

J.F. PARGOOD

Series I, vol. 24, p. 671

Greenwood, Mississippi

Sunk at Greenwood.

J.J. CRITTENDEN U.S.S. • Stone Fleet

Series II, vol. 1, p. 111

Purchased May 19, 1863

Paid for but never in naval service.

J.P. SMITH • Steamer

November 7, 1862

Series I, vol. 19, p. 329

Bayou Cheval, Louisiana

See Osprey

J.W. PINDAR • British Schooner

November 17, 1862

Series I, vol. 8

JACKSON • Rebel Ram

Report of the Sect. of War VII,
p. 1246

Columbus, Georgia

On the 16th April 1865, Gen. Upton, with about 400 dismounted men, assaulted and carried the breast works of Columbus, saving by the impetuosity of his attacks, the bridges over the Chattahoochee and capturing 52 field guns in position, besides 1,200 prisoners.

The rebel ram *Jackson* nearly ready for sea and carrying an armament of 6-7'' guns, fell into our hands and was destroyed as well as the Navy yard, foundries, the arsenal and armory, sword and pistol factory.

Report of the Sect. of War VII
p. 142

Thence, a forced march direct on Columbus and another on West Point, both of which places were assaulted and captured on the 16th. At the former place, we got 1,500 prisoners and 52 field guns, destroyed two gunboats, the navy yard foundries, arsenal, many factories and much other public property.

JACKSON C.S. • Gunboat

Series I, vol. 22, p. 259

Columbus, Georgia

32 miles below Columbus on a shoal and badly burned amidships.

Guns, engines and armor are in her bottom partly melted by fire.

JACKSON C.S.S. • Side Wheel River Steamer, Tug

Series II, vol. 1, p. 257

New Orleans, Louisiana

Sunk by Confederates at fall of New Orleans.

2 pivoted S.B. 32#

JACOB BELL U.S.S. • Sidewheel Steamer

November 6, 1865

Series II, vol. 1, p. 111

At sea

Tonnage: 229

Length: 141' 3'' Beam: 21' Depth: 8' 1''

Battery:
1 - VIII Dahlgren S.B.
1 - 32# - 32 cwt.
1 - 30# rifle
1 - 12 Heavy S.B.

Lost while being towed to New York by U.S.S. *Banshee*.

JACOB MUSSELMAN • Steamer

January 6, 1863

Series I, vol. 24, p. 136

Memphis, Tennessee

Ran her to Bradley Landing, 15 miles above that point - probably close to Arkansas side.

Stripped.

JAMESTOWN

Series I, vol. 8, p. 69

Ft. Darling, Virginia
James River

Sunk in barrier above.

JAMESTOWN C.S.S. • Sidewheel Steamer

May 1862

Series II, vol. 1, p. 257

James River, Virginia
Drewry's Bluff

Battery:
2 - Guns

JANE • Schooner

Ex. Doc. 253-(279)-295
40th Cong., 2nd Sess.

Rio Brazos, Texas

October 1863, off Rio Brazos.

Destroyed by *Tennessee*

Series I, vol. 20, p. 632

of Nassau, New Providence

Explosion heard at Galveston, 30 miles distant.

JANE WRIGHT • Sloop

August 16, 1861

Series I, vol. 4, pp. 616, 624

Potomac River

Left Washington down river about 1 hour after sunrise near Smith's Point (Smith's Isl.)

Also T.W. Riley probable vicinity.

Smith's Point opposite Aquia Creek Landing.

River is 3 1/2 mile wide.

JEFFERSON DAVIS • Privateer

*Military & Naval History
of the Rebellion*, p. 62 (Western Pub.)

St. Agustine, Florida

Former Slaver *Echo*, full rigged brig.

32# amidships on pivot and on each side
a 32 # and 12 #.

Crew: 260

Prizes listed

August 17, grounded crossing bar at St. Augustine, Florida.
6:30 Sunday morning—grounded on north breakers starboard. Guns thrown overboard to lighten but caused her to bilge—all small arms saved in lighter boats.

The brig became a total loss.

The Civil War in America, p. 430

Ran aground at the entrance to the port of St. Augustine and was lost.

JOHN ALEXANDER U.S.S. • Schooner, Stone Fleet

Series II, vol. 1, p. 114

Purchased August 13, 1861, at Baltimore, Maryland.

JOHN F. CARR • Reb. Gunboat, Steamer

January 1, 1864

Series I, vol. 20, p. 743

Matagorda Bay, Texas

Matagorda Peninsula

Driven on by north gale—aground in the bay in the morning. The Reb. Steamer was ashore and destroyed by fire.

Union troops landed at Smith's Landing, 7 miles below mouth of the Caney, to cut off Reb pickits on Peninsula.

Union troops retreated down beach from Reb gunboat shelling and embarked them about 15 miles from Pass Cavallo.

While getting under way, lost anchor and 45 fathoms of chain (U.S. Sloop *Monongahela*) in 2 1/2 fathoms.

Natural driftwood Redan of fight, 20 miles above.

Draft: 4'

Battery:
1 - 18#
1 - 24# Howitzer

JOHN McHALE U.S.S. • Canal Boat, Stone Fleet

Series II, vol. 1, p. 115

Purchased July 19, 1864, at Philadelphia, Pennsylvania.

Tonnage: 122

Bought with 60 tons of stone on board and sent to Commodore Dorin at Baltimore, Maryland.

JOHN MITCHELL U.S.S. • Canal Boat, Stone Fleet

Series II, vol. 1, p. 115

Purchased July 19, 1864, at Philadelphia, Pennsylvania.

Tonnage: 114

Sent to Baltimore, Maryland.

JOHN WALSH • Steamer

Series I, vol. 25

Yazoo River, Mississippi
(Greenwood)

15 miles of Ft. Pemberton from mouth.

Sunk on bar.

JOHN WARNER • Steamer

May 5, 1864

Series I, vol. 26

Red River, Louisiana

See *City Belle.*

JOHN WESLEY • Schooner (Center Board)

November 1, 1861

Series I, vol. 6, p. 382

Hog Island

In route to Hampton Roads.

At 3:15 p.m., passed outer buoy on Chincoteague bar.
Steered S. under all sail; wind N.E. by N., fresh at 4:00 p.m., gave course nothing to west S.S.W. At 7:00 p.m., shortly after struck Hog Isl, to lee and breakers to windward.

Schooner total loss on enemy's coast—armament destroyed. Breakers at a distance N. of wreck. Escape direction sand shoal, New Inlet ship shoal, Smith's Island.

Cargo: wood

JOSEPH H. TOONE

October 12, 1861

Series I, vol. 16, pp. 715, 728

Mississippi River
Slightly above head of the passes.

Leaky prize vessel from which they were coaling drifted on to the western bank with the three fire rafts after attack of Confederate Ram.

Jos. H. Toone

JOSEPHINE • Sloop

March 5, 1863

Series I, vol. 19, p. 649

Mobile, Alabama

Tonnage: 40 or 50

Aroostock at Station, 5 or 6 miles east of Ft. Morgan. Discovered sail close to beach trying to run into Mobile Bay. Beached and destroyed by gunfire and sea making breach over her.

JOSEPHINE TRUXILLO • Schooner

December 10, 1863

Series I, vol. 20

JOSIAH A. BELL C.S.S. • Gunboat, Cotton Clad Steamer

Series II, vol. 1, p. 257

Sabine Pass, Texas

Acquired and fitted out at Sabine Pass.

Battery: October 27, 1863
1 - 32#

Series I, vol. 19, p. 394

December 7, 1862: 2 - 64#, said to be rifled

Series I, vol. 19, pp. 559, 564–65

Cotton clad: 2 - 24# field pieces
<u>Uncle Ben</u>: 1 - 68# rifle

Flagship, 2nd Squadron, Magruder Fleet

January 23, 1863

Action with *Morning Light*—

1 - 8'' Columbiad bored as 6'' rifle under Lt. Dowling and on Ben.
2 unserviceable 12#, improperly mounted and with no shells to inspire confidence of men.

JUANITA • Mexican Schooner

Ex. Doc. 253-(279)-295
40th Cong., 2nd Sess.

San Luis Pass, Texas

April 11, off San Luis Pass, Texas, destroyed by *Virginia*.

Series I, vol. 21, p. 180

April 11, 1864

Prize—Light wind S.W.E. dispatched for New Orleans, April 11, 10:00 p.m.

April 12, discovered two miles distant inside the line of breakers with her head toward beach and nearly out of water—being of very light draft—abandoned.

JUBILEE U.S.S. • Stone Fleet

Series II, vol. 1, p. 115

Purchased November 28, 1861, at Portland, Maine.

Tonnage: 233

JUDAH

September 14, 1861

Series I, vol. 16, p. 670

Pensacola, Florida

Moored to the navy yard wharf.

Armed with a pivot and 4 broadside guns.

While burning, set free and drifted down opposite Ft. Barrancas, where she sunk.

Series I, vol. 16, p. 674

Note from Gideon Wells.

JULIA • Schooner, Blockade Runner

January 24, 1862

Series I, vol. 17, p. 77

Mouth of Mississippi River

Tonnage: 130

Bound out with cotton.

Remains grounded inside the bar at the mouth of the South Pass—also, unidentified afire and aground at S.E. pass.

JULIA BAKER • Schooner

March 11, 1864

Series I, vol. 9

JULIANA • Sloop

Series I, vol. 19, p. 639

Galveston, Texas

Seized and sunk by officer and crew of *Owasco*.

While in Galveston and since has gone to pieces—compensation claimed $300 by Mr. Nicholas Drovet, Sr. (French citizen).

JULIET U.S.S. (No. 4)

Series I, vol. 24

Isl. No. 10

Grounding of

Sold.

JULIUS

February 12, 1862

Series I, vol. 22, p. 821

Tennessee River at Florence

Burned to prevent capture.

K

KATE • Schooner, Blockade Runner of Nassau, New Providence

April 2, 1862

Series I, vol. 7, p. 196

Wilmington, North Carolina

They could not fetch into Lockwood's Folly Inlet—the wind fresh from N.E. Beached with all sails set.

Cargo: Salt

Fired and shelled

U.S.S. *Mount Vernon* returned to anchor at Bald Head, 13 miles

Borne three different names: *Leonora, Lucy C. Holmes* and *Kate*

KATE • Steamer

Cutting out of August 1, 1863
Ashore July 12

Series I, vol. 9, p. 120

Smith's Isl., North Carolina (?)

Tonnage: 344

Double-screw schooner rigged

Iron steamer driven on shore at full speed south end of Smith's Isl.

Burned 3 hours, plus XI & IX shells fired through her.

Sold.

KATE BRUCK C.S.S. • Schooner

Series II, vol. 1, p. 257

Chattahoochee River, Georgia

Sunk to obstruct

Battery: 2 guns

KATE DALE • Sloop

October 16-17, 1863

Series I, vol. 17, pp. 570, 573-79

Hillsboro River, Florida

Also *Scottish Chief*

Act. Rear Adm. Theodorus Baily and Capt. Semmes by armed expedition from U.S. Gunboat *Tahoma* and *Adela*—they were loaded with cotton and ready to sail—men landed at Ballast Point, Old Tampa Bay—line of march taken up for river—the vessels were on the opposite bank—2 miles above us—both vessels fired.

Ballast Point—about 5 miles below the town of Tampa.

Boats light draft—not over 4'

Western shore of bay

KEARSARGE U.S.S.

February 2, 1864

Series II, vol. 1, p. 119

Roncador Reef, approximately 220 E. of Nicaragua

13° 5'' N. Lat.
80° W. Long.

Battery: June 19, 1864
1 - 28# rifle
2 - XI Dahlgren S.B.
4 - 32# 42 cwt.

November 30, 1864
2 - XI Dahlgren SB
1 - 30# Parrott Rifle
1 - Light 12#
4 - 32#
4 - 32 cwt

October 1, 1865
Remove light 12#

Length: 201' 4''   Beam: 33' 10''   Depth: 16'   Draft: 13' 5''   Aft.: 14' 3''

KENSINGTON U.S.S. • Ship, Stone Fleet

Series II, vol. 1, p. 119

Purchased October 28, 1861

Tonnage: 357

KEOKUK U.S.S. • Twin Screw Steamer, Monitor, Iron

Sunk April 8, 1863, off south end of Morris Island, South Carolina

Series I, vol. 14, p. 213

Tonnage: 677

Length: 159' 6''   Beam: 36'   Depth: 13' 6''   Draft: 8' 6''

Battery:
2 - XI 11'' Dahlgren S.B.

Commander A.C. Rhind

Guns removed by C.S. May 7, 1863, by unbolting the turrents and taken off underwater and at night to remove them.

Series I, vol. 14, pp. 23, 37, 57,
74, 80, 86

At a distance of 550 yards of Ft. Sumter, close battle for 30 minutes, struck 90 times and hull pierced 19 at and just below waterline—Turrets pierced. Submerged to top of smokestack.

Two fractures in starb. bow and large one on port bow.

Sank in 17' water, about 1000 yards from Morris Island. Her armament; 2 XI inch Dahlgren taken out—C.S. Rep., May 24, 1863

3 1/2 miles from Ft. Sumter and 3/4 mile from Morris Isl.

Two turrets and 1 gun each.

Series I, vol. 14, p. 677

September 28, 1863—terms of contract for raising agreed.

Military & Naval History
of the Rebellion, p. 449

Charleston, South Carolina

Attack on Ft. Sumter. Within 550 yards of fort, struck 90 times, 19 piercing her at and below the water line—withdrew from action after 1/2 hour and got her to anchor out of range of fire. Kept afloat by pumps but sank next morning.

6 April 1863—side and turrent armor 5 1/2'' thick.

Inside the bar near Charleston.

Series I, vol. 15, p. 577

Stono Inlet, South Carolina

July 19, 1864—woodwork of structure to raise ironclad destroyed by worms.

KEY WEST U.S.S. (NO. 32) • Stern Wheel Steamer, Wood

Burned November 4, 1864

Series I, vol. 27, p. 284

Johnsonville, Tennessee

Tonnage: 207

Length: 156'   Beam: 32'   Depth: 4' 6''

Battery:
6 - 24# Howitzers
1 - 12# Rifle
2 - 24# S.B.

Recovered as of June 29, 1865, by A.V.C. Rogers of U.S.S. *Kate.*

1 - rifled brass 12#

KINGFISHER U.S. • Bark

March 28, 1864

Series I, vol. 15, pp. 383, 388

St. Helena Sound, South Carolina
Near Otter Isl.
Ashepoo River

Grounded on Combahee Bank

Started to move around into Coosaw Channel (between Combahee and Pelican Banks) at low tide, 6' water alongside, burying herself in sand.

All public property saved.

KINGFISHER U.S. • Bark, Wood

Wrecked March 28, 1864

Series I, vol. 15, pp. 384–88

St. Helena Sound, South Carolina

At St. Helena Island

Tonnage: 451

Length: 121' 4''   Beam: 28' 8''   Depth: 14' 4''

Battery:
4 - VIII 8'' Dahlgren S.B.
1 - 20# rifle
1 - light 12#

Grounded on Combahee Bank—had started for Coosaw Channel, put people close ashore on Otter Isl.

Copper bottomed and struck hard, starboard guns underwater.

Carried 4 to 6 fathoms till of S.E. point of Otter Isl. and Black Buoy on lower end of Combahee Bank, bore S. by E., 600 or 800 yards distant—water shoaled and put helm hard a starboard—headway 3 or 4 knots and tide about 1/2 flood, wind and tide on port beam.

KINGSTON • Side Wheel Steamer

July 24, 1864

Series I, vol. 5, p. 470

Chesapeake Bay

Tonnage: 200

Got aground on Diamond Marshes between Smith's Point and Windmill Point on the Virginia side.

Boarded and burned by Rebels—in charter to U.S. Government

KNICKERBOCKER • Steamer

February 15, 1865

Series I, vol. 5, p. 508

Smith's Point, Virginia

Between Smith's Point and Fleet's Point, Virginia.

Aground within 250 yards of beach.

Wreck entirely destroyed.

KOBB C.S. • Transport Steamer

Series I, vol. 22, p. 671

Florence, Alabama

Kane Creek near Florence, Alabama.

Heard they were sunk and had been raised but had seen no trace and doubt report— March 24, 1862, *Lt. Commanding Wm. Gwin, U.S. Gunboat Tyler*

KOSCIUSKO U.S.S. • Steamer

March 25, 1863

Series II, vol. 1, p. 123

Vicksburg, Mississippi

In passing batteries

Component of Ellet Marine Brigade

Called the *Lancaster* and changed to *Kosciusko*.

L

L. and R. SMITH • Schooner

November 23, 1864

Series I, vol. 11, p. 95

21 miles eastward of Cape Henry

Cargo: 353 tons of coal

L.C. RICHMOND U.S.S. • Ship, Stone Fleet

Series II, vol. 1, p. 123

Purchased October 25, 1861, at New Bedford, Massachusetts

Tonnage: 341

LAFAYETTE • Sloop

Series I, vol. 17, p. 208

Lost at sea.

Captured St. Andrews Bay, Florida, 4 April 1862.

Sprung a leak and foundered at sea while on way to Key West, Florida, from St. Andrews Bay.

LANCASTER • Ram

*Military & Naval History
of the Rebellion*, p. 345

Vicksburg, Mississippi

On March 25th, the Ram *Lancaster* was lost in attempting to run the batteries at Vicksburg in order to gain the fleet of Admiral Farragut below. The *Switzerland* got through badly cut up.

Series I, vol. 24, p. 515

She was struck with a shot and tumbled to pieces—she was a rotten, unserviceable vessel and would have sunk had she run into anything.

LANCASTER NO. 3 • **Ellet Ram**

March 25, 1863

Series I, vol. 20, pp. 20, 23–24, 30

Vicksburg Batteries
Vicksburg, Mississippi

Sunk near the lower end of our canal, blown up—sank rapidly—set ashore crew and set fire to upper works.

When opposite mouth of canal, Lt. Col. Ellet came alongside in a yawl.

Pulled through shell and grape nearly 2 miles to offer assistance to *Switzerland.*

LANCASTER U.S.S.

March 1863

Series I, vol. 23, p. 277

Mississippi River
Vicksburg, Mississippi

Instantly sunk by large ball entering her stern which appeared to have destroyed all her bottom timbers.

LAPWING • **American Bark**

Captured March 28, 1863
Destroyed June 20

Series I, vol. 2, p. 407

Also known as C.S. Bark *Oreto* tender to C.S.S. *Florida.*

Series I, vol. 3

Burned by own men when failing to meet C.S.S. *Florida* on Long. 30°, low on provisions.

Off Barbados, West Indies

Series II, vol. 1, p. 258

Burned and abandoned, June 20, 1863.

Battery:
2 - Howitzers

LAUNCH NO. 6 C.S.S. • **Steamer**

April 24, 1862

Series II, vol. 1, p. 258

Battery:
1 - Howitzer

LAUREL HILL U.S. • **Wharf Boat**

August 12, 1862

Series I, vol. 19, p. 150

Mississippi River
Baton Rouge, Louisiana

Prize wharf boat sank this morn. to upper deck, parted her fasts and drifted down the river.

LAVENDER U.S.S.

June 12, 1864

Series I, vol. 10, p. 200

Cape Lookout Shoals

From Delaware to Charleston, South Carolina

At 3:00 p.m., Cape Hatteras light bore N. distance 5 miles from which I took departure to clean C.L.S. Steering S.W. by S. until 6:00 p.m., the vessel going 8 m.p.h., I then changed course to S.W. 1/2 S.— at 10:30, sounded 9 1/2 fathoms— wind heavy from N.E., at 11:00, made breakers ahead and on both bows—total wreck.

LAVENDER U.S.S. • **Screw Steamer, Copper Fastened**

Wrecked June 13, 1864

Series I, vol. 10

Cape Lookout, North Carolina

Acting Master J.H. Gleason

Tonnage: 173

Length: 112'   Beam: 22'   Depth: 7' 6''

Battery:
2 - 12# rifles
2 - 24# Howitzers

LAVINA LOGAN U.S.S. • **Steamer**

September 23, 1864

Series II, vol. 1, p. 125

Mississippi River

Tonnage: 145

LEBANON • Steamer

May 24, 1864

Series I, vol. 26

Mississippi River, near Gaines Landing, Arkansas

Near Ford's Landing below Bayou Macon

Stores removed and burned.

Capt. Jacobs, Comp. F, 4th Regiment

LECOMPT • Confederate Pilot Boat

Ashore May 24, 1865

Series I, vol. 22

Near Galveston, Texas

Protect entrance to Matagorda Bay.

LECOMPTE • Confederate Guard Schooner

January 11, 1865

Series I, vol. 21, p. 773

Galveston, Texas

Arrived off Bolivar Point.

The Schooner *Belle* (cut out) was lying at 1/4 mile of Ft. Jackson and at 1 mile from Ft. Green and less than 400 yards from Confederate Guard Schooner *Lecompte*.

LENORA

December 30, 1861

Series I, vol. 6, p. 786

V.C. Roanoke Isl.

Boiler removed.

LENOX • Federal Bark

June 8, 1863

Series I, vol. 20
Series II, vol. 2, p. 530

LENOX • **Federal Bark**

June 8, 1863

Series I, vol. 20, p. 828

Mississippi Sound

Burned between Pass A'L'Outre and Mobile.

LEONIDAS U.S.S. • **Bark, Stone Fleet**

Series II, vol. 1, p. 126

Purchased November 27, 1861, at New Bedford, Massachusetts.

Tonnage:　231

LEVANT U.S.S. • **Sloop of War Ship**

Series II, vol. 1, p. 126

Lost in Pacific Ocean

Tonnage:　792

Length:　132' 3''　Beam:　35' 3''　Depth:　15' 9''　Draft:　16' 6''

Battery:
20 gun

LEWIS U.S.S. • **Stone Fleet**

Series II, vol. 1, p. 126

Purchased October 28, 1861, at New London, Connecticut.

Tonnage:　308

LEWIS WHITMAN and *ONEIDA* U.S.S. • **Gunboat**

August 7, 1862

Series I, vol. 19, pp. 121, 138,
139

Mississippi River

50 to 100 feet of bank going up.
Collision with *Lewis Whitman*, Army Transport, Steamer

I was turning the 35 miles point and I saw a light up the river—ordered man at wheel to port his helm—*Whitman* altered course across river—ordered helm hard a-port which fetched me within 100 feet of bank.

We were on right hand side coming up and she was on right hand side going down—struck us on port bow—Pilot of *Oneida*.

Awakened by crash, was on deck in time to see her sink—Lieut. Preble, U.S.N.

LEXINGTON U.S.S.

Series I, vol. 22

Grounding of in Tennessee River.

Sold at auction.

LIBERTY • Barge

Series I, vol. 5

LILY • Steamer

April 28, 1863

Series I, vol. 24, pp. 584, 589, 594, 686

Mouth of Yazoo River, Mississippi

Sunk May 3, 1863, collision with *Choctaw* in Yazoo River.

Tonnage: 50

No guns
Sank in 10 fathoms—current swept her on the ram of the Choctaw—nothing saved from her—cook trapped below—tomorrow recon of Chickasaw bayou in prep. for attack on Hayne's Bluff.

Night of 29 April, at Chickasaw Bayou. Right bank—in sight of enemy camp on bluffs leading to Vicksburg.

LINDEN (NO. 10) U.S.S.

Sunk February 22, 1864

Series I, vol. 25, pp. 774–75

Arkansas River, below Pine Bluff

Snagged 15 miles from mouth of Arkansas River.

Machinery raised.

Tonnage: 177

Length: 154' Beam: 31' Depth: 4'

Battery:
6 - 24# Howitzers

A transport Ad. Hines—8 miles below Pine Bluff, 8' water, full of stores, sank and the *Linden* went to his assistance—guns, stores and ammunition removed.

A church bar, Arkansas River—400 yards of Ad. Hines.

Starboard lead gave 3'
Port lead gave 4'

Struck stump on port bow and tore out 90'. Opened deck to get at what ammunition and stores were still below—were removing boilers when rise to as much as 12' & 14' around her.

Abandoned.

LINWOOD

July 22, 1861

Series II, vol. 2, p. 162

Cape Hatteras, North Carolina

Ran aground near (Ft. Clark?) the camp.

6,000 bags of coffee—arms found, transferred to ordnance.

LINWOOD • Bark

July 16, 1861

Series I, vol. 6, pp. 67, 78

Cape Hatteras

6 miles N. of Hatteras Inlet.

Cargo of coffee—Rio de Janeiro to New York

Stranded 400' from beach, drawing 15'

LITTLE ADA • Steamer, Blockade Runner

March 25, 1864

Series I, vol. 15, pp. 374–84

South Santee River, South Carolina
Suwanee

Afterward U.S.S. *Little Ada*

Riddled by Confed. after capture to drive off Union troops.

Not sunk or destroyed.

LITTLE MAGRUDER • Steamer

January 7, 1863

Series I, vol. 8, p. 410

Pamunkey River, Virginia
White House

Indian town, 5 miles up river
Across the river, 1 1/2 miles to the White House overland.

Also, 2 sloops, 2 barges, 4 pontoon boats, a small steamer, a large scow used as a ferry boat.

LITTLE REBEL C.S.S.

Series I, vol. 26

Mississippi River

Grounding of April 4, 1864

Refloated

Series II, vol. 1, p. 258

Captured by Fed. at Memphis, Tennessee, June 6, 1862.

LIVERPOOL • Schooner

April 10, 1862

Series I, vol. 12, pp. 677, 679

Georgetown, South Carolina

Nassau—on shore during blockade of Georgetown by U.S.S. *Keystone State.*

150–180 ton burden and deeply loaded.

Outside of the point of North Inlet.

LIVINGSTON C.S.S. • Man-of-War, Side Wheel Steamer

June 26, 1862

Series II, vol. 1, p. 258

Yazoo River, Mississippi

Length: 180'   Beam: 40'   Depth: 9' 6''

Battery:
6 guns

Series I, vol. 22, p. 844

Commodore Hollins—I think all guns and ammunition left at Fort Pillow.—Before committee C.S. Congress investigating C.S. Navy.

LIZZIE • Blockade Runner, Sloop

August 1, 1862

Series I, vol. 7, p. 612

Wilmington, North Carolina

Captured and destroyed as being unseaworthy.

4 miles from shore, N.E. on New Inlet.

LONESTAR • Schooner

October 14, 1862

Series I, vol. 19, p. 228

Taylors Bayou, Texas
of Sabine Lake

Burned enemy's barracks and schooner near railroad bridge, also destroyed (2 1/2 miles from town).

Barracks about 5 miles from pass.

Sabine Lake

LOTUS • Schooner

Series I, vol. 13

Wreck of, January 15, 1863

North Isle, South Carolina

LOTUS • Schooner of Boston

January 15, 1863

Series I, vol. 13, pp. 512, 657

North Island, South Carolina
Vic. Winyah Bay

Cargo: Sutlers stores, 1/4 removed—also a large quantity of matter sent by Adams Express Company to Port Royal.

Sailed December 23 from New York

Ran ashore on North Island Beach.

Order for every assistance in saving cargo.
Agent of Express Company arriving February 10, 1863.

LOUISA • Schooner

November 24, 1864

Series I, vol. 21, p. 755

San Bernard River, Texas

Chased ashore on the bar—totally wrecked in heavy S.E. gale that night.

LOUISA • Schooner

February 18, 1865

Series I, vol. 22, p. 53

Aransas Pass, Texas

Chased ashore on morning of 16th and sunk in shallow water.

Cargo: baggage, cordage, wines and crockery

Ex. Doc. 253-(279)-295
40th Congress 2nd Session

February 18, 1865, Aransas Pass by *Penobscot.*

Set on fire and sunk

E.A.K. Benham, Lieut. Comm.
U.S. Gunboat *Penobscot*

I chased these vessels (*Louisa* and *Mary Agnes*) ashore on the morn of the 16th.

LOUISA • Schooner, Blockade Runner

August 11, 1861

Series I, vol. 6, p. 86

Cape Fear

200 tons out of Wilmington

Standing over S. side of shoal endeavoring to reach the river—closed in 5 or 6 has chase and he chose another channel but ran upon a reef near the lighthouse, distant about 3 miles from fort, soon breeched.

Cargo: coffee, supposed

LOUISA REED of NEW YORK

Series I, vol. 7, p. 735

Vic. James River

Boarded by Rebels—captured, taken and boat fired.

LOUISIANA • **Confederate Ram**

*Military & Naval History
of the Rebellion*, p. 199

Just as the battery got abreast of Ft. St. Phillip, it blew up with tremendous noise
and sank immediately.

LOUISIANA C.S.S. • **Ironclad Steamer**

April 28, 1862

Series I, vol. 18, pp. 149, 202,
242, 287, 288, 294–302, 304,
309, 310, 312–15, 318–20, 369–
71, 433, 444, 824, 830, 834, 836,
844

Mississippi River
Fort Jackson, Louisiana

Bow guns, 1 rifled, 7'' and 2 - 9'' shell
Star broadside, 1 rifled, 6'' and 2 - 8'' shell

Commanding Officer McIntosh

Total armament: 7 - 32'' cannon
Stern 2 - 8' and 1 - 7''
Port 1 - 9'' smooth bore

5 port
5 Starboard
3 forward
3 aft
16 total heavy guns

Tonnage: 1,400

Length: 264'   Beam 62'

Commander John K. Mitchell took over after Comm. McIntosh fatally wounded.

Map showing location of sinking—p. 433

Vessel fired and 10,000# powder exploded casemate of railroad iron and deck
boiler iron.

Small arms thrown overboard near western shore anchorage

Quarantine.

5 miles above forts

Battery:
2 - 7'' rifles
3 - 9'' shell guns
4 - 8'' shell guns
7 - 32#

LOUISIANA U.S.S.

Series I, vol. 11, pp. 207–45

Explosion near Ft. Fisher, North Carolina, December 24, 1864

Record of explosions
1830, the Steam Frigate *Fulton*—the first vessel of this character ever built (finished and in service in 1814), was injured by the explosion of her mag. While moored on the flats at the navy yard—the vessel had timbered side several feet thick, floated on two hulls, with water wheels between them.

Length: 143' 2''   Beam: 27' 3''   Depth: 8' 1''   Draft: 8' 6''

Loaded with powder and blown up.

LUELLA

Before March 25, 1863

Series I, vol. 24, p. 289

Lost arms and clothing by sinking of that vessel.

Probably Army Transport.

LYDIA FRANCES • Brig

May 6, 1861

Series I, vol. 6, p. 78

Hatteras Cove

Cargo: sugar

Cuba to New York

LYDIA FRANCIS • Schooner

Military & Naval History
of the Rebellion, p. 83

Hatteras Inlet, North Carolina

Wrecked about 1st of May, 1862, on the coast near Hatteras Inlet.

Master Daniel Campbell

LYNN BOYD • Confederate Steamer

Series I, vol. 22, p. 821

February 8, 1862

Near Paris, Tennessee River
Mouth of Duck River

Burned to prevent capture.

LYNN HAVEN U.S.S. • Stone Fleet

Series II, vol. 1, p. 130

Sunk as an obstruction at outlet of Chesapeake and Albemarle Canal.

Paid for but never in naval service.

LYNX • Blockade Runner

Series I, vol. 27, p. 627

35 bales cotton from wreck of Blockade Runner *Lynx*, received from U.S.S. *Niphon* and Gov. Buckingham—October 6, 1864.

LYNX • Blockade Runner, Side Wheel Steamer, 2 Stacks

September 25, 1864

Series I, vol. 10, p. 479

Vicinity of Half Moon Batt.

North of Ft. Fisher, North Carolina

Vicinity 4 miles north of Ft. Fisher.

Exit through Swash Channel

Carried $50,000 in gold—saved.

Wilmington Daily Journal of the 26th carries full account.

LYNX • Steamer

Series I, vol. 10

September 25, 1864

M

McCLELLAN

Series I, vol. 5, p. 400

Armed with 25#'s

Captured with Tug *Titian* while laying cable.

1 - 23#.

McRAE C.S.S.

April 28, 1862

Series I, vol. 18, pp. 287, 295,
302, 312, 331–34, 345, 346, 440,
445, 697, 722, 757, 792, 795,
796, 805

Lieut. Commanding Thomas B. Huger

6 light 32# Smoothbore Broadside
1 - 9'' shell gun pivoted amidships

Burst 9'' pivot shell gun in action.

Lieut. Read, CSN, brought wounded to New Orleans.

Anchored off Julia St., as near inshore as possible, at 8:30 p.m. The ship
commenced to drag; the cable was veered its entire length; 50 fathoms. I had no
other anchor to let go and it was found impossible to bring her up. I started the
engines and sheered over to the point near the 2nd district ferry landing, where the
water was shoaler in going across the river. The ship rested on something under the
water—when she drifted off and brought up a short distance below.

Sank a mile or two below anchorage off New Orleans.

McRAE C.S.S.

April 28, 1862

Series II, vol. 1, p. 259

Mississippi River, Mississippi

6 - light 32# S.B. broadside guns
1 - 9'' shell gun pivot amidships

Former *Marquis de la Habana*

M.C. ETHERIDGE

February 10, 1862

Series I, vol. 6, p. 617

Plymouth, North Carolina
Elizabeth City
Pasquotank River
Evidently storeship for rebel fleet.

Black Warrior (?)

MADGIE U.S.S.

October 13, 1863

Series I, vol. 15, p. 34

Frying Pan Shoals

Sank 18 fathoms while under tow N. of U.S.S. *Fahkee.*

Frying Pan Shoals lightship by compass N.W. 12 miles distant.

Payroll and effects saved.

MADGIE U.S.S. • Screw Steamer, Wood

October 11, 1863—foundered

Series I, vol. 15, p. 34

Rolled heavily to starboard and sank in 18 fathoms, off *Frying Pan Shoals.*
Lightship bearing by compass N.W. 12 miles distant.

Of the effects of the ship, only the chronometer and 3 boats saved.

Tonnage: 220

Length: 122' 10''   Beam: 22' 7''   Depth: 8' 5''

Battery: May 4, 1863
1 - 30# Parrott rifle
1 - 20# Parrott rifle
2 - 24# Broadside Howitzers
1 - light 12# S.B.

Act. Mast. Woodbury H. Polleys

Left Charleston bar—north—in tow U.S.S. *Fahkee* at 5 p.m.

At 8:45, the *Madgie* having entirely filled, rolled heavily to starboard and sank in 18 fathoms—the *Frying Pan Shoals* lightship bearing by compass N.W., 12 miles distant.

Of the effects of the ship, only the chronometer and 3 boats (books, papers, funds) saved.

Acting Ensign Webb Commanding *Fahkee.*

Series I, vol. 9, p. 231

Officer and crew saved and but little else. Frying Pan Shoals Light Ship then bearing by compass N.W. 12 miles the Madgie lurched heavily to starboard and sank in 18 fathoms.

MAGENTA • Confederate Steamer

Series I, vol. 25, p. 133

Yazoo River, Mississippi

MAGNOLIA • Steamer

March 10, 1863

Series I, vol. 24, pp. 266, 295–99, 541

Tallahatchie River, Mississippi

Our position 20 miles from 1/2 mile wide neck of land (Ft. Pemberton), a dozen miles above Greenwood by water.

Mabbie Mary Keene

I have but two boats, the *Kerne* and *Magenta.*

Natchez around also.

MAGNOLIA U.S. • Gunboat

Harper's Weekly
August 16, 1862, p. 515

Captured British steamship *Memphis*, July 31, 1862.

Prop. 800 tons, carrying 1575 bales, $500,000.

MAHASKA U.S.S.

Series I, vol. 8

Destruction of vessels in Ware and Severn River, Virginia.

Series I, vol. 7

Grounding of vessel.

Sold.

MAJESTIC U.S.S. • Ship, Stone Fleet

Series II, vol. 1, p. 132

Purchased December 2, 1861, at New Bedford, Massachusetts.

Tonnage: 297

MANASSAS C.S. • Ram

April 24, 1862

Series I, vol. 18, pp. 142, 149, 154, 175, 182, 188, 193–95, 198, 205, 206, 218, 220, 223, 287, 295, 302–4, 335–45, 357, 358, 383, 385, 400, 416, 418, 420–22, 721, 760, 769, 792, 805, 809, 814, 819, 822, 823

Former *Enoch Train*; also privateer

Commander, Lieut. A.F. Warley
Ran the bow onto a steep part of bank—filled up—slid off and sank.

1 - 32# Carronade in bow

Series II, vol. 1, p. 259

Tonnage: 387

Length: 143' Beam: 33' Depth: 17' Draft: 11'

MANDERSON • Bark

May 26th

Series I, vol. 17, p. 456

West Pass, St. George's Sound, Florida

On shore from gale.

MANHASSET U.S. • Coal Schooner

September 19, 1863

Series I, vol. 20, p. 841

C.S. saved everything, October 5, 1863.

Ashore in gale.

High and dry on beach, 10 miles to westward of Sabine Pass.

Rebs in possession.

MANIGAULT • Confederate Steamer Scow

July 12, 1863

Series I, vol. 14, pp. 719, 738

Charleston, South Carolina
Behind Morris Isl. (?)
Vincent's Creek

Hit by shells and fired in attack on fort on batt. *Wagner.*

Mouth of creek.

MAPLE LEAF U.S. • Army Steamer, Transport

April 1, 1864

Series I, vol. 35, p. 397

St. John's River, Florida

Torpedo

Wreck of *Maple Leaf* at McIntosh's Point.
Near Jacksonville

Mr. Bennett commenced operation with little success.

Recovery started with little success.

Series I, vol. 15, p. 316

A large, double-stack, sidewheel steamer is sunk opposite the mouth of Doctor's Lake, 15 miles above Jacksonville. She is supposed to be the *Maple Leaf*, sunk by torpedo at 4 o'clock this morning.

Off Mandarin—going down the St. John's from Palatka—bow blown off.

MARCIA U.S.S. • Bark, Stone Fleet

Purchased December 10, 1861, at Portland, Maine.

Tonnage: 343

MARGARET & REBECCA U.S.S. • Canal Boat, Stone Fleet

Series II, vol. 1, p. 134

Purchased July 18, 1864, at Philadelphia, Pennsylvania.

Tonnage: 125

MARGARET SCOTT U.S.S. • Ship, Stone Fleet

Series II, vol. 1, p. 135

Purchased November 30, 1861, at New Bedford.

Tonnage: 330

MARIA J. CARELTON U.S.• Mortar Schooner

April 19, 1862, sunk

Series I, vol. 18, pp. 359, 365,
403, 409–11, 416, 424, 430

White Oak and Chestnut

Charles Jack—Master—at 9 o'clock, on 2nd morning, April 19, sunk by rifled shot passed through deck, magazine and bottom when found sinking—hauled onto bank and saved many stores and also arms saved but she finally slipped off bank and into deep water and nothing left visible but upper rail—as she went down, her motor was fired at the enemy for the last time in 2nd division under command of Lieut. W.W. Queen on northeast shore. The headmast one 3680 yards from Ft. Jackson. M.J.C. second in line—fort plainly visible from this position—(3900 yards to 4500). Map, p. 362.

Moved *Queen* to south bank, ahead of all, 2 a.m., 19th, they were all on the right bank and 20 mortars distance from Ft. Jackson, 3010 to 4100 yards.

Tonnage: 178

Length: 98' Beam: 27' Depth: 7' 8''

Battery:
1 - XIII in Mortar
2 - 12# rifles

MARIA THERESA U.S.S. • Stone Fleet

Series II, vol. 1, p. 135

Purchased October 31, 1861, at New Bedford, Massachusetts.

Tonnage: 330

MARIE BANKS • Schooner

Series I, vol. 8

February 3, 1863

Cape Henry

Went ashore 3 miles southeast of Cape Henry Light.

Cargo: 364 coils rigging and some stuff for Ft. Monroe.

Schooner full of water.

MARINER • Steamer

July 2, 1864

Series I, vol. 26

St. Francis River, Arkansas

High and dry on bar near mouth of St. Francis River. Burned by soldiers commanded by Capt. McCoy - private property and no stores aboard—aground 30 days.

Series II, vol. 1, p. 259

Possible C.S. Privateer *Mariner* Screw Steamer prop.

Tonnage: 135

Battery: July 25, 1861
2 - 12#
1 - rifle

MARION • Reb Steamer

April 6, 1863

Series I, vol. 16, pp. 386, 402, 412

Ashley River
Charleston, South Carolina

Obstructions placed (torpedoes) between Sumter and Moultrie.

20 torpedoes put down from Broad Street to Shute's Folly on Cooper River.

Sunk in the Ashley the night before the attack on Sumter.

Near Wappoo Creek.

MARION • Schooner

March 14, 1864

Series I, vol. 21, p. 136

Off Galveston, Texas

12 or 18 ton burden.

Prize schooner of U.S.S. *Aroostook.* Cargo taken off (salt and iron). Dismantled rigging and blocks—cut hole in deck, fired 24# shot, caved her to fill, capsize and sink.

Series I, vol. 21, p. 142

At anchor in gale.

Series I, vol. 21, p. 810

In 4 1/2 fathoms.

MARTHA WASHINGTON and
Unknown Large Schooner

October 11, 1861

Series I, vol. 4, p. 709

Off Potomac River
Quantico Creek, Virginia
(Known also as Dumfries Creek)

Fired—close to shore.

MARY • British Sloop

Captured January 19, 1864
Loss January 22

Series I, vol. 17, p. 637

Indian River Inlet, Florida

Off Indian River Inlet. Sailed for Key West. About dark—1/2 hour after sailing, discovered taking water very fast and immediately turned back and soon filled. Let go anchors and 1 cable parted and drifted rapidly on beach. Wind blowing on a strong breeze—the sloop went well up on beach. Cotton nearly all saved.

MARY • Schooner, Blockade Runner of Nassau

October 13, 1863

Series I, vol. 15, p. 35

Off Morris Isl.
St. Simon's

Off the mouth of Jekyl Creek.

Order.

When raised to send to Port Royal and cargo to Washington.

Standing in towards St. Simon's.

MARY AGNES • Schooner

February 18, 1865

Series I, vol. 22, p. 53

Aransas Pass, Texas

See *Louisa*, schooner

Cordage & Wines

Ex. Doc. 253-(279)-295
40th Cong., 2nd Session

By *Penobscot*, set on fire and sunk.

MARY ANN • Confederate Schooner

October 1862

Series I, vol. 19, p. 227

Lake Calcasieu
Burned.

MARY ANN • Confederate Schooner Cotton

November 26, 1862

Series I, vol. 19

Ex. Doc. 253-(279)-295
40th Cong. 2nd Sess.

Lat. 26° 22' N., Long. 97° W.

MARY ANN • Sloop

December 8, 1864

Series I, vol. 21

Ex. Doc. 253-(279)-295
40th Cong. 2nd Sess.

Cotton

Off Pass Cavallo, Texas, by *Itasca*. Sloop destroyed—Cotton sent to New Orleans.

MARY ANN • Sloop

December 8, 1864

Series I, vol. 21, p. 756

Galveston, Texas
Pass Cavallo

Cargo (21 bales) removed and mast and beams.

Could not fire—underwater.

MARY ANN U.S.S. • Canal Boat, Stone Fleet

Series II, vol. 1, p. 137

Purchased July 19, 1864, at Philadelphia, Pennsylvania.

MARY BOWERS • Blockade Runner, Sidewheel Steamer

August 31, 1864

Series I, vol. 16, p. 37

Charleston, South Carolina

Struck the wreck of the *Georgiana* off Long Island and sank—she was discovered by the Outside Fleet at daylight.

Running in.

Series I, vol. 15, pp. 658–59

English Sidewheel Iron Steamer.

The vessel is lying on the wreck of or some vessel as there is deep water all around her—no cargo aboard—her bell, marked 1864, binnacle and compass and two kedge anchors saved—U.S. Frig. *Wabash*, Capt. J. DeCamp

Off Charleston, South Carolina 8/1/64

3 fathoms, 3/4 miles from shore between Rattlesnake Shoal and Long Island.

Nothing but coal and gunny sacks.

MARY BOWERS • British Steamer, Blockade Runner

August 31, 1864

Series I, vol. 15, pp. 658–59

Off Charleston, South Carolina

Lies in 3 fathoms—3/4 miles from shore between Rattlesnake Shoals and Long Island.

Hailed from Glasgow, last from Bermuda, bound into Charleston—probably struck on a wreck, as deep water all around.

Sidewheel iron steamer, almost entirely submerged—impossible to save anything except Bell (1864), binnacle and compass and two kedge anchors.

Lone boy (14 yrs.) survivor knows of no cargo.

MARY E. KEENE • Steamer

Series I, vols. 23, 24, 25

Yazoo River, Mississippi

MARY E. PINDAR • Prize Schooner

Capt. September 22, 1861

Series I, vol. 6, pp. 641, 693

Believed lost at sea on way to Hampton Roads

Captured with 50 casks of lime on board.

Federal Point bears S. W. by W. 1/2 W distant 12 miles.

Anchored and abandoned as crew escaped to beach.

MARY FRANCES U.S.S. • Schooner, Stone Fleet

Series II, vol. 1, p. 137

Purchased August 13, 1861.

No record tonnage.

MARY JANE • British Schooner

Destroyed June 18, 1863

Series I, vol. 17, p. 477

Clearwater, Florida

Run on the beach on a small key near Clearwater, Florida.

Lat. 28° N., Long. 82° 53' West.

Portion of cotton cargo saved.

MARY JANE • Sloop

February 24, 1863

Series I, vol. 8, p. 567

Back Creek, Virginia

Tonnage: 30

MARY LINDA U.S.S. • Canal Boat, Stone Fleet

Series II, vol. 1, p. 137

Purchased July 16, 1864, at Philadelphia, Pennsylvania.

Tonnage: 116

MARY LOUISA • **Sloop**

March 27–28, 1862

Series I, vol. 12, pp. 666–68

Bull's Bay, South Carolina

Fired.

MARY NEVIS • **Confederate Sloop**

Captured January 25, 1862

Series I, vol. 17, pp. 66–69, 84–86, 133

Bayes Pass, Florida
1/2 way between Clearwater Bay (Harbor) and Tampa Bay.

Bayes Pass near house of Mr. Girard (Pilot), 5 1/4 hours to Clearwater.

Grounded on bar—bilged—everything of value removed and burned.

Spitfire Schooner and Sloop *Caroline* sunk in Passage Key Channel (inlet)—8' on south side of Tampa Bay by U.S. Bark (Gunboat) *Ethan Allen*, March, 1862—Act. Vol. Lieut. Comdg. W.B. Eaton.

MARY OLIVIA • **Sloop**

Series I, vol. 17, pp. 202, 204–05

Apalachicola, Florida

On the bar A.R., burned 7' water, with *Cygnet* and *New Island*.

MARY PATTERSON • **Steamer**

June 16, 1862

Series I, vol. 23

White River, Arkansas

MARY WILLIS • **Schooner**

December 22, 1861

Series I, vol. 5, p. 14

Potomac River, Virginia

Loaded with wood—struck by batteries at Boyd's Hole—run on Flats opposite, about 17 miles from Fredericksburg, Virginia.

Hope to get off.

MATAGORDA (former *ALICE*) • Rebel Steamer

July 7, 1864

Series I, vol. 27, p. 679

Velasco, Texas

July 8, 1864—at 12:30 p.m., weighed anchor at Galveston Bar—shaped course for San Luis—at 3:30, when passing wreck of Rebel Steamer *Matagorda* (driven on beach at midnight of 7th and set fire to).

Series I, vol. 21, p. 151

C.S. report, March 22, 1864—High on the beach—about 18'' in the sand.

MATAGORDA • Rebel Steamer

July 8, 1864

Ex. Doc. 253-(279)-295
40th Cong. 2nd Sess.

Galveston, Texas
San Louis Pass, Texas

Off coast of Texas by Kanawha and others.

Destroyed.

Run ashore and shelled—burned and complete wreck.

Cargo: cotton

Series I, vol. 21, p. 782

About 7 miles N. and E. of San Louis Pass.

MATILDA • Schooner

Ex. Doc. 253-(279)-295
40th Cong. 2nd Sess.

Matagorda Bay, Texas

Matagorda Bay by Henry Janes, etc., wrecked.

MATTIE CABLER U.S.A.T. • Steamer

March 20, 1865

Series I, vol. 27, p. 130

22 miles below Nashville.

Supposed attempted recovery, April 1, 1865.

MAUREPAS C.S.S. • Sidewheel River Steamer

June 15, 1862

Series I, vol. 23

White River, Arkansas

Series II, vol. 1, p. 259

Near St. Charles, Arkansas, to obstruct river.

Battery:
5 guns

MAZEPPA

Series I, vol. 26, pp. 604, 624

Tennessee River

With 700 tons freight from Cincinnati, was captured and burned at Ft. Heiman, 2 miles this way (Johnsonville) from Fort Henry on the opposite side of river.

All stores saved.

MECHANIC U.S.S. • Stone Fleet

Series II, vol. 1, p. 140

Purchased November 13, 1861, at Newport, Rhode Island.

Tonnage: 335

MERRIMAC C.S. #2
YOUNG MERRIMAC C.S.
RICHMOND C.S. • Ironclad Steamer

Series I, vol. 8, p. 207
Series I, vol. 7, pp. 590-620

Built in Gosport Navy Yard.

Length: 150' Beam: 32'

Frames 2' apart C. to C.
Sides 8'' - 10'' at heel and 6 1/2 at head, wales 5'', bottom plank 4''

Top and roof, yellow pine, 13'' angle up and down 35°

Yellow pine 5'' fore and aft
Oak Plank 4'' up and down
Iron 2'' fore and aft
Iron 2'' up and down

26'' thick

6 guns

MERRIMACK

June 26, 1861

Series I, vol. 5, pp. 748, 801

Burned to water's edge—taken into Dry Dock—pronounced worthless. Machinery all destroyed.

May 30, 1861, have *Merrimack* up and just pulling her into Dry Dock.

MERRIMACK

Harper's Weekly
March 22, 1862, pp. 183–85

Newport News, Virginia

4 - 11'' navy guns on each side and 2 - 100# Armstrong guns at bow and stern.

Engagement with *Monitor* and *Minnesota* reported.

Running down *Cumberland* and *Merrimack* and *Monitor* in fight.

Series I, vol. 7, p. 797

Lighten in the bight of Craney Isl.

MERRIMACK C.S.S.

Harper's Weekly
February 15, 1862, p. 100

10 - 100#'s Armstrong guns

MERRIMACK U.S.S. • Sidewheel Iron Steamer

February 15, 1865

Ex. Doc. 253-(279)-295
40th Cong. 2nd Sess.

Series I, vol. 12, pp. 38–41, 43

Tonnage: 684

Foundered at sea, February 15, 1865, in N.E. gale.

Lat. 29° 11' N., Long. 79° 12' W.

Act. Master Late Commander Wm. Earle when abandoned. Nothing saved but 4 boats and chronometer and boats turned over to Naval Authorities at Baypoint, South Carolina.

Saving vessel U.S. Mail Steamer *Morning Star*, Capt. Nelson, out of New Orleans for New York.

Length: 230' Beam: 30' Depth: 11' Draft Frwd.: 8' 4'' Aft.: 8' 6''

Battery:
1 - 30# Parrott rifle
4 - 24#'s
1 - heavy 12#

MERRIMACK (VIRGINIA)

*Military & Naval History
of the Rebellion*, p. 225

Hampton Roads, Virginia

Blown up by crew near Craney Isl., 1/2 past 4 a.m., 9th March 1862.

Near batteries at Sewall's Point.

Series II, vol. 1, p. 271

Blew up, 4:58 a.m., May 11, 1862.

C.S.S. *Virginia*, Scr. Ironclad Ram

Tonnage: 3,200

Length: 275' Beam 38' 6'' Depth: 27 1/2' Draft: 22'

Battery: 10 Guns
2 - 7'' rifle pivot
2 - 6'' rifles
6 - 9'' Dahlgren in broadside
2 - 12# Howitzers on deck

MESSENGER U.S.S. • Bark, Stone Fleet

Series II, vol. 1, p. 142

Purchased November 16, 1861, at Salem, Massachusetts.

Tonnage: 216

METEOR U.S.S. • Ship, Stone Fleet

Series II, vol. 1, p. 142

Purchased November 4, 1861, at Mystic, Connecticut.

Tonnage: 324

MIDNIGHT U.S. • Bark

Series I, vol. 9, p. 703

Pass Cavallo, Texas

Battery:
6 - 32#
1 Parrott pivot 20#

66 men

250 ton burden

7' draw light.

Stationed at Pass Cavallo, Texas.

Series II, vol. 1, p. 144

Sold November 1, 1865

MILLEDGEVILLE • Steamer

December 21, 1864

Series I, vol. 16, p. 502

Savannah, Georgia
Savannah River

Burned to water's edge and sunk in the middle of the river to prevent capture at fall of Savannah.

MILLEDGEVILLE C.S.S. • Ironclad Steamer

January 17, 1865

Series I, vol. 16, pp. 468–69, 502

Agusta, Georgia

Steamer constructed by Mr. Willink.

Was burned to water's edge and sunk in middle of river.

Little was lost in her.

Series II, vol. 1, p. 260

Burned to water's edge and sunk in the river at Savannah, Georgia, December 1864.

MILWAUKEE U.S.S. • River Monitor

Sunk March 27, 1865, by torpedo

Series I, vol. 22, pp. 67, 71

Screw steamer of wood and iron with double turret—Monitor

Tonnage: 970

Battery:
4 - XI Dahlgren S.B.

Spanish Fort—below Blakely River—had steamed in (Blakely River) as far as we had bouyed the channel, but in dropping back with the current stern, foremost struck a torpedo and sank.

To within 1 1/2 miles of the lower fort on the left bank of river.

MILWAUKEE U.S. and *OSAGE*• River Monitors

*Military & Naval History
of the Rebellion*, p. 704

Mobile, Alabama

Spanish fort—at the head of Mobile Bay.

The communications between the city and the fort was cut off by the fleet, with the loss of the *Milwaukee* and *Osage*, blown up by torpedoes.

At the same time, the fleet got under way and proceeded up the way to Howard's Landing, below the fort. The *Metacomet, Stockdale, Milwaukee, Cincinnati, Albatross, Winnebago, Genesee* and *Osage* were ordered in towards shore and opened a cannonade which the enemy did not return.

MINGO U.S.S.

November 1862

Series II, vol. 1, p. 144

Cape Girardeau, Missouri

Tonnage: 300

Stern wheel steamer ram

MINHO • Blockade Runner

October 20, 1862

Series I, vol. 13, pp. 396, 408

Charleston

About 3/4 mile distant from Ft. Moultrie, aground and apparently a complete wreck.

On the spit off Moultrie.

MINNAHO • Rebel Steamer

October 27

> *Harper's Weekly*
> November 15, 1862, p. 723

The Rebel steamer was chased and driven ashore at the same time. She was bound for Charleston with stores for Rebels. Others taken in to Port Royal.

MISSISSIPPI C.S.S.

April 25, 1862

> Series I, vol. 18
> Series II, vol. 1

No gun or ammo on board when set on fire by her officers to prevent capture.

Tonnage: 1,400

Length: 260' Beam: 58' Depth: 15' Draft: 12' - 12.5', when completed 14'

MISSISSIPPI U.S.S. • Sidewheeled Steamer

March 14, 1863—11 p.m.— 2 a.m.

> Series I, vol. 19, pp. 664, 669,
> 686, 693, 695, 769
> Series II, vol. 1

Mississippi River
Port Hudson

Sunk at Port Hudson, Mississippi River, on March 14, 1863.

Abandoned and blown up. Capt. Melancton Smith commanding. Sunk by Confederate batteries.

Tonnage: 1,732

Length: 225' Beam: 40' Depth: 23' 6''

Battery:
1 - X'' Dahlgren pivot S.B.
19 - VIII 63 cwt.
1 - 20# Parrott rifle

Steamer ran aground, abandoned and burned.

Grounded abreast the Batt. (last and most formidable) having gained the turn— within gun range and shelled by 3 batteries.

Got afloat at 3 a.m. and drifted down river—blowing up with terrific concussion at 5:30 a.m.

VIII and X guns.

Monongahela grounded on west shore near turning point.

Got off.

Waited for *Mississippi* to drift past a- anchored in 6 1/2 fathoms abreast Profit Isl., also, grounded on Thompson's (Thomas) Point—astern of her, the *Mississippi* also aground.

Came down close to west bank.

Blew up about 10 miles below Profit Isl.

MINESOTA S.S.

*Military & Naval History
of the Rebellion*, p. 224

Hampton Roads
Newport News, Virginia

Left Ft. Monron on approach to action. Within a few miles, the ship got aground, also Frigate *St. Lawrence*.

About 3 miles below Newport News.

Monitor carried 11'' Dahlgren throwing 168# shot.

Floated and sold.

MINNESOTA • Steamer

May 2, 1863

Series 1, vol. 24

Memphis, Tennessee
Argyle Landing

May 2-9, 1863—Greenville, Mississippi

3 miles above Greenville.

Battery on Mississippi Shore—below Isl. #82.

MIST • Steamer

October 15 (?), 1863

Series I, vol. 25, p. 520

Mississippi River

MOBILE • **Rebel Steamer**

Series I, vol. 25

Yazoo City
Yazoo River

A screw vessel ready for plating.

Destroyed.

MOBILE C.S.S. • **Screw Steamer**

May 1863

Yazoo River, Mississippi

Burned by Confederates.

Ready for plating when destroyed.

4 guns

MODERN GREECE • **Blockade Runner, Steam Prop.**

June 27, 1862

Series I, vol. 7, p. 514

Wilmington, North Carolina
Off New Inlet

1,000 ton burden.

Beached within 1/2 mile of the Fort Color Slate—full of water and gradually settling. Total wreck, while cargo will be partially secured by Rebels.

Cargo 1,000 tons of gunpowder, some rifled cannon and other arms and equipment, together with bales of clothing and spirituous liquors—clothing and liquor saved but not one pound of powder or cannon.

Run ashore 1/2 mile N of Batt. on Federal Point.

MODERN GREECE • **Blockade Runner, Steamer**

Series I, vol. 17, p. 214

New Inlet, Delaware (?)

176 ton sloop

Series I, vol. 8, p. 88

Run ashore near New Inlet.

Cargo: Powder, arms, whiskey, 500 stand arms, 6 Whitworth. Cannon saved—
much remains.

2 Whitworth guns set up 1/4 mile apart. Situated on the ridge of Sand Hillocks on
Oak Island. Fired on *Marantasas* and *Genesee*.

MONITOR U.S.S.

Series I, vol. 7, p. 483

James River

Temperatures

At anchor June 13, 1862.

Galley 156° 8-12 164° 12-4
Engine R. 128° 12-4

Door in bulkhead open. Hatch open, blowers slow.

June 14, under way 150°, 146° 10-12, Galley

138° Eng. R. Blower Fast
Oak deck in shade 90° in sun 125°

Berth deck 120°

MONITOR U.S.S. and *CANNON*

Series I, vol. 6, p. 604

Dahlgren—"in no case ought a projectile weighing over 170# be fired from a XI-
inch gun."

MONTAUK

February 1863

Series I, vol. 16, p. 387

Ft. McAllister

When attacking Ft. McAllister.

Sold.

MONTE CHRISTO • Schooner, Cotton

Ex. Doc. 253-(279)-295
40th Cong. 2nd Sess.

July 10, 1862, Coast of Texas by Arthur.

Destroyed by Rebels.

MONTE CHRISTO • Sloop

Lamar, Texas

Series I, vol. 19, p. 302

Burned by enemy while we were securing the cotton.

MONTEZUMA U.S.S. • Ship, Stone Fleet

Series II, vol. 1, p. 150

Purchased November 29, 1861, at New London, Connecticut.

Tonnage: 424

MORGAN C.S.S. • Steamer, Side Wheel

1865

Mobile, Alabama

Series II, vol. 1, p. 260

At fall of Mobile, Alabama

Length: 202' Beam: 38' Draft: 7' 2''

Battery:
1 - 7'' rifle
1 - 6'' Rifle in pivot
2 - 32# rifles
2 - 32# long S.B.

MORO • Steamer

Series I, vol. 24, p. 224

Red River

Coming down river.

Cargo: 110,000 lbs. pork, 500 hogs and large quantity salt.

Set on fire about 15 miles above mouth Red River by *Queen of the West*.

MOSHER

Series I, vol. 18, p. 295

Ft. Jackson and Ft. Phillip, Louisiana

Unarmed tug pushing fire raft during battle and Ft. Phillip and Ft. Jackson sunk instantly by broadside from Sloop of War—Capt. Sherman

Tonnage: 49, unarmed

MUSADORA U.S.S. • Canal Boat, Stone Fleet

Purchased July 16, 1864, at Philadelphia, Pennsylvania.

Sent to Baltimore, Maryland.

Tonnage: 123

MUSCLE • Steamer

Series I, vol. 22

MUSCOGEE C.S. • Center Wheel, Steamer, Ironclad

Series II, vol. 1, p. 260

Burned at the close of the war.

Battery:
6 gun

MYSTIC U.S.S.

Series I, vol. 8

Destruction of schooner by September 26, 1862.

Sold.

N

NAN-NAN

February 24, 1864

Series I, vol. 17, p. 654

East Pass
Swanee River, Florida

6# of fire power. Plenty of ammunition.

Cotton deck cargo

Got aground afnd was fired.

Side wheel walking beam, iron steamer.

The barrels and rammers of a quantity of musket were also taken from wreck.

NANSEMOND C.S.S. • **Steam Wood**

April 4, 1865

Series II, vol. 1, p. 261

Richmond, Virginia

Tonnage: 80

Burned at evacuation of Richmond, Virginia.

Battery:
2 - gun

NARCISSUS U.S.S.

December 7, 1864

Series II, vol. 1, p. 155

Wrecked January 4, 1866, at Egmont Key, Florida.

Screw Steamer, Wood

Tonnage: 101

Length: 81' 6''   Beam: 18' 9''   Depth: 8'   Draft: 6'

Battery:
1 - 20# Parrott rifle
1 - heavy 12#

NARCISSUS U.S.S. • **Steam Tug**

December 7, 1864

Series I, vol. 21, p. 752

Mobile Bay
Dog River Bar

All guns, small arms and ammo saved.

Raised December 28, 1864.

NASHVILLE • **Confederate Steamer, Privateer**

March 2, 1863

Series I, vol. 13, p. 696

Ogeechee River, Georgia

By U.S.S. *Montauk*—under guns of Ft. McAllister.

Grounded in Seven Mile Reach.

Large pivot gun mounted abaft her foremast.

Exploded from heat of fire of ship burning.

Magazine exploded, shattering her in smoking ruins.

Series I, vol. 13, p. 221

Map with wreck.

Also known to Confederates as *Rattlesnake*.

NASHVILLE • Ironclad Ram

Series I, vol. 22, p. 255

Mobile, Alabama

Still remains aground 40 miles above Mobile.

Length: 271'   Width: 95 1/2' over whls   Beam: 62 1/2'   Depth: 13'
Draft: 10' 9''

Battery:
3 - 7'' Brooke rifles
1 - 24# Howitzer

NASHVILLE • Privateer

*Military & Naval History
of the Rebellion,* p. 446

Savannah, Georgia

February 1, 1863—Lying under the protection of Ft. McAllister (shoal water 1,400 yards) watching an opportunity to run blockade. The river had been staked and torpedoes across the channel.

On the morning of the 27th, a recon discovered her aground. In 20 minutes she was in flames from exploding shells and 1/2 hour later her magazine blew leaving no trace.

NASHVILLE • Rebel Steamer

August 24, 1864

Series I, vol. 21, p. 530

Mobile, Alabama
Near Dog River Bar?

We discovered the Rebels had sunk the *Nashville*, the vessel intended for an ironclad, across the channel, completely obstructing it.—August 16, 1864.

NASHVILLE • Rebel Steamer, Brig., Sidewheel Steamer

February 28, 1863

Series 1, vol. 13

Wassaw Sound, Georgia
Ogeechee River

Destroyed by fire of U.S. Gunboat *Montauk* in the lower part of Ogeechee River.

Former Blockade R. *Thomas L. Wragg*, subsequently Privateer *Rattlesnake.*

Tonnage: 1,221

Length: 215' 6''   Beam: 34' 6''   Depth: 21' 9''

Battery:
? - 26# rifles

NASHVILLE • Steamer

February 28, 1863

Series I, vol. 13

Formerly C.S.S. *Nashville*; also known as *Thomas L. Wragg* and *Rattlesnake.*

Sold.

NATCHEZ • Steamer (River)

Series I, vol. 25

Yazoo River, Mississippi

NATHANIEL TAYLOR U.S.S. • Schooner

Series II, vol. 1, p. 155

Petit Bois Channel, Alabama

Purchased May 19, 1863.

Sunk.

NAUGATUCK

Harper's Weekly
April 26, 1862, p. 267

Length: 101' Width: 22' Depth: 9'

Built in 4 compartments—end 2, filled with water in battle.

Draws 9', empty 4 1/2.

Constructed 4 1/2' depth, 20'' thick, extending 18'' thick.

Battery:
1 - 100# rifled
2 - 12# Howitzers

NEAPOLITAN • Bark

Harper's Weekly
August 16, 1862, p. 527

Morocco, Africa

Burned within three miles of the coast of Morocco, by Sumter on way to Gibraltar.

NELLIE

June 25, 1862

Series I, vol. 13, p. 142

Charleston, South Carolina

The cargo of the *Nellie* was pretty much saved and they have been removing the machinery.

NEPTUNE

Series I, vol. 17, p. 575

Hillsboro River, Florida

Sunk in Hillsboro River, near Tampa, Florida.

NEPTUNE • Confederate River Steamer, Wood

January 1, 1863

*Military & Naval History
of the Rebellion*, p. 311

Galveston, Texas

Jan. 1, 1863, ran into *Harriet Lane* and was so disabled, was obliged to back in on the flats where she sank in 8' water.

Series I, vol. 19, pp. 448, 450,
475

Armed two small brass pieces.

Backed in on the flats in 8' near the scene of action.
Federal Naval force gunboats.
Westfield, Harriet Lane, Clifton, Owasco, Corypheus and *Schem*, 1 broken down—army transports *Saxon, M.A. Bardman.*

Federal lost *Westfield—Harriet Lane* and 2 coal barks, *Caralto* and *Elias Pike.*

All saved including guns, except killed in battle.

NETTLE U.S.S. • Steamer Tug

October 20, 1865

Series II, vol. 1, p. 158

Tonnage: 50

Run down by ironclad and lost.

Original name: *Wonder*

NEUSE C.S. • Ram, Ironclad Sloop

1865

Series I, vol. 12, pp. 67, 76

New Berne, North Carolina

Near Kinston, North Carolina

Ram burned on way after evacuating.

Series II, vol. 1, p. 261

At approach of Sherman's Army

2 - guns, November 5, 1864

NEW ENGLAND U.S.S. • Ship, Stone Fleet

Acquired November 30, 1861, at Gloucester, Massachusetts

Tonnage: 375

NEW ERA #5

February 28

Series I, vol. 24, pp. 387, 396

Mississippi River

Scuttled in the middle of the river.

(Near Biggs House) Col. Char. R. Woods.

Check position for correctness.

Fleet below Yazoo River and above Red River.

NEW IRONSIDES U.S.S. • Bark, Screw Steamer, Ironclad

December 19, 1866

Series II, vol. 1, p. 159

League Isl. Navy Yard

Tonnage: 3,486

Length: 230' Draft for.: 15' 8''

Battery: October 1864
2 - 150# Parrott rifles
2 - 60# Parrot rifles
14 - XI Dahlgren S.B.

NEW ISLAND • Schooner

Series I, vol. 17

See *Mary Olivia* Sloop

NEW LONDON U.S.S.

May 10, 1864

Series I, vol. 21

Calcasieu Pass, Louisiana

Loss of boat.

Sold.

NEWBURY PORT U.S.S. • Ship, Stone Fleet

Series II, vol. 1, p. 158

Acquired November 30, 1861, at Gloucester, Massachusetts.

Tonnage: 341

NIGHT HAWK • Blockade Runner

September 29, 1864

Series I, vol. 10, pp. 492, 493, 497

New Inlet, North Carolina
Federal Shoals

Boarded, few articles saved and set afire.
300 tons burden—bound in—general cargo.

No. 1 Station mound light bearing W. 1/2 S. in 4 1/2 fathoms.

From station, saw steamer at S.E. standing in toward New Inlet.

Niphon being in 5 fathoms, mound light bearing W. by S., gave chase—causing her to run ashore on Federal Shoals.

About 1/2 mile from Ft. Fisher.

Saved chron., one boat, one pair night glasses.

Did eventually float off.

NIGHT HAWK • Steamer

September 29, 1864

Series I, vol. 10

NIGHTINGALE U.S. • Clip Ship

Series I, vol. 16, p. 729

Mississippi River

Aground outermost east mud lumps South West Pass.

NOBLE U.S.S. • Bark, Stone Fleet

Series II, vol. 1, p. 162

Acquired December 2, 1861, at Sag Harbor, New York.

Tonnage: 275

NORMAN • Schooner

November 14, 1863

Series I, vol. 20, pp. 675–76

Pensacola, Florida

5 miles W.S.W. of Pensacola bar. Made out 3 vessels steering for Pensacola. They separated—hauled out to sea. The *Norman,* captured by James Duke and 10 men, made out for land upon us heaving in sight and he beached and burned her.

Started for Perdido River.

NORTH CAROLINA • Rebel Gunboat

February 6, 1862

*Military & Naval History
of the Rebellion*, p. 137

Fort Henry
North Carolina

Largest gunboat sunk.
Resisting Gen. Burnside.

NORTH CAROLINA C.S.N. • Ironclad

Series I, vol. 10, p. 509

Wilmington, North Carolina

Sunk near Wilmington; a blockade runner ran afoul of her wreck and immediately sunk. Report of September 28, 1864.

NORTH HAMPTON

Series I, vol. 8, p. 69

Ft. Darling, James River, Virginia

Sunk in barrier above.

NORTH HEATH • Steamer, Blockade Runner

December 21, 1864

Series I, vol. 11, p. 785

Order for sinking of, in New Inlet, North Carolina

Just beyond the New Inlet Rip.

NUECES • Bark

December 5, 1861

Series I, vol. 16, p. 867

Galveston, Texas

C.S. *Obstruction*

Towed into channel between Hitchcock's Shoal and the East Point, sank in 5 1/2 fathoms.

In line between Bolivar Point Lighthouse and Market House Steeple.

NUTFIELD • Steamer

February 4–5, 1864

Series I, vol. 9

NUTFIELD • Paddle Wheel, Blockade Runner

February 4, 1864

Series I, vol. 9, pp. 459, 482

New River Inlet

Mouth of New River Inlet

Enfield rifles, munitions and merchandise,

—Battery of 8 Whitworth rifled guns and quantity of pig lead thrown over during chase.

February 5—removed Enfields and quinine and compasses and set her on fire—in action with *Florida*, thoroughly shelled and destroyed.

Chased 60 miles by *Sassacus*, got within long range 10 miles from here - under fire 1 hour, sp. 12 knots.

Purser saved from drowning.

O

O.M. PETTIT U.S.S.

Series II, vol. 1, p. 164

Sunk by collision.

Raised and sold at Bay Point, South Carolina, September 2, 1865.

OCEAN WAVE

Series I, vol. 8, p. 288

Neuse River, North Carolina
(more than 4 miles below Kinston, probably 6)

Sunk on a snag but will be raised without difficulty.

On expedition against *Goldsboro*.

OCONEE C.S.S.

August 18, 1863

Series I, vol. 14, p. 494

At sea

Known also as *Everglade* and C.S.S. *Savannah*

Cargo: cotton

ODD FELLOW • Schooner

June 11, 1863

Series I, vol. 5, p. 285

Coan River

Burned inside by boat from Coeur de Lion.

ONEIDA U.S.S. • 3 Masted Schooner, Screw Steam Wood Sloop

January 24, 1870

Series II, vol. 1, p. 165

Yokohama Bay

Run down and sunk by P. & O. Steamer *Bombay*.

Length: 201' 5'' Beam: 33' 10'' Depth: 16' Draft for.: 6' 8'' Aft.: 8' 11''

Battery:
3 - 30# Parrott rifles
2 - IX Dahlgren S.B.
4 - 32# 33 cwt.
1 - light 12# Howitzer

Wreck sold to Tatcho-bo-nai-yo.

ORATE

Harper's Weekly
November 15, 1862, p. 733

Florida

John Maffit, Capt.

View

Running Mobile Blockade, chased by U.S. Steam Sloop *Oneida*.

ORION U.S.S. • Schooner, Stone Fleet

Series II, vol. 1, p. 166

Acquired August 13, 1861, at Baltimore, Maryland.

ORR C.S.

February 7 & 8, 1862

Series I, vol. 22, p. 782

Tennessee River
Up Tennessee River

Arrived off foot of Panther Creek Isl.

Flagship fired on Ft. Henry

Passed burning steamer
2 steamers burning near Florence, Ala.

February 8, 1862, Paris, Tennessee—three of our steamers burned to prevent capture. *Sam Orr, Appleton Belle*, and *Lynn Boyd* at mouth of Duck River.

Also, *Lexington, Conestog*a.

OSAGE U.S.S.

Sunk March 29, 1865

Series II, vol. 1, p. 167

Blakely River, Alabama

Sunk by torpedo.

Raised and sold November 22, 1867, public auction including—*Calhoun, Tennessee, Nashville* for $20,467.10.

OSAGE U.S.S.

Series II, vol. 1
Series I, vol. 22

Monitor.

Entrance Blakely River, Alabama

Raised July 15, 1865.

OSCEOLA U.S. • Transport, Steamer

November 2, 1862

Series I, vol. 1, p. 389
Series I, vol. 12, pp. 288, 293

A government transport with DuPont's Fleet, shipwrecked at Georgetown, South Carolina; crew prisoners in Richmond until last Sunday and are now here in Washington and want passes home—Hon. S.C. Fessenden, U.S. House of Repre. to Assnt. Sect. of Navy.

Also Union Steamer.

Sold.

OSPREY • Steamer

November 7, 1862

Series I, vol. 19, p. 329

Bayou Cheval, Louisiana

About 9 miles from Grand Lake and J.P. Smith, burned, having been run hard ashore and employed as shelter for party making bowie knives, buckshot and bullets.

OSTEGO U.S.S.

December 9, 1864

Series I, vol. 11, p. 162

Roanoke River, North Carolina
Off Jamesville

Sank in 2 1/2 fathoms—stripped.

Above Plymouth, North Carolina

OSTEGO U.S.S. • Schooner, Double-end Sidewheel Steamer

Sunk December 9, 1864

Series II, vol. 1, p. 168

Roanoke River

Battery recovered and disposed of.

Tonnage: 974

Length: 9'

P

PALMETTO STATE C.S. • Ironclad Sloop

1865

Series I, vol. 16, p. 459

Charleston Harbor, South Carolina

First Lieutenant W.H. Ward

3 guns as of November 5, 1864.

Same style Battery as *Chicora*

Burned by Confederates at evacuation

Battery:
10 - 7'' rifles (4 each broadside, 1 bow and 1 stern).

PAMLICO C.S.S. • Sidewheel River Steamer

1862

Series II, vol. 1, p. 262

Lake Ponchartrain, Louisiana

Battery:
2 guns

PARGOUD • Confederate Steamer

Series I, vol. 25

Yazoo River, Mississippi

PASSAIC U.S. • Ironclad

Harper's Weekly
November 29, 1862, p. 758

Trying her gun at the Palisades.

2 - 15'' gun, weight each 42,000, balls 425#

PATAPSCO U.S. • Ironclad (Monitor)

January 15, 1865

Series I, vol. 16, p. 171

Charleston Harbor

Near entrance to lower harbor

600 to 800 yards below Sumter and below it.

800 yards from Sumter and 1200 yards from Moultrie.

Exactly in a line due N., tangent to extreme course of low water mark on Morris
Island.

300 yards N. of Lehigh Buoy (placed on the extreme end of the point making out from Morris Isl.) in 5 fathoms.

Court of Inquiry.

700 yards from Sumter on the west side of the channel.

2 guns

PATHFINDER • British Schooner

November 2, 1862

Series I, vol. 8

Little River Inlet, North Carolina

2 miles west of Little River Inlet.

Cargo: Salt, boots, shoes, olive oil, cutlery, liquors

Fired.

PATRICK HENRY C.S.S. • Sidewheel Steamer

April 4, 1865

Series II, vol. 1, p. 262

Richmond, Virginia

Tonnage: 1,300

Draft: 9.4' Forward, 10.2' Aft.

Battery:
4 guns

PATRIOT U.S.S. • Schooner, Stone Fleet

Series II, vol. 1, p. 171

Acquired August 13, 1861

PATRIOT OF NASSAU • Blockade Runner, Centerboard Schooner

August 27, 1862

Series I, vol. 13, p. 253

Mosquito Inlet, Florida

Ashore 12 or 15 miles south—bilged and stripped.

PAW PAW

August 6, 1863

Series I, vol. 25, p. 344

Walnut Bend, Mississippi River
Hardin's Point, Arkansas

Formerly *Fanny.*

Lower end of Walnut Bend, Hardin's Point, Arkansas Shore.

The vessel was secured with Hawsers around the upper part of casemate to keep her from sliding off the bank into deep water which was 3 fathoms on the outside of vessel.

Nearly everything removed.

Raised before September 16, 1863.

PENNSYLVANIA U.S.S. • Ship of the Line

Burned April 20, 1861

Series II, vol. 1, p. 174

Tonnage: 3,241

Length: 247'   Beam: 59' 6''   Depth: 54' 10''

PENSACOLA U.S. • Sloop of War

Harper's Weekly
February 1, 1862, p. 76

Potomac River

Pictured passing Rebel batteries on Potomac, January 11, 1862.

PERI U.S.S. • Ship, Stone Fleet

Series II, vol. 1, p. 175

Acquired November 29, 1861, at Portland, Maine.

Tonnage: 265

PERIWINKLE U.S.S. • Two Masted Schooner, Screw Steamer

Series II, vol. 1, p. 176

Arctic

Tonnage: 383

Length: 140' Beam: 28' Depth: 12' Draft: 10' 6''

Battery:
2 - 24#

Lost in Arctic Regions, Hall's Expedition.

Former *America* for 80,000 from John W. Lynn.

PETEE • Sloop

March 10, 1863

Series I, vol. 17, pp. 383–84

Indian River Inlet, Florida

6 ton of Savannah from Nassau.

Cargo: salt

PETER DEMILL U.S.S. • Bark, Stone Fleet

Series II, vol. 1, p. 176

Tonnage: 300

Acquired November 9, 1861, at New London, Connecticut

PETER HOFF U.S.S.

March 7, 1864

Series I, vol. 9, pp. 535, 537, 781

New Inlet, North Carolina

Sunk March 6, 1864, by collision on coast with U.S.S. *Monticello* of North Carolina.

Thrown overboard from wreck as she sat.

30# Parrott rifle on forecastle, 12# Howitzer from under 5 1/2' low tide.

Main deck gun could not be got at 5' water over her spar deck.

4 1/2–5 fathoms, 1 mile south of Sheep Head Rock, S. of New Inlet Bar.

Vessel total loss.

30#

Tonnage: 800

Length: 210' Beam: 28' Depth: 15'

200 yards of wreck is 4 1/2 fathoms—Ft. Fisher bearing N. 1/2 E., Bald Head S.W. by W. 1/2 W.

Off of Zeek's Isl.

Series I, vol. 10, p. 275

U.S.S. *Cherokee*, July 15, 1864, struck upon a wreck supposed to be U.S.S. *Peter Hoff*—mound light bearing by compass N. 1/2 W., and Bald Head Light S.W. 3/4 W.

PETREL C.S. • Privateer

July 28, 1861

Series I, vols. 1, 6, pp. 51, 112, 818

Former *Aiken*, Revenue Cutter

Tonnage: 82

2 Guns

William Perry, Commanding

July 28, 1861—Off Charleston, at 6:00 a.m., commenced chasing sail off Leebow. At 10, came up with her, when she hoisted Confederate flag and fired a gun. Beat to quarters and commenced firing. The schooner fired 3 shots, one of which passed through the mainsail and took a splinter out of the main yard. The schooner hauled down her flag after receiving 2 shots, one of which struck her bows, and she sunk from the effects of it at 10:30. Got out the boats and picked up the crew. She proved to be the *Petrel* of Charleston.—Capt. H.Y. Purviance, U.S.S. *St. Lawrence*

Military & Naval History of the Rebellion, p. 61 (Western Pub.)

Sunk by broadside of U.S. Frigate *St. Lawrence*, July 28. Sunk by three guns; two grape and one 32# round shot amidships below—W.L.

December 1862, Boutelle discovered this was Ex United States Coast Survey ship. Where was he?

Former revenue cutter *Aiken* surrendered to Confederates in Charleston Harbor and the crew volunteered under New Government. This vessel had run the blockade— was no sooner at sea than she fell in with U.S. Frig. *St. Lawrence*, 1861.

Among the first to take letters of Mark (William Perry, Capt.)

Schooner rigged.

Tonnage: 82

Series I, vol. 6, p. 219

32° 30' N., 79° 09' W.

PETREL U.S.S. • Tinclad, Wood

April 30, 1864

Series II, vol. 1, p. 176

Above Yazoo City, Mississippi

Tonnage: 226

Former *Duchess*, December 22, 1862.

Series I, vol. 26, pp. 251, 252

3 or 4 miles above Yazoo City, all guns, ammunition and valuables removed by Rebs before burned.

Capture of *Petrel*.

Map.

PEVENSEY • Steamer, Blockade Runner

June 9, 1864

Series I, vol. 27, p. 700

Beaufort, North Carolina

On beach about 7 miles to westward of Beaufort.

Of London from Bermuda, bound to run blockade at Wilmington, North Carolina.

Valuable cargo of arms and assorted goods.

PEVENSEY • Blockade Runner

June 9, 1864

Series I, vol. 10, p. 137

Named *Penversey* in abstracts of April 16, 1864.

9 miles west of Beaufort, North Carolina.

Cargo: Arms, blankets, shoes, clothing, lead

7 Whitworth Tompions tied together—possibility of guns being under musket boxes.

Vessel and cargo a total loss.

PEYTONA • Confederate Steamer

Series II, vol. 1
Series I, vol. 25

Yazoo River, Mississippi

PHANTOM • Blockade Runner

September 23, 1863

Series I, vol. 9, pp. 215–16, 222

Wilmington, North Carolina
New Inlet

Run ashore and destroyed (iron propeller).

Near Rich Inlet.

Bound in—cargo: arms, medicine

Ashore: Lat. 34° 13' N.
          Long. 77° 50' W.

PHILIPPI U.S.S. • Sidewheel Steamer

Destroyed August 5, 1864

Series I, vol. 21, pp. 506, 600

Tonnage: 311

Length: 140' Beam: 24' Depth: 9' 10''

Battery:
2 - 12# rifles
1 - 20# Parrott rifle
1 - 24# Howitzer

Formerly *Ella*.

Lead read 1/4 less 3.

Chart of wreck.

PHOENIX C.S.S. • Ironclad, Floating Battery

1865

Series II, vol. 1, p. 262

Mobile, Alabama

Destroyed by Confederate at fall of Mobile, Alabama.

Battery:
6 guns

PHOENIX U.S.S. • Ship, Stone Fleet

Series II, vol. 1, p. 177

Tonnage: 404

Purchased November 9 at New London, Connecticut.

PICKET U.S. • Gunboat

Harper's Weekly
September 27, 1862, p. 611

September 6

Washington, North Carolina

Gunboat *Louisiana.*

Gunboat *Picket* was blown up by accidental explosion of her magazine—Capt. Nichols.

219 killed, 6 wounded

Tonnage: 400

6' water
4 Guns
2 - 12# Wiard

PICKET BOAT #2

September 26, 1864

Series I, vol. 10, p. 483

Bergen Point, New Jersey

Sunk for two days.

Cargo: ammo

Refloated and arrived at New Brunswick, New Jersey.

PICKET BOAT #2 • Small Steamer

October 8, 1864

Series I, vol. 5, p. 486

Great Wicomico River, Virginia

The wreck of *Picket Boat* in sight up Rising Creek—one of the small ones making off from the river.

Rebels took 12# Howitzer and 12 prisoners.

PICKET BOAT NO. 2 U.S.

October 8, 1864

Series I, vols. 5, 10

Known as *J.E. Bazely* and U.S.S. *Beta.*

By Commodore Read, U.S.S.

PICKET BOAT #2 U.S.

October 8, 1864

Series I, vol. 10, pp. 539, 540
Series I, vol. 5, p. 486

Wicomico Bay, Virginia

Between Potomac and Rappahannock River.

Left Baltimore, #1 engine broke and towed, arrived Annapolis. Left next day #1 still in tow. Wind S.E. and freshing. Made harbor under eastern shore—at 3:30 p.m., wind shifted S.W.. Compelled to run across into West River. Left early morning, October 7, arriving Point Lookout at 6 p.m. Made repairs and started for Ft. Monroe. Wind blowing, took refuge again. Attacked by Guerrillas—slipped cable. Grounded on sand bar. Threw everything over on bow to lighten, to no avail—fired forward—Captain Pilot.

Put into mouth of reason Creek. To keep Rebels from boarding, slipped cable and attempted to cross a point—grounded—expended all ammo and fired.

PICKET BOAT NO. 2 U.S.S.

October 18, 1864

Series II, vol. 1, p. 178

Great Wicomico River, Maryland

Crew captured and boat destroyed.

Possibly recovered.

PICKET BOAT NO. 3 U.S.S. • Screw Steamer

February 19, 1865

Series II, vol. 1, p. 178

Cape Fear River (Mouth)

Retrieved—cut adrift and drifted to sea.

PILGRIM U.S.S. • Canal Boat, Stone Fleet

Series II, vol. 1, p. 179

Acquired July 18, 1864

Tonnage: 126

Sent to Baltimore, Maryland.

PINK U.S.S.

September 23, 1865

Series I, vol. 22, p. 250

Dauphin Island, Alabama
On passage from New Orleans to Mobile.

Fresh gale from N.E.

Supposed vessel to be E. of Sand Isle.

Struck, bilged.

PIONEER • Sloop

Ex. Doc. 253-(279)-295
40th Cong. 2nd Sess.

Rio Grande, Texas

Rio Grande, February 20, 1864, by Portsmouth

Destroyed.

PLYMOUTH U.S.S. • Ship, Sloop of War

April 20, 1861, burned and scuttled

Series II, vol. 1, pp. 180, 263

Norfolk Navy Yard

Battery:
20 guns

C.S.S.

Burned at evacuation of Norfolk, 1862.

Battery: 22 guns

Series I, vol. 5, p. 806

Arrangements being made to raise.

POCAHONTAS • Army Steamer

January 19, 1862

Series I, vol. 6, p. 583

Hatteras Inlet, North Carolina

Burnside Exp., Battle of Roanoke Isl.

Ashore 20 miles above Cape Hatteras.

19 of 103 horses saved—all 60 crew saved.

POCAHONTAS U.S.S. • Screw Steamer, 2nd Class Sloop

Series I, vol. 9, p. 108

Hatteras, North Carolina

Was lost on the Cape and all the horses except 19 perished.

Between January 13 and 28, 1862.

Tonnage: 694

POLK C.S.S. • Side Wheel River Steamer

1862

Yazoo River, Mississippi

Burned

Battery:
7 Guns

PONTCHARTRAIN C.S.S. • Side Wheel River Steamer

Series II, vol. 1, p. 263

Arkansas River, Arkansas

Burned to avoid capture.

Battery: 5 guns

Former *Lizzie Simmons.*

PORT LEON (Old)

Destroyed 1843

Series I, vol. 17, p. 500

St. Marks, Florida

POTOMAC U.S.S. • Ship, Stone Fleet

Series II, vol. 1, p. 183

Acquired November 1, 1861, at Nantucket, Rhode Island.

Tonnage: 356

POWERFUL • Steamer

December 19–20, 1863

Series I, vol. 17, pp. 607-9, 616

Mouth of Suwanee River, Florida

Anchored in the channel leading to the mouth of the Suwanee, 1 1/2 miles distant. Fired, being almost surrounded by oyster beds. No cargo—personnel—anything found aboard.

PREBLE U.S. • Ship, Sloop

April 27, 1863

Series I, vol. 20, p. 162

Pensacola, Florida

While lying at anchor off the town of Pensacola.

Tonnage: 556

Burned accidentally—W.F. Shankland, Act. Mast.

Battery:
10 - 32#
2 - VIII# 63 cwt.
1 - 32# 43 cwt.
6 - 32#

PRESTO • Blockade Runner, Iron Vessel, Steamer

February 2, 1864

Series I, vol. 15, pp. 262–66

Off Ft. Moultrie, South Carolina
On Sullivan's Isl.

Close under the batteries of Moultrie.

In flames.

On Sullivan's Isl., just to the right of Fort Moultrie.

Off Wagner Buoy, max. 2,350 yards to ship.

PRINCE ALBERT • Blockade Runner

August 1864

Series I, vol. 10, p. 477

Charleston, South Carolina

Lost entering harbor.

Aground off Moultrie, bound in.

Set on fire and destroyed by shells from *Catskill* and battery on Morris Isl.

PRINCE OF WALES • Schooner

December 24, 1861

Series I, vol. 12, pp. 428–30

Off Georgetown, South Carolina

Cargo: salt and oranges

At North Inlet—9 miles to the north of the entrance to Georgetown.

Passed into North Inlet (entrance) after running 1/4 mile inside Point. Ran aground.
Crew escaped.

Towed her out of creek or channel. Aground channel, 150 yards beach.

PRINCE OF WALES • Steamer

Series I, vol. 25

Yazoo River, Mississippi

PRONY H.I.M.S.

November 5, 1861

Series I, vol. 6

PUSHMATAHA • Rebel Schooner

October 7, 1863

Series I, vol. 20, p. 615

Off Calcasieu River, Louisiana

From Havana with cargo of rum, claret and gunpowder—taken off—Cayuga in 2
fathoms as close to boat as she could get. Burned to water's edge.

PUSHMATAHA • Schooner and Sloop

October 7, 1863

Series I, vol. 20, p. 615

While off Calcasieu River, Louisiana, saw both under sail and both some distance
from the mouth of the river near the lake—made sail to the eastward and stood for
her (a Schooner trying to get into Mermentau River)— she went ashore 3/4 miles
from the beach—I sent 1 boat to the vessel already aground and another sail made
on the starboard bow to the eastward working inshore, wind offshore. Rain squall
came up and lost sight. Cleared and in range of bow gun. After firing 1 shell near,
she went about and immediately blew up, leaving nothing but burning fragments
(Cayuga within 3/4 to 1 mile of her.)

Q

QUEEN CITY U.S.S. • Gunboat, Side Wheel Steamer, Wood

June 24, 1864

Series II, vol. 1, p. 187

Clarendon, Arkansas
White River

Tonnage: 212

Battery:
2 - 30# Parrott rifles
2 - 32# 42 cwt.
4 - 24# Howitzers
1 - heavy 12#

Series I, vol. 26, pp. 424–25, 428,
429, 432, 433, 418, 502

Lies about a mile below the town in 2 fathoms. Most completely burned and blown up. Casemates have tumbled in on the guns—they are all there except one 24# Howitzer—which we are endeavoring to raise. June 28, 1864, C. Bache

Her anchor, chain and buoy saved.

Raised 2 - 32# Parrotts and 1 - 32#.

Remaining guns have fallen in and cannot raise until water falls more—June 28, 1864

3 guns reported removed by Rebs; the 2 - 30# and 1 - 32#.

Shelby captures her—we removed 1 - 24# and 1 12#.

Her armament was 4 - 32#, 4 - 24# and 1 - 12#

Covered 1 1/4'' iron.

50 stand of small arms.

Rebs removed all small arms, most ammunition, a 12# Howitzer, paymaster stores, but fearing other gunboats would come, they burned it.

The exchange has succeeded in raising another of Q.C. guns, making 7 in all that we now have from that vessel. The remaining 2 are still in deep water from falling through deck. August 9, 1864.

QUEEN OF THE WAVE • British Steamer

Ashore February 24, 1863
Destroyed March 7, 1863

Series I, vol. 13, pp. 687, 746

Vicinity Winyah Bay
North Santee River, South Carolina
Near Georgetown, South Carolina

Driving ashore and destruction of British Steamer off the mouth of river.

Ran ashore near the mouth of the North Santee—abandoned, set on fire, destroying great part of cargo—broke up by bad weather and destroyed by set explosives.

Portion of cargo—tin sheets, bottles of quinine, morphine, opium and calico.

Rept. ammo and clothing.

QUEEN OF THE WEST

February 22, 1863

Series I, vol. 24, p. 383

Gordon's Landing
Red River

Grounded 100 miles up river under Battery of Ft. Taylor—not fired because of wounded on board—abandoned.

Series I, vol. 20, pp. 64, 65, 134

Compelled them to destroy the *Queen of the West* in the contest for the possession of the Butte-a-la-Rosie on Grand Lake, Louisiana.

Diana, Hart and *Queen of the West* destroyed and their armament captured.

Came from Chicot Pass—burning wreck drifted 2 or 3 miles down the lake where she grounded and shortly exploded—saved 1 - 30# Parrott Rifle, 1 - 20# Parrott rifle, 3 - 12# Brass field pieces

Series I, vol. 23, p. 276

"A full history of what was accomplished by this boat would make one of the most interesting features of the war"—James Brooks, Capt. and Act. Quartermaster, Chief Quart. U.S. Ram Fleet and Miss. Marine Brigade.

QUEEN OF THE WEST

DESOTO • Tender

Military & Naval History
of the Rebellion, p. 340

Black River

Grounded on bar and captured near Fort Taylor. River makes abrupt bend to North opposite is long bar making necessary to hug south shore because strong eddy.

Fort Taylor located 40 miles from mouth on south bank just above a bend, its guns commanded.

DeSoto, after losing 2 rudder, blown up about 20 miles below.

Series I, vol. 24, p. 383

U.S. Army Steamer

Drifted down 15 miles, scuttled and burned.

QUEEN OF THE WEST U.S.S. • Ram

April 14, 1863

Series I, vol. 20

On Atchatalaya River, Louisiana

Captured by Confederacy.

Iron protected steam ram

Series II, vol. 1, p. 263

Captured from Fed. on February 14, 1868.

Battery:
1 - 30# Parrott
1 - 20# Parrott
3 - 12# Howitzers

Series I, vol. 24, p. 224

February 9, 1863

Armament - 12 brass 12# as said by released prisoners.

Military & Naval History
of the Rebellion, p. 367

Previously captured, blown up and destroyed on Lake Chetimacha up the Atchafalaya in the vicinity of Irish Bend, about 3 miles west of Franklin— On this retreat, they destroyed the gunboat Diana and the transports *Gossamer*, *Newsboy* and *Era #2*, at Franklin.

So rapid was the pursuit that the enemy was unable to remove the transports at New Iberia and 5 with all stores and ammunitions were destroyed with an incomplete iron-clad gunboat.

QUINNEBAUGH U.S. • Transport

July 20, 1865

Series I, vol. 12, p. 171

Beaufort, North Carolina

Loaded with troops, left port this date, 7:30 and 8:45, she struck on reef off Shackleford Banks.

—In crossing the bar.

R

R.B. FORBES U.S.S. • Twin Screw Steamer, Wood

February 25, 1862

Series I, vol. 6, pp. 664, 668, 673

Currituck Inlet, North Carolina

Wrecked about 4 miles south.

Saved as much of government property as possible and fired.

On shore 25 miles south of Cape Henry.

All chronometers, small arms, spy glasses, put on board *Young America*.

Series II, vol. 1, p. 188

Tonnage: 330

Length: 121' Beam: 25' 6'' Depth: 11' 7 1/2'' Draft: 12' 3''

Battery:
1 - 30# Parrott rifle
2 - 32# 57 cwt.

R.J. BRENCKINRIDGE C.S.S.

Series I, vol. 18, pp. 249–52, 291, 296, 305-6

Known also as *Gen. Brenckinridge*.

R.J. LOCKLAND • Steamer

Series I, vol. 25

Yazoo River, Mississippi
Greenwood

15 miles off Ft. Pemberton from mouth.

Sunk on bar.

RACCOON • **Blockade Runner**

Series I, vol. 14, p. 367

Vicinity of Charleston, South Carolina

Run ashore on Drunken Dick.

Trying to get out.

RACER • **British Schooner**

Series I, vol. 8

Abandonment.

Series I, vol. 15, pp. 615–19

August 1, 1864

Off Bull's Bay, South Carolina

Racer Brit. Sloop

RACER U.S.S. • **Sail Mortar Schooner**

Series II, vol. 1, p. 188

Tonnage: 252

Length: 105' Beam: 28' 10'' Depth: 9' 6'' Draft: 9' 10''

Sold, September 27, 1865.

RALEIGH C.S. • **Ram, Ironclad Sloop**

May 7, 1864

Series I, vol. 10
Series II, vol. 2
Series I, vol. 12

Cape Fear River, North Carolina
New Inlet, North Carolina
Wilmington Bar

Flag Officer Wm. Flynch crossed Wilmington Bar on returning. Got aground—all arms saved—4 guns.

> Series I, vol. 12, p. 38

Map of wreck of *Raleigh*, north portion of New Inlet, North Carolina, due west of south most point of Ft. Fisher Point, 1/2 mile in Cape Fear River.

> Series II, vol. 1, p. 263

April 30, 1864

November 30, 1863

4 Guns.

> Series I, vol. 9, p. 714

On shore 8 miles up river. It is thought she will not get off.

Draws 16'

> Series I, vol. 10, p. 24

Report of Sec. of C.S.N.—guns, iron, equipment, saved.

RANGER • Blockade Runner

> Series I, vol. 10, p. 518

Cape Fear River, North Carolina
Off Western Bar Entrance

From Piney Point to Westward as far as the wreck of Blockade Runner *Ranger*—September 25, 1864.

RANGER • Steamer, Blockade Runner

January 11, 1864

> Series I, vol. 9, pp. 402, 405, 437

Lockwood's Folly Inlet

Beached and burning 1 mile west of this inlet. Sand hills which were high and near.

Loaded for C.S. *Government.*

Some muskets and carpenters tools taken off by C.S.

RAPPAHANNOCK C.S.S.

Series I, vol. 3

Abandonment—former *H.B.M.S. Victor*, afterwards Steamer *Beatrice*.

Series II, vol. 1, p. 264

Was in France and never to sea at end of war.

RARITAN U.S. • Ship

April 20, 1861

Series I, vol. 4
Series II, vol. 2, p. 110

Gosport Navy Yard
Norfolk, Virginia
Scuttling and abandonment of vessel.

The Frigate *Raritan* has disappeared altogether.

Whatever is left of her is out of sight in the deep water channel.

Wreck sold 1867.

RATTLER U.S.S. • Steamer, Wood

December 30, 1864

Series I, vols. 26, 27, pp. 769–71

Off Grand Gulf, Mississippi

During gale, S.E. shifted to N.—parted chains and was blown on left bark on Mississippi side.

Everything saved except 2 - 30# Parrotts—spiked. Burned to waters edge by enemy scouts. Acting Master Commanding N.B. Willets

Tonnage: 165

Battery:
2 - 30# Parrott rifles
4 - 24#
2 - 24#

RATTLESNAKE C.S. • Privateer, Steamer

February 28, 1863

Series I, vol. 16, p. 354

Charleston Harbor, South Carolina
Lying near Breach Inlet

Series I, vol. 1, p. 818

Fitted out Charleston—Master T. Harrison Baker Comm., November 5, 1862

Tonnage: 1,204

Battery:
6 guns

Formerly *Nashville*
Destroyed by U.S. Monitor *Montauk*, Commander John L. Worden, U.S.N.

Series II, vol. 2, p. 603

Turned over to John Frazer and Co., at Charleston, South Carolina as merchant vessel—all guns and armament removed—named *Thomas L. Wragg.*

REBECCA SIMS U.S.S. • Ship, Stone Fleet

Series II, vol. 1, p. 189

Acquired October 21, 1861, at Fair Haven, Massachusetts

REINDEER • Schooner

October 3, 1861

Series I, vol. 16, pp. 734, 842

San Louis Pass, Texas

4 ton schooner.

Sunk as worthless.

Fri. eve. she took a salt vessel nearly under our jaws and wantonly sunk her (Letter from Velasco).

Sold.

RELIANCE U.S.S.

September 2, 1863

Series I, vol. 5, p. 344

Port Royal, Virginia

Stripped and scuttled.

RENALDO

Series I, vol. 25, p. 400

Harrisonburg
Natchez

Captured and burned.

REPUBLIC • Confederate Steamer

Series I, vol. 25

Yazoo City
Yazoo River

Being fitted for a ram with railroad iron plating.

Destroyed.

RESOLUTE

Series I, vol. 18, p. 296

Mississippi River

Aground on west bank one mile above Ft. Jackson.

Burned after taking as much of the property on board as practicable.

Capt. Hooper.

Series II, vol. 1, p. 191

Sold.

RESOLUTE C.S.S.

December 12, 1864

Series I, vol. 16, pp. 486, 490

Savannah River

Going downstream, passed mill at Tweedside (below Argyle Island) and fired on from bluff (near Broad River) 1,000 to 1,200 yards distant—kept on to 800 yards in turning to retire C.S.S. *Macon* and C.S.S. *Sampson*—struck *Resolute*, became unmanageable and drifted ashore.

Armed with muskets only.

RESOLUTE C.S.S. • Gunboat

April 24, 1862

Series II, vol. 1, p. 264

Mississippi River

RESOLUTE C.S. • Tender, Sidewheel Steamer

December 12, 1864

Series I, vol. 16, pp. 469, 477,
485, 486, 489

Savannah, Georgia
Savannah River
Below Argyle Island

After passing Mill at Tweedside, situated on a back river some distance—we were opened upon by one or more light batteries of Parrott guns posted upon a bluff in a bend in the river which we had to approach head on and commanding the channel. C.S. *Sampson*, *Resolve*, *Macon* proceed to 800 yards and returned fire. Hit twice by battery, one her wheel, disabling her, ran into twice, while vessels retiring and drifted ashore.

Saw a fire in direction of her and thinks she was fired.

Armed with muskets only.

Above Back River.

Series II, vol. 1, p. 264

Used as transport and tender and residence for crew of *Savannah*.

REVENGE • Schooner

July 21, 1863

Series I, vol. 20, p. 406

Calcasieu Lake, Louisiana

20 ton.

To reconnoiter 2 small vessels at anchor up near the lake—several miles from the bar and aground—scuttled her.

Cargo: 18 hogs heads of sugar, 200 hides and small quantity of mineral salt

RICHARD O'BRYAN • English Schooner

Series I, vol. 19, p. 88

Off Galveston, Texas

Destroyed near Galveston by *Rhode Island*, July 25, 1862.

Found in communication with shore to south of Sabine River and destroyed.

RICHARD O'BRYAN • English Schooner

July 4, 1862

Series I, vol. 27, pp. 449, 704

San Luis Pass, Texas

English Schooner from Jamaica to Matamoros.

Having made a schooner some 7 miles eastward of San Luis Pass—stood for her soon afterwards. She came to anchor about 1/2 mile from beach—upon approach of the *Rhode Island*, she got underway and was run on shore. Ground abreast was somewhat higher and covered with thick brushwood.

She was bilged and abandoned.

Assorted cargo: Large amount of drugs.

Fired by boat crew after taking boat load cargo.

Inside bay nearly a mile across neck of land, Richard O'Bryan of Kingston.

RICHARD O'BRYAN • Schooner

July 4, 1862

Series I, vols. 19, 20, 27

By U.S.S. *Rhode Island.*

RICHARD VAUX U.S.S. • Canal Boat, Stone Fleet

Series II, vol. 1, p. 192

Acquired July 16, 1864, at Philadelphia, Pennsylvania.

Tonnage: 120

Sent to Baltimore, Maryland.

RICHMOND C.S.S. • Ironclad

April 4, 1865

Series II, vol. 1, p. 265

Richmond, Virginia

Scuttled by Confederates.

Length: 180'   Draft: About 16'

Battery:
4 guns

Same as *Merrimack.*

ROANOKE • Iron Screw, Gunboat Tug

April 4, 1865

Harper's Weekly,
August 23, 1862, p. 536

6 - 15'' Dahlgren

Tonnage: 65

Battery:
2 guns

Out of commission.

ROB ROY • Schooner

March 2, 1865

Series I, vol. 17, p. 825

See *Havana.*

ROBERT E. LEE C.S. • Steamer,. Iron Sidewheel

Series I, vol. 9, pp. 263, 276, 278,
279, 283, 289, 290

Cape Lookout Shoal

 (Possibly concealed Specie)

November 5, 1863—Letter written by order of Maj. Gen. Peck, informing me the
Steamer *R.E. Lee* was about to leave Wilmington, North Carolina, with mail for
Gen. Magruder and funds to pay troops in Texas. —Com. D. Lynch, Ord. Sch.
Arletia

November 9, 1863—*R.E. Lee* captured.

When about 20 miles Beaufort Bar, steamer standing S. and E (sighted N. and E.)
at daylight, gave chase but Cape Lookout Shoal to east of her and had to shape
course across our bows—out of Bermuda number of passengers and large crew—
arms and army clothing for cargo—no papers found. Shortly after, she stopped.
7:30, C.S. *Flag* raised a few moments and then burned.

Left Wilmington, October 3, 1863.

Arrived Hamilton Bermuda, October 24, 1863

November 16, 1863—If captured C.S. agent in north ordered to purchase and send
 to Halifax to recover.

Supposedly left Hamilton at 6:00 a.m., Nov. 4.

14 miles S.S.W. from Beaufort Bar.

Treasure said to be in Keelson.

Condemned.

Purchased by Navy, name changed to *Ft. Donelson*, January 1864.

Sold at New York on October 25, 1865.
900 ton.

September 7, 1863, supposed disbursement money for trip to Texas $10,400.

ROBERT FULTON • Steamer

October 7, 1863

Series I, vol. 25, p. 450

Red River, Louisiana

See *Argus*.

ROBERT WILBUR and Unknown Schooner

Series I, vol. 5, p. 148

Nomini Creek (R.), Virginia

Up the creek within about 5 miles. Destroyed 2 schooners that could not be gotten out. About 5 miles up hidden in small bay, fired *Robert Wilbur*.

Also, small schooner partly hauled up on beach opposite small brick church.

ROBIN HOOD U.S.S. • Ship, Stone Fleet

Series II, vol. 1, p. 193

Acquired October 20, 1861, at Mystic, Connecticut.

Tonnage: 395

ROLLING WAVE U.S.S. • Canal Boat, Stone Fleet

Series II, vol. 1, p. 194

Acquired July 19, 1864, at Philadelphia, Pennsylvania.

Tonnage: 112

Sent to Baltimore, Maryland.

ROSALIE

Series I, vol. 20, p. 741

ROSE • British Steamer

June 2, 1864

Series I, vol. 15, pp. 467, 513, 517

Near North Inlet, South Carolina
Off Georgetown

South end of Pawley's Island where she ran ashore near the wreck of another steamer and some buildings on the beach. No cargo except some cases and barrels of liquors and small stores. Nothing saved and ship consumed by fire by the U.S.S. *Wamsutta* crew.

ROSE OF LONDON • British Steamer

June 2, 1864

Series I, vol. 15, p. 467

North Inlet, South Carolina
South end of Pawley's Island

Ran ashore near wreck of another steamer and some buildings on the beach.

ROSINA • Sloop

April 15, 1864

Series I, vol. 21

San Louis Pass, Texas
Galveston, Texas

Standing down the beach, stood toward her run aground on 13th. Fired by crew of U.S. *Virginia* of 15th—removed mast rigging and anchors.

ROVER • Schooner

October 20, 1863

Series I, vol. 15, p. 59

Murrell's Inlet, South Carolina

1/2 mile up the inlet, 50 ton former Charleston Pilot Boat.

Set fire and destroyed.

ROVER C.S. • Schooner

October 17, 1863

Series I, vol. 15, p. 59

Murrell's Inlet, South Carolina
1/2 mile up the inlet.

50 ton.

Cargo: cotton

Set fire and destroyed.

ROWENA

Series I, vol. 24, p. 587

I refer you to Prichett's letter to Greer for an account of the sinking of the *Rowena*. She was snagged between St. Louis and Cairo.

Series I, vol. 25, p. 364

Before August 7 or 9, 1863

Be careful none of the beef sunk in the *Rowena* goes below or is used.

ROYAL • Shoal Light Boat

Series I, vol. 8, p. 117

Off New Berne, North Carolina

Raised about 1st week of October, 1862.

ROYAL YACHT

November 7–8, 1861

Series I, vol. 16, pp. 755, 757, 759, 762

Off Galveston Bar, Texas

Total destruction by fire.

Carried 1 - 32# on a circle—appeared nightly off the entrance to the harbor.

Guarding the channel and the Bolivar and Ft. Point forts.

Anchored near Bolivar Point.

C.S. Report—C.S.S. *Gen. Rusk* anchored 2 miles from yacht of *Pelican Spit.* Extinguished the fire and towed, securing her to wharf in Galveston.

Carried 12# gun.

Anchored.

N. 1/2 E. from Central Wharf at Galveston, distant about 4 miles.

9# gun

Chartered to Confederates October 9, 1861, for $1,350. Owner Thomas Chubb.

ROYAL YACHT • Armed Rebel Schooner - Fire Arms

Ex. Doc. 279
40th Cong. 2nd Sess.

Galveston, Texas

Galveston, November 7, 1863, by expedition from *Santee*—vessel burnt.

Series I, vol. 16, pp. 759–60

Burned 'tween decks—not sunk.

Armament placed aboard *Gen. Rusk* (12#, small arms and ammo) towed to Galveston.

Originally anchored off Bolivar Point, N. 1/2 E. from Central Wharf at Galveston.

Distant about 4 miles.

RUBY • Steamer

June 28, 1863

Series I, vol. 14, p. 301

Charleston, South Carolina
Folly Isl., off the head of

Rebels are wrecking.

RUDOLPH

Series I, vol. 16, p. 386

Mobile, Alabama
Mobile Bay Area

It is probable *Tecumseh, Milwaukee* and *Osage* and *Tinclad* sunk by torpedoes.

RUDOLPH U.S.S. (No. 48) • Sidewheeled Steamer, Wood Tin Clad

April 1, 1865

Series I, vol. 16, pp. 396, 432

Ent. Blakely River, Alabama
Mobile, Alabama

Stern wheel

Tonnage: 217

Battery:
2 - 30# Parrott rifles
4 - 24# Howitzers

Destroyed by torpedo while attacked Rebel forts.

Series I, vol. 22, p. 73

Sank in 12' water.

RUNBER S.S.

Series II, vol. 2, p. 784

Europe
Wrecked in Angra Bay, Island of Terceira.

Articles for submarine defense.

S

S.C. JONES • Mortar Schooner

July 18, 1862

Series I, vol. 19, pp. 27, 28, 133

Mississippi River
Above Vicksburg, Mississippi

Just out of gunshot of enemy on right bank of river and about a mile above the *Brooklyn.*

With the exception of the *S.C. Jones* lying aground about a mile above us and on the same side—on fire and shortly after, blew up.

25 yards out—powder set to blow mortar into deep water nearby.

The enemy's lower mortar fleet, thinking we were about to attack them, burned one of their vessels, which was aground below the city.

SABINE U.S. • Frigate

May 1, 1861

Series I, vol. 4, p. 153

Discharge

The crew is a good one and has served faithfully through a cruise which has been long and unpleasant. Since they came on board in 1858, they have had liberty on shore but once for 24 hours—H.A. Adamas, Capt.

SACHEM • Small Screw Steamer

Sabine Pass, Texas

Formerly C.S. *Vessel*, September 1862.

Surrendered—September 3, 1863, at Sabine Pass by Acting Volunteer Lt. Amos Johnson.

Tonnage: 197

Length: 121'   Beam: 23' 6''   Depth: 7' 6''

Battery:
1 - 20# Parrott rifle
4 - 32# 57 cwt.

*Military & Naval History
of the Rebellion*, p. 480

September 8, 1863, *Sachem,* followed by the *Arizona*, advanced up the east channel to draw the fire of the forts while the *Clifton* advanced up the west channel—the *Granite City* stayed to cover *Gen. Weitzel*—abreast of the fort they were both disabled, white flags raised, by eight guns (3 rifled) and in 20 minutes were taken in tow by the enemy.

Series I, vol. 20, p. 559

C.S. Lieut. Dowlings (Davis Guards) Report of Sabine Pass Expedition.

47 men of *Texas* captured *Clifton* and *Sachem* of 13 guns total and 350 crew and drove off 15,000 troops commanded by Weitzel Gen. and Major Gen. Franklin.

Clifton, 8 gun, Schachem, 5

SACRAMENTO U.S.S. • Screw Steamer, Wood Sloop

June 19, 1867

Series II, vol. 1, p. 196

Tonnage: 1,367

Length: 229' 6'' Beam: 38' Depth: 16' 7'' Draft For.: 7' 10'' Aft.: 8' 10''

Barkentine to Top Gallant

Total wreck on shoal off the mouth of the Kothapali, a branch of the Godavery River, Madras Dist.

Latitude: 16° 53' N., Longitude: 82° 23' E

Battery:
2 - IX Dahlgren S.B.
1 - 60# Rifle
2 - 24# Howitzers
1 - 12# rifle
1 - 12# S.B.

SAGINAW U.S. • Side Wheel Steamer

3 a.m., October 29, 1870

Series II, vol. 1, p. 197

Ocean Isl. Reef

Lauriel Wood

Battery: June 23, 1863

1 - 50# Dahlgren Rifle

1 - 32# 42 cwt.

2 - 24# rifle

Tonnage: 453

Draft For.: 3' 7''   Aft.: 4' 5''

SALLIE WOOD • Mail Boat

July 1862

Series I, vol. 19, pp. 56, 75

Mississippi River

Fired into and burned on her way up to Memphis, Tennessee.

Written from Vicksburg, Mississippi.

Ran one transport ashore above (Vicksburg) and burned her—mail taken with interesting accounts of Arkansas—Earl Van Dorn, Maj. Gen. C.S.

SALLIE WOOD U.S.S.

August 1862

Series I, vol. 24, p. 212

Isl. #82, Mississippi River

Robbed and burned.

SALLIE WOOD U.S.S. • Naval Transport

July 21, 1862

Series I, vol. 27, p. 293

Isl. #82 in Mississippi River

Captured and burned July 17, 1862.

Sunk at the foot of Isl. #82—July 17, 1865—she has been so long ashore the sand entirely covers. Mr. Llewellyn, a citizen residing near wreck says anything valuable has long since been removed.

Series I, vol. 23, p. 272

From this point, the Rebels crossed over a peninsula to another opposite Island #82, where they burned the *Sallie Wood.*

SAM GATY **Steamer**

Series I, vol. 25, p. 442

Mississippi River
Skipworth's Land, Mississippi

Getting off all government property. Sunk just above us to her boiler deck. The *Champion* (#5) can do nothing toward saving her—October 1, 1863.

SAM HOUSTON • **Schooner**

Captured July 7, 1861

Series I, vol. 16, pp. 550, 575,
588, 595, 597, 607, 614, 631,
645, 659, 682, 734, 768, 805,
812, 817, 842, 861

Galveston, Texas

66 ton

By U.S.S. *South Carolina* off Galveston—Commander James Alden

Sold.

SAM KIRKMAN

February 12, 1862

Series I, vol. 22, p. 821

Tennessee River at Florence
Burned to prevent capture.

SAM YOUNG **U.S.A. • Steamer**

Series I, vol. 25, p. 339

May be on Tennessee River

Above White River, I found the *Sam Young* with prisoners from Yazoo City—hard aground—I presume the Rebels have burned her by this time—August 3, 1863.

SAMPSON **C.S. • River Steamer, Side Wheel**

Series I, vol. 16, pp. 459, 496

Savannah River, Georgia

1st Lieut. T.B. Mills

Wood Gunboat

1 gun as of November 5, 1864.

2 guns, 11 officers and 30 men as of January 5, 1865.

Not sunk.

SAMUEL ORR • Steamer

February 7, 1862

Series I, vol. 22

SAN JACINTO U.S.S. • Screw Steamer

Wrecked January 1, 1865

Series I, vols. 17, 22

Great Abaco, Bahama Isl.
(On No Name Cay) Green Turtle Cay

Wood

Removal of material from wreck. Struck reef about 14' N.W. of Elbow Cay—Capt. Richard W. Meade

Tonnage: 1,567

Wrecked at No Name Cay and wreck sold May 18, 1871, at Nassau.

Battery:
1 - 100# Parrott rifle
10 - IX'' Dahlgren S.B.
1 - 20# Parrott rifle
1 - heavy 20#
1 - light 20#
1 - 24# Howitzer
1 - 12#

Series I, vol. 22

Removal of wreck of U.S.S. *San Jacinto.*

U.S. *Trefoil* sent to take on board all material remaining on the key.

SANFORD U.S. • Army Transport

December 10, 1862

Series I, vol. 19, pp. 401, 417

Carysfort Light, Florida

About 1 1/2 south of light, ran on reef—wind N. standing S.W.— ran close by Carysfort Light S. of Turtle Harbor.

Large quantities of government property thrown overboard soon after she struck.

Got off again without loss, December 14, 1862.

SARAH

May 28, 1863

Series I, vol. 5, p. 85

Great Wicomico River, Virginia (?)

Destroyed eastern branch of river.

SARAH • Schooner

May 1, 1862

Series I, vol. 12, pp. 793, 800

Bull's Bay, South Carolina

Wind (light) from S.E.— could not get out of Bay, tripped anchor and ran ashore— fired and burned rapidly—launch about 2 miles from her.

Hailing from Nassau, N.P.

SARAH BIBBEY U.S.S. • Schooner, Stone Fleet

Series II, vol. 1, p. 200

Acquired August 3, 1861.

SARAH BLADEN • Schooner

December 11, 1863

Series I, vol. 20, p. 856

Bayou Bunfouca

43 ton.

And Barge *Helena.*

SARAH M. KEMP U.S.S. • Schooner, Stone Fleet

Series II, vol. 1, p. 701

Acquired August 13, 1861, at Baltimore, Maryland.

SARAH MARGARET • Schooner

June 11, 1863

Series I, vol. 5, p. 285

Coan River

Burned inside by boat from Coeur de Lion.

SARAH MARY OF NASSAU N.P. • **Sloop**

June 27, 1864

Series I, vol. 15, p. 541

Off Mosquito Inlet, Florida

On the beach near the mouth of Horse Isl. Creek.

SARANAC U.S.S. • **Side Wheel Steamer**

June 18, 1875

Series II, vol. 1, p. 201

Vancouver Isl.

Wood

Seymour Narrows

Tonnage: 1,446

Length: 215' 6''   Beam: 37' 9''   Depth: 26' 6''

Battery:
1 - XI Dahlgren S.B.
8 - VIII rifles 55 cwt.
2 - 30# Parrott rifles
2 - 12#

SATELLITE U.S.S. • **Sidewheeled Steamer, Tug**

September 2, 1863

Series I, vol. 5, p. 345

Port Royal, Virginia
(1/2 mile below)

Destruction of wreck.

Wood

Tonnage: 217

Length: 120' 7''   Beam: 22' 9''   Depth: 8' 6''

Battery:
1 - VIII'' 55 cwt.
1 - 30# Parrott rifle

1 - 32# cannon lost overboard while dismantling

SAVANNAH • Stone Fleet

Series I, vol. 12, p. 418

Savannah, Georgia

Loaded with granite—sunk in narrow channel above Tybee Light.

25 vessels.

SAVANNAH C.S.

December 21, 1864

Series I, vol. 16, p. 484

Savannah, Georgia
Screven's Ferry

Vicinity—crew and last boats landed at Ferry Wharf after firing the ship.

Probably the *Isondiga* and *Georgia.*

SAVANNAH C.S. • Ram

Series I, vol. 16, p. 289

Savannah River, Georgia

Appear entirely destroyed by explosion of her magazine; I may recover her guns—March 11, 1865.

SCHULTZ • Steamer

February 19–20, 1865

Series I, vol. 12, p. 186

James River, Virginia
Chaffin's Bluff

Blown up by torpedo just below Bluff at Bishop's, 60 yards from south bank.

SCIOTA U.S.S. • Screw Steamer, Gunboat

Sunk April 14, 1865

Series I, vols. 20, 22

Mobile Bay Area, Alabama

Wood

Raising and condition of by torpedo, April 14, 1865.

U.S.S. *Antona*, July 14, 1863.

Wreck sold at public auction October 15, 1865.

Tonnage: 507

Length: 158' Beam: 28' Depth: 12' Draft Fwd: 5' Aft.: 7'

Battery:
1 - 20# Parrott rifle
2 - 24# Howitzers
1 - XI Dahlgren S.B.
1 - heavy 12# SB

Series I, vol. 20, pp. 389, 485

July 14, 1863

Rammed by U.S.S. *Antona* in Mississippi River. Sank near E. Bank in 12' water. 8 miles N. of quarantine (68 miles below New Orleans).

August 26, 1863, raised and lying here at New Orleans.

SCOTLAND • Steamer

Series I, vol. 25, p. 133

Yazoo River, Mississippi
Greenwood

15 miles of Ft. Pemberton from mouth.

John Walsh
R.J. Lockland, Golden Age,
Scotland

Sunk on a bar—fired and destroyed all except what was under water.

SCOTTISH CHIEF • Steamer

October 16–17, 1863

Series I, vol. 17, p. 570

See *Kate Dale*

SCUPPERNONG • Schooner

June 10, 1862

Series I, vol. 7, p. 487

Indiantown, North Carolina
North River

A short distance below the bridge, partly laden with oak timber.

Burned.

SEA BIRD C.S.S. • Coal Schooner, Side Wheel River Steamer

February 10, 1862

Series I, vol. 9, p. 38

Elizabeth City, North Carolina

2 Guns

Second ship that name Neuse River, May 23, 1863.

Cargo of coal transferred to 2nd Schooner.

U.S. Army Steamer *Allison* scuttled her to prevent use after finding her near another boat aground and on fire with 50 ton coal.

Possible vicinity Wilkinson's Point.

Sold.

SELMA C.S.S. • Side Wheel Wood Steamer, Gunboat

August 5, 1864

Series II, vol.1 p. 266

Ent. Mobile
Capt. Battle
Mobile Bay

Length: 252'   Beam: 30'   Depth: 6'   Draft: 6'

Battery:
2 - 9''
1 - 8''
1 - 6'' rifle, all in pivot

February 5, 1863—sunk in 8' water at entrance to Mobile, Alabama.

February 13, 1863—raised and repaired.

SERETA • Schooner of Nassau

June 8, 1862

Series I, vol. 7, p. 466

Shallotte Inlet
Inside

Salt, fruit, etc.—destroyed by fire set by 2 boats from U.S.S. Gunboat *Penobscot*.

SHARP • Confederate Steamer

Series I, vol. 25

Mississippi River
Sunflower River

SHARP • **Rebel Steamer**

Series I, vol. 25, p. 756

Yalobusha River

Burned to prevent falling into Union hands.

SHAWSHEEN (SHESHONEE) • **Sidewheeled Steamer, Tug Gunboat**

May 7, 1864

Series I, vol. 10, p. 26

James River, Virginia
Turkey Bend

By Confederate batteries at Turkey Bend.

Tonnage: 180

Length: 118' Beam: 22' 6'' Depth: 7' 3''

Battery:
1 - 20# Parrott rifle
1 - 30# Parrott rifle
1 - 12# Howitzer rifle (Dahlgren)

Series I, vol. 10, p. 27

Body of Act. Eng. Char. Ringot (in temporary command) interred in family burial ground of Mr. Watkins of Watkins' Landing about a mile above (in Curles Neck).

Attack battery on north bank—backed ashore on south bank.

Shawsheen set ablaze by Reb and magazine blew.

Series I, vol. 10, p. 29

Left Flagship *Malvern* at 10:30; 2 miles above Chaffin's Bluff to proceed to Chaffin's farm to search for torpedoes—at 11:20, anchored off farm in 6' water, we drawing 5 1/2'.

Battery opened fire from woods on cliff.

Series I, vol. 10, p. 30

C.S. Report

Battery encountered *Shawsheen* of Turkey Isl.

Nothing removed save prisoners.

An hour before party from boat had fired house and corn houses of Robt. Taylor adjoining.

SHEPHERD KNOPP U.S.S. • Sailing Ship

May 18, 1863

Series II, vol. 1, p. 207

Cape Haiten on Coral Reef

Under Act. Vol. Lieut. H.S. Eytinge, Commanding.

Tonnage: 838

Length: 160' 10'' Beam: 33' 8'' Depth: 22' 3'' Draft Light: 13'

SHINGISS • Steamer

July 9, 1862

Series I, vol. 23, p. 255

Mississippi River

Struck a snag and sank about 7 miles below Ft. Pillow.

SIDELL U.S.A.

Series I, vol. 24, p. 19

Cumberland River
Above Harpeth Shoals

Old ferryboat with a field piece.

Adm. Porter remarks as to Quarter Master Corp.

Recovered starboard gun from wreck of *Sidell*.

SIDNEY C. JONES U.S. • Mortar Schooner

July 15, 1862

Series I, vol. 19, p. 712

Grounded in attack of Vicksburg batteries.

Tonnage: 245

Length: 98' Beam: 27' Depth: 7' 8''

Battery:
1 - XIII inch mortar
2 - 32# 57 cwt.
2 - heavy 12# S.B.

#13 aground and on fire—blew up—Westfield brought 3 mortar boats up—placed foremast near burning wreck on left bank.

SIGNAL U.S.S.

Series I, vol. 26, pp. 113, 119, 135

Red River
Below Alexandria

Abreast an almost perpendicular bank (left bank going down).

Guns removed by Rebs.

SIGNAL U.S. • Gunboat, *COVINGTON* and *WARNER* • Transports

Report of the Sect. of War
Vol. II, p. 1, 299

We received news on the morning of the 6th of May 1865 of the destruction of the gunboats and transport. The enemy had established a battery near Marksville supported by a large infantry force.

Ft. De Russy is below the batteries 3 miles from Marksville for the defense of the Red River.

SIGNAL U.S.S. (NO. 8) • Stern Wheel Steamer

May 15, 1864

Series I, vol. 26
Series II, vol. 1

Commanding—Act. Vol. Lieut. Edward Morgan, U.S.N.

Wood

Battery:
2 - 30# Parrott
2 - 12# Rifled Dahlgren
4 - 24# Howitzers

All captured by Col. Baylor, C.S. Army.

May 5, 1864, by shore batteries about 20 miles below Alexandria.
Tonnage: 190

Length: 157' Beam: 30' Depth: 4' 4''

Battery:
3 - 32# 42 cwt.
4 - 24# Howitzers
2 - 12# Dahlgren rifle Howitzer

SHRAPNEL C.S.S. • Tender

April 4, 1865

Series II, vol. 1, p. 267

Richmond, Virginia

Burned by Confederates.

SMITH BRIGGS U.S.A.• Gunboat

January 31, 1864

Series I, vol. 10, p. 218

Smithfield, James River
Close proximity to Smithfield

Captured and destroyed.

Series I, vol. 9, pp. 425, 430

On Pagan Creek, about 5 miles.

Magazine exploded.

Beyond around a point of land.

On peninsula formed by Nausemond River and Pagan Creek to within 2,000 yards
of Smithfield, may be 250 yards from wharf below town.

SMOKER • British Iron Vessel

September 18, 1863

Series I, vol. 20, p. 595

Tampico, Mexico
While engaged loading a British vessel outside the bar with 80 bales of cotton taken
from the *Sarah*, was stranded on the beach, all of which will be a total loss.

SOLEDAD COS alias *ANNA TAYLOR* • Schooner

Series I, vol. 17, p. 35

Was wrecked at Sabine Pass, Texas.

Crew of 9.

Captured September 11, 1861.

Series I, vol. 16, pp. 665–66, 734,
749

Has center board and draws 3' water.

SOMERFIELD U.S.S. • Schooner, Stone Fleet

Series II, vol. 1, p. 210

Acquired August 13, 1861.

SOMERSET • Schooner

June 8, 1861

Series I, vol. 4, p. 507

Breton's Bay, Maryland

Captured in Breton's Bay and had been engaged in carry provisions. Towed close to Virginia shore and burned.

SOMERSET, DUKE OF

Series I, vol. 4

Capture and destruction.

SOPHIA • British Schooner

March 3, 1864, captured.

Series I, vol. 15, pp. 349–54

At sea
May 8, 1864

Latitude 38° 30' N.
Longitude 69° W

Did not say destroyed.

Crew and cargo transported to Italian Bark *Aurora*.

SOPHIA • British Schooner

Captured March 3, 1864
Loss May 8, 1864

Series I, vol. 15, p. 349

At Sea

Latitude 38°, 30' N., Longitude 69° W.

Found ashore N.E. part of Egg Isl. (Altamaha Sound). Prize sailed March 26 with overtaking heavy weather and loss at sea.

SOPHIA • Large British Bark

November 4, 1862

Series I, vol. 8, p. 194

Masonboro Inlet, North Carolina.

Aground on the beach about 2 1/2 (3 1/2) miles west to 4 miles S.W. of Mas. Inlet—in breakers—not over 300 yards out.

Cargo: salt, saltpeter, soda ash, 3 brass field pieces, gun carriages, trucks, small arms

5 prisoners removed and boat fired effectively—enveloped in flames.

Burned to water's edge—some cargo may be saved.

Also morning of 6th, another bark and schooner ran ashore at our approach and totally destroyed by surf—also schooner derelict partially burned, loaded with rosin.

SOPHIA • Prize Schooner

May 8, 1864

Series I, vol. 15, p. 350

At Sea

Boat unloaded on to Italian Bark *Aurora*.

Latitude 38°, 30' N., Longitude 69° W.

Capt. Dominico Chirico.

SOUTH AMERICA U.S.S. • Bark, Stone Fleet

Series II, vol. 1, p. 211

Acquired November 7, 1861, at New Bedford, Massachusetts.

Tonnage: 606

SOUTHERNER U.S.S. • Schooner, Stone Fleet

Series II, vol. 1, p. 211

Acquired August 13, 1861, at Baltimore, Maryland.

SOUTHFIELD

May 16, 1864

Series I, vol. 10, p. 640

Plymouth, North Carolina
One mile below town

Have succeeded in raising 2 - IX Dahlgren guns and 1 - 100# Parrott and hope to succeed in getting the others.

SOUTHFIELD • Gunboat

Plymouth, North Carolina

Sunk by the *Albermarle* (iron clad ram), Roanoke River, April 18, 1864.

The ram first struck the *Miami* and *Gliding*.

Off struck the *Southfield* on her left side crushing in six or eight square feet.

The *Southfield* rapidly sunk.

The federal gunboats were anchored in the river opposite the town.

Series II, vol. 2, p. 745

On the night of the 19th instant the ironclad screw sloop *Albermarle* of 2 guns.
Commander Cooke—with about 100 men, descended the Roanoke River in
cooperation with Gen. Hoke, passed the batteries near Plymouth, received their fire
and attacked their steam gunboats, sinking the *Southfield,* 6 gun, 117 men, only 8
were saved.

Miami of 12 guns escaped.

Series I, vol. 10, pp. 86, 406

May 24, 1864

The guns of the *Southfield* have been raised. One has been sent away and 2 are on
the wharf ready for transportation, thinks they are evacuating the place.

SOUTHFIELD U.S.S. • Sidewheel Steamer, Double-end Wood Ferry

Sunk April 19, 1864, by C.S. Ram *Albermarle.*

Series II, vol. 1, p. 212

Plymouth, North Carolina

Raising of guns by Confederates.

Wreck of U.S.S. *Southfield.*

Tonnage: 750, 781

Length: 200' Beam: 34' Depth: 11' 8'' Draft: 6' 6''

Battery:
1 - 100# Parrott rifle
3 - IX inch Dahlgren S.B.
1 - 12# S.B.
2 - IX inch Dahlgren S.B.

117 men

Chas. W. Flusser, Commanding, was killed aboard.

SOUTHWIND U.S.S. • Schooner, Stone Fleet

Series II, vol. 1, p. 212

Acquired August 13, 1861, at Baltimore, Maryland.

SPARKLING SEA • Transport, and *SWAN* • Steamer

January 14, 1863

Series I, vol. 17, p. 352

And Swan (Steamer).

Key West, Florida

Between Key West and Indian River on coast about a day out due to gale. Everything on board lost.

Reported by U.S. *Sagamore*.

SPRAY • Schooner

March 3, 1865

Series I, vol. 12, p. 61

Cape Lookout, North Carolina

Rescue of crew.

U.S.S. *Rhode Island* on passage from Beaufort to Hampton Roads discover Schooner on shoals about 11 miles S.S.E. of Cape Lookout.

Spray of Egg Harbor, New Jersey—Israel G. Adams Mast.

Load of coal for army.

Series I, vol. 27, p. 711

March 2, 1865, discovered.

Struck February 28.

On reef 10 miles S.E. by E. from Cape Lookout Lighthouse.

Vessel a total loss.

Left Ft. Monroe for Beaufort, North Carolina.

SPRAY C.S.S. • Steamer, Gunboat, Tug

Series II, vol. 1, p. 267

St. Mary's River, Florida

Battery: 2 gun

Sunk by Confederates.

SPUNKIE

February 9, 1864

Series I, vol. 9, p. 473

Ft. Caswell

Ashore broadside, bow west, on the beach a short distance west of Ft. Caswell.

Bound in with blankets, shoes, provisions.

Principal portion of cargo removed.

Broken in two and a wreck.

ST. MARY C.S.S. • Side Wheel River Steamer

Series II, vol. 1, p. 265

Yazoo River, Mississippi

Burned.

2 guns.

ST. MARY'S

February 9, 1864

Series I, vol. 15, p. 279

McGirt's Creek, Florida
St. John's River

Jacksonville, Florida

ST. MARY'S • Steamer

February 11, 1864

Series I, vol. 12, pp. 638, 640,
643

St. John's River, Florida

Discovery and raising of vessel.

At the head of Dunn's Lake.

Haw Creek up St. John's River, 140 miles from Palatka.

Series I, vol. 15, pp. 276–81,
288, 423

Cedar creek above Jacksonville, March 6, 1864
McGirt's Creek.

Small rifled gun found ashore at abandoned camp.

ST. NICHOLAS

April 19, 1862

Series I, vol. 5, pp. 34, 37

Fredericksburg, Virginia

Burned at evacuation.

Supposed to have 2 guns—may have been removed.

Former U.S. Steamer *Star of the West.*

ST. PHILIP C.S.S.

Series II, vol. 1, p. 265

Fort Pemberton, Mississippi

Former U.S. *Star of the West.*

Sunk at Ft. Pemberton above mouth of Yalobusha, in Tallahatchie, Mississippi, as an obstruction.

ST. PAUL • Steamer

April 16, 1865

Series I, vol. 27

Hatcher River, Tennessee
Morgan's Landing

About 40 miles from mouth.

STAG • Rebel Steamer

Series I, vol. 7, pp. 440, 711

Blackwater River
Franklin, 20 miles up

Two schooners and steamer *Stag* sunk a short distance below railroad depot.

1/4 miles from Railroad bridge.

STAR C.S.S.

Series I, vol. 18, pp. 249, 250,
252, 270, 291, 297

STARS & STRIPES • Steamer

October 2, 1861

Series I, vol. 6, p. 280

North Carolina

Abandoned towing stone vessels from Old Point to Hatteras Inlet to be sunk as obstructions.

Also one schooner.

To be sunk in Oregon Loggerhead and Ocracoke inlets (on bulkhead not outer bar).

STAR OF THE UNION U.S.S.

November 6, 1862

Series I, vol. 6, p. 689

To the east of Bogue Inlet.

Run ashore November 1, 1862, in S.E. gale.

Communicated with shore under flag of truck.

Two steamers ashore off Charleston and 2 off Hatteras.

December 18, wreck of *Union* fired.

STAR OF THE UNION or SOUTH • Iron Side Wheel Steamer

November 1, 1861

Series I, vol. 6, p. 416

Bogue Island

Ashore on Bogue Isl. (Banks), 20 miles west of Beaufort.

Cargo: horses, provisions and hay.

Run ashore in leaky condition, broke in two.

STAR OF THE WEST

Series I, vol. 4, p. 165

Seized in New Orleans, April 28, 1861, by Gov. Moore of Louisiana.

Belonged to Morgan's Texas Line.

Spoke Edith, of Harwich, Massachussetts—she reported *Star of the West* had attempted to enter the harbor (Charleston, South Carolina) on the (January 1861) 10th instant, but being fired into put to sea again—U.S.S. Sloop *Brooklyn*.

STAR OF THE WEST C.S.S.

March 20, 1863

Series I, vol. 24, pp. 266, 271, 671

Greenwood
Tallahatchie River

Sunk below rafts at Ft. Pemberton, 3 miles from Greenwood by land.

Also, Chillico, the 11 inch shells hit steamboat just beyond fort below Greenwood.

Sunk alongside of raft to keep it from going downstream—she had never been converted to an ironclad and the machinery is still all in her.

Series I, vol. 25, pp. 133, 756,

June 1, 1863

Sunk, blockading completely the *Yalobusha*—must be an error.

Opposite Ft. Pemberton.

September 9, 1862, report of Maj. Gen. Van Dor, C.S.A.

I commanded Capt. Brown to take the ark.

Series I, vol. 19, p. 137

Through the raft of the Yazoo and sink *Star of the West* in the passage. Capt. Brown substituted a vessel of inferior quality.

STEPHEN YOUNG U.S.S. • Brig, Stone Fleet

Series II, vol. 1, p. 214

Acquired November 27, 1861, at Boston, Massachusetts.

Tonnage: 199

STEPHENY • Barge

December 10, 1863

Series I, vol. 20

STEVENS • Rebel Gunboat

Series I, vol. 20, p. 824

New Iberia, Louisiana

Unfinished and sunk about 2 miles below.

STING RAY • British Schooner

May 22, 1864

Series I, vol. 21, p. 296

Velasco, Texas

Beaching about 2 miles west.

STONEWALL • Schooner

October 14, 1862

Series I, vol. 19, p. 228

Taylor's Bayou, Texas
Off Sabine

Burned enemy's barracks and schooner near railroad bridge also destroyed.

2 1/2 miles from town.

Barracks about 5 miles from Pass.

Sold.

STONEWALL JACKSON • Steamer

April 12, 1863

Series I, vol. 14, p. 126

Charleston, South Carolina

Formerly *Leopard*.

While attempting to run in, beached on Long Island, burned to water's edge.

Cargo: several pieces field artillery, 200 barrels of salt peter, 40,000 army shoes, large assortment of merchandise.

Under protection of Char T. Haskell, Jr., Capt. battery.

STONO C.S.S.

1865

Series II, vol. 2, p. 530

Charleston, South Carolina
Fort Moultrie, South Carolina

The *Stono* was stranded on the breakwater near Ft. Moultrie.

Cargo: cotton

Series II, vol. 1, p. 267

Burned by Confederates at evacuation of Charleston, 1865.

Forme*r Isaac Smith*.

Series I, vol. 14, p. 494

Chased by enemy, stranded on beach water by Ft. Moultrie.

Cargo: cotton

STORMY PETREL

December 7, 1864

Series I, vol. 11, p. 754

Off Federal Point.
Ft. Fisher, North Carolina
New Inlet, Cape Fear River

Capt. Donaly, Sellers, pilot, Langham, operator, grounded well out on south breakers.

December 9, N.E. gale came up last night and this morn *Stormy Petrel* was a complete wreck.

Power, low and co. sent 50 Negroes to try to save cargo - some cloth saved.

Series I, vol. 11, p. 745

Grounded well out in south breakers.

Trying to come in—some cargo of cloth salvaged.

SUMTER C.S.S.

Harper's Weekly
August 16, 1862, p. 525

Prop.— Bark rigged carrying 5 guns.

4 - 32# and 1 - 68# on pivot

Captain Semmes

Commissioned June 3, 1861.

June 29—a field Howitzer 12# added to *Sumter*. Later thrown overboard to trim ship.

Series I, vol. 9, p. 229

Before Oct. 5, 1863—Bermuda Gazette

C.S. *Sumter*, alias *Gibraltar*, in Charleston Harbor. She was fired into by Ft. Moultrie. Rebel mistaking her for Fed. *Man of War*.

630 persons on board—all but 20 saved.

Series II, vol. 1, p. 268

Sold.

SUMTER U.S.S. • Ironclad Steamer

August 1862

Series II, vol. 1, p. 216

Bayou Sara, Louisiana
Mississippi River

Tonnage: 400

Battery:
1 - 32# 42 cwt.
1 - 32# 60 cwt.

Got ashore and abandoned.

Most machinery stolen at low water and when wrecked.

Good only for old iron.

SUWANEE U.S.S. • Schooner, Iron Side Wheel Steamer

July 9, 1868

Series II, vol. 1, p. 217

Shadwell Passages

Double end, 2 mast schooner.

Tonnage: 1,030

Depth For.: 8' 2''   Aft.: 9'

Battery:
2 - 100# Parrott R.F.
4 - IX Dahlgren S.B.
1 - Light 12 S.B.
2 - 20# Dahlgren R.F.

SWALLOW • Steamer

August 19, 1862

Series I, vol. 2, 3 p. 307

Memphis, Tennessee

Ashore 10 or 12 days, 22 miles below this place. Boarded by guerrillas and burned.

SWITZERLAND U.S.S. • Ram

March 25, 1863

Series II, vol. 1, p. 218

Vicksburg Batt.

Tonnage: 500

SYKES

June 18, 1863

Series I, vol. 20, p. 235

Plaquemine, Louisiana

SYLVANUS • British Blockade Runner

January 2, 1864

Series I, vol. 15, p. 219

About 1 mile inside up the Doboy Sound, Georgia.

Cargo: salt, spirits and cordage

From Nassau, N.P.

Cargo and ship apparently abandoned.

SYLVANUS • British Schooner

January 2, 1864

Series I, vol. 15, p. 220

Doboy Sound, Georgia

Sunk by U.S. *Huron*—shot through and run aground.

1st sighted 3/4 mile off *Huron* anchorage.

Up the sound with light N.N.E. breeze.

Water rose above deck and let go anchor.

Cargo: Salt, spirits, cordage

T

T.W. RILEY • Sloop

Series I, vol. 4

TACONY C.S.S. • Bark

Burned June 25, 1863

Series II, vol. 1, p. 268

Captured by C.S.S. *Clarence*, June 12, 1863.

TALOMICO C.S.S. • Sidewheel Steamer

1863

Series II, vol. 1, p. 268

Savannah Harbor, Georgia

2 guns—accidentally sunk

TAWAH U.S.S. (NO. 29) • Sidewheeled Steamer, Wood

November 4, 1864

Series I, vol. 27, p. 284

Near Johnsonville, Tennessee

Sunk and burned to prevent capture.

Former *Ebenezer*.

Guns taken from wreck.

Many parts recovered from her in 1865.

Tonnage: 108

Length: 114'   Beam: 33'   Depth: 3' 9''

Battery:
2 - 30#
4 - 24#
2 - 12# Wiard rifles

Recovered as of June 29, 1865, by A.V.L. Rogers of U.S.S. *Kate*.

4 - 24# Howitzers
2 - rifled steel 12#

TECUMSEH U.S.S. • Screw Steamer

August 5, 1864

Series I, vol. 21, p. 818

Ft. Morgan
Mobile Bay Area, Alabama

Single Turret Monitor of Wood and Iron.

Sunk by torpedo at battle of Mobile Bay.

Commander Craven was drowned.

Arrived overdue, August 4, 5:45 p.m.
Sank 7:22 a.m., August 5.

Tonnage: 1,034

Draft loaded 14' light

Battery: July 1864
2 - XV Dahlgren S.B.

*Military & Naval History
of the Rebellion*, p. 646

Ft. Morgan, Mobile Bay Pass, Alabama

At about 7:00 as the head of the column came abreast of the fort, the latter opened fire—at 7:40, while the firing was at its height and the fleet making rapid progress in spite of the obstructions in its path, the Monitor *Tecumseh* struck a torpedo, which blew a large hole through her bottom, just under the turret, and almost immediately she filled with water and sank.

About 200 yards from the fort.

Some Famous Sea Fights
pp. 204, 213–14, 225

Within six hundred yards of the Fort.

Gaines made for Fort Morgan and ran aground.

Rebel Gunboat—6 guns

Series I, vol. 21, p. 725

200 or 300 yards from wharf in S.W. direction in 7 fathoms with 3 fathoms over her —November 9, 1864.

TENEDOS U.S.S. • Bark, Stone Fleet

Series II, vol. 1, p. 221

Tonnage: 245

Acquired October 16, 1861, at New London, Connecticut.

TEXANA • Bark

June 8, 1863

Series I, vol. 20, p. 828
Series II, vol. 2, p. 530

Mississippi Sound

Captured and burned June 9th—assorted cargo—by Acting Master James Duke (C.S.N.) out of Mobile by Pass A'L'Outre towards sea in captured Federal steam prop. *Boston.*

TEXAS C.S. • Steamer

November 13, 1861

Series I, vol. 16, pp. 768, 820

San Louis Bar, Texas

Destruction of Schooner

The U.S.S. *Sam Houston* chased a schooner of 60 or 70 ton off San Louis bar causing her to run ashore on the breakers—entirely destroyed as there was a heavy surf running and sea breaking entirely over her.

THEODORE STONEY • Schooner

February 14, 1862

Series I, vol. 12, pp. 547–50

Bull's Bay, South Carolina

Off.

THISTLE • Steamer

Series I, vol. 26, p. 501

Paducah, Kentucky

Sunk about 60 miles above Paducah in 8' of water with $10,000 worth of Navy tobacco on board—do all you can to save and protect Government property—August 8, 1864.

THOMAS JEFFERSON C.S.S. • Sidewheel Steamer

May 1862

Series II, vol. 1, p. 269

James River, Virginia
Drewry's Bluff

THOMAS WATSON • Merchant Ship

October 15, 1861

Series I, vol. 6, pp. 323, 325, 326.

Charleston, South Carolina

Aground on Stono Reef—burned to water's edge.

Cargo: Salt, blankets, no arms

1 1/2 miles from Rebel Battery; northeastern side of Stono Breakers.

Among articles on board was an iron 9 pounder, together with small quantity of ball, which was thrown overboard.

THOMPSON U.S.S.E.D. • Schooner, Stone Fleet

Series II, vol. 1, p. 76

Purchased at Baltimore, Maryland, August 13, 1861.

TIGRESS U.S. • Army Steamer, Transport

April 22, 1863

> *Military & Naval History*
> *of the Rebellion*, p. 346

Vicksburg, Mississippi
Mississippi River

April 22, 1862—The *Tigress* received a shot in her hull below the waterline, and sunk on the Louisiana shore after passing the last of the batteries.

> Series I, vol. 24, pp. 604, 630

Received 15 shots.

She rounded to at Johnson's Plantation, 3 1/2 miles below Vicksburg. Grounded and sank breaking amidships—total loss.

April 23, 1863—The wreck of one of the boats in sight near Brown & Johnston's— smoke stack and one wheelhouse out of water.

TIGRESS U.S.S. • Tug

> Series II, vol. 1, p. 224

Indian Head
Potomac River

Run down by steamer.

Raised and sold, November 22, 1862.

TIME C.S.

February 12, 1862

> Series I, vol. 22, p. 821

Tennessee River at Florence

$100,000 worth of Government stores.

TIMOR U.S.S. • Ship, Stone Fleet

> Series II, vol. 1, p. 224

Tonnage: 289

Acquired October 30, 1861, at Sag Harbor, New York.

TITAN U.S.A. • Tug

March 5, 1864

Series I, vol. 9, p. 530

Piankatank River, Virginia
Freeport, Eastern Shore

Captured Cherrystone Inlet—22 miles up river.

Burned to water's edge.

Series I, vol. 5, pp. 400, 402, 611

Rifles—no cannon

Captured with *McClellan* Steamer.

March 7, 1864—lying above Haley's Farms, on the opposite side.

TOM HICKS

July 9, 1861

Series I, vol. 16, p. 578

Off Galveston, Texas

27 tons

Scuttled.

Cargo: lumber—owned at Calcasieu Bay, Louisiana

Galveston to Port Lavaca
Capt. Charles Wells

Lumber, 15,000 ft., transferred to U.S.S. *South Carolina*.

Ex. Doc. 253-(279)-295
40th Cong., 2nd. Sess.

Schooner.

Lumber.

July 9, 1861—Galveston by South Carolina.

Sunk.

TORPEDO C.S. • Prize, Boat

June 7, 1865

Series I, vol. 16, p. 344

Cape Hatteras

While being towed north after being raised from Cooper R., Charleston, where sunk at evacuation.

TORPEDO C.S.S.

April 4, 1865

Series II, vol. 1, p. 269

Richmond, Virginia

By Confederates.

Taken to Norfolk, Virginia, as prize much injured.

TROPIC • **Confederate, Side Wheel Steamer**

January 18, 1863

Series I, vols. 13, 27

Off Charleston, South Carolina

Formerly *Huntress.*

Former C.S.S. *Huntress* used as Blockade Runner *Tropic.*

Tonnage: 500

Length: 230'

Battery: 1 gun

TROPIC C.S. • **Steamer**

January 18, 1863

Series I, vol. 13, p. 516

Charleston, South Carolina

Former *Huntress.*

South side of blockade—found steamer in flames.

TRUXILLO • **Schooner**

December 10, 1863

Series I, vol. 20, p. 856

On Bayou Lacomb, Louisiana.

37 ton

And Barge *Stepheny.*

TULIP U.S.A.T.

Series I, vol. 4

Rappahannock River, Virginia
Ragged Point

TULIP U.S.S. • Screw Steamer, Tug

November 11, 1864

Series II, vol. 1, p. 226

Ragged Point, Virginia

Destroyed by boiler explosion.

W.H. Smith, Act. Master Commanding

Tonnage: 183

Length: 97' 3''   Beam: 21' 9''   Depth: 9' 6''   Draft: 8' loaded

Battery:
1 - 20# Parrott rifle
2 - 24#
2 - heavy 12#

TUSCALOOSA C.S.S. • Ironclad, Steamer, Floating Battery

Series II, vol. 1, p. 269

Mobile, Alabama

4 Gun

Sunk 12 miles above Mobile in Spanish River.

TUSCARORA C.S.S. • Side Wheel River Steamer

November 23, 1861

Series II, vol. 1, p. 270

New Orleans, Louisiana

Accidentally burned.

1 - 32#
1 - 8'' Columbiad

Series I, vol. 22, p. 804

While coming up river, discovered afire 15 miles this side of Helena (Memphis paper)— explosion of shells set slave quarters on fire at Mr. Harbett's (Harbert's) Plantation—magazine at stern underwater having been run aground.

TWO BROTHERS • Schooner

September 2, 1863

Series I, vol. 5, p. 345

Port Royal, Virginia

47 ton

U

UATEREE U.S.S. • Side Wheel Steamer, Iron Gunboat

August 13, 1868

Series II, vol. 1, p. 237

Arica, Peru

Stranded by tidal wave, August 13, 1868.

Sold.

UNCLE BEN C.S.

June 24, 1863

Series I, vol. 20, p. 830

2 - 12# iron guns
1 - 12# Mountain Howitzer

UNDERWRITER U.S. • Gunboat

February 2, 1864

Series I, vol. 9, pp. 439, 449, 453, 458, 468

Off Newbern, North Carolina

Captured and blown up at anchor in Neuse River. Set fire and retreated under a fire from battery on shore—stripped off everything they could carry off.

Above our line of works—burned to the water's edge, then Ft. Stevenson opened on the vessel.

Positioned to command and the plain outside our line of works.

Boat not worth raising.

Battery:
2 - VIII' 55 Hundred weight
2 - 12# Howitzers could not be found

Lying aground off Foster's Wharf within a few hundred yards from General quarters.

Recovered 1 - 12# Howitzer, anchor and chain—U.S.S. *Hetzel*, February 7, 1864.

UNDERWRITER U.S.S. • Sidewheeled Steamer

February 2, 1864

Series I, vol. 12, p. 181
Series I, vol. 9, pp. 439–54

Captured and destroyed by Confederates in Neuse River, North Carolina.

Tonnage: 341

Length: 170'   Beam: 23' 7''   Depth: 8' 1''

Battery:
2 - VIII inch 55 cwt.
1 - 12# rifle
1 - 12# S.B.

Series I, vol. 4, p. 699

Bottom coppered—October 1, 1861.

*Military & Naval History
of the Rebellion*

Newbern, North Carolina

The Steamer was aground but so lay as to cover a portion of the fortifications between Ft. Anderson and Fort Stevens at Newbern.

Captured and destroyed February 1–2, 1864.

Series II, vol. 2, pp. 648, 744

4 guns and crew of 85.

Taken by Capt. Wilson and detachment of C.S. Marines and Col. J. Taylor Wood, C.S.A.—boarded and captured but could not hold and burned her.

33 officers and 220 men, inclusive.

UNDINE • Gunboat

July 25, 1864

Series I, vol. 26, p. 489

Tennessee River
Clifton, Tennessee

Which went down on a snag on the Tennessee River. She was finally raised and got afloat by the exertions of her officers.

UNDINE U.S.S. (NO. 55) • Tinclad

Captured by Confederates and burned November 4, 1864 on Tennessee River.

Series I, vol. 26, pp. 489–91, 605, 609, 622

Tennessee River on west Shore
1 mile above Reynoldsburg Island
Near Johnsonville

Captured by Confederates and burned.

Guns taken from wreck.

Sinking of, July 25, 1864.

Paris landing 40 miles below Johnsonville and 4 miles this way from Ft. Heiman.

Fired and abandoned by enemy without their being able to remove a gun from her.

Gunboats *Key West* and *Elfin* and *Tawah* and all (1) transports fired (the water being of insufficient depth to submerge them below main deck and scuttling) at Johnsonville.

Carried 8 - 24# Brass Howitzers

Gunboats fired—bend opposite upper batteries.

All articles of value recovered. AVL—G.W. Rogers, U.S.S. *Rate*, August 1865.

UNION • Steamer

November 12, 1861

Series I, vol. 6, p. 478

Vicinity of Bogue Inlet

A great number of people gathered around the wreck removing valuables—fired upon.

UNION U.S. • Army Steamer

Series I, vol. 12, pp. 288, 291–93, 828

North Carolina Coast

Driven ashore on coast of North Carolina.

Dest. Port Royal, South Carolina.

Series I, vol. 19, p. 620

February 19, 1863—Had 4,000 in specie on boat.

New Orleans to Galveston—arrived February 23.

UNION U.S. • Transport

April 3, 1863

Series I, vol. 8, p. 703

Off Wilmington, Delaware

From Hilton Head, South Carolina, to Beaufort, North Carolina, engines bad condition, hull working—going to pieces, removed crew—XI inch shells fired into her and sank 1/2 mile from beach.

UNITED STATES U.S. • Frigate

Series II, vol. 1, p. 229
Series I, vol. 5, p. 806

Norfolk, Virginia

Abandoned.
Pumping out by Confederates.

Ordered to be docked and broken up—December 18, 1865.

Prepared for School Ship C.S.

9 - 9'' guns of 9,000#
16 - 32#s of 51 cwt pounds (Columbiads)

V

VANDERBILT U.S.

Harper's Weekly
November 22, 1862, p. 747

Cost nearly one million for Commodore V. by Jeremiah Simpson, 5 years ago.

Tonnage: 5,268

Length: 340'   Beam: 49'   Depth of Hold: 33'

2 engine 2,500 H.P.

12 - 9'' Dahlgren, 6 to a side
2 - 100# Parrott, 1 forward and 1 aft.

Ram solid 50' from bow.

Capt. Baldwin

VARUNA U.S.S. • Screw Steamer

Sunk April 24, 1862, below New Orleans, Louisiana.

Series I, vol. 18

Mississippi River

Raising of *Varuna*.

2 - 8'' 55 cwt.
2 - 30# Parrott guns
8 - 8'' guns in broadside
6 - 8'' 63 cwt.

Tonnage: 1,300

160 men.

VELOCITY U.S. • Schooner

Series I, vol. 19, p. 566

Sabine Pass, Texas

Captured January 23, 1863, mounted 2 brass Dahlgren, 12# Howitzers.

Heavy Model 1858.

U.S. Armed Schooner *Fairy*, former *Velocity*.

VENUS • Steamer, Blockade Runner

October 21, 1863

Series I, vol. 9, p. 248

New Inlet

On beach above Ft. Fisher, complete wreck.

Iron hull.

In-bound.

Cargo: Lead, drugs, dry goods, bacon, coffee

Going 14 knots when went ashore.

Length: 265'

Tonnage: 1,000

Drew 8'

Hebe, Douro and *Venus* within short distance of each other.

VENUS and Transports • River Steamer

November 4, 1864

Series I, vol. 26, p. 612

Johnsonville, Tennessee

Burned with *Undine* and seven other transports; *Tawah, Key West, Elfin,* Transports *Cheeseman* and *Venus.*

VESTRA • Steamer, Blockade Runner

January 11, 1864

Series I, vol. 9, p. 402
Series I, vol. 10

Lockwood's Folly Inlet

Fine double prop. beached and on fire between Tubbs and Little River Inlet.

4 miles below and west of Tubbs Inlet.

500 ton iron.

Draw: 8'

Complete wreck, having removed only anchors and 5' water in her.

Exactly like the *Ceres.*

VICKSBURG • Confederate Wharf Boat

March 30, 1863

Series I, vol. 20, p. 36

Mississippi River
Below Warrenton Battery, Mississippi

had broke loose from that city, floated ashore opposite where *Hartford* and *Albatross* anchored — Rebels came down and burned her.

Machinery taken out (Hulk).

VICTORIA • Rebel Steamer

November 28, 1862

Series I, vol. 19, pp. 380, 386

Off Last Isl., Louisiana

Blown up 2 weeks ago.

Cargo: Arms, ammo, clothing

Ran into Atchafalaya—got on shore—found U.S. in possession—they set fire and she blew up.

VIOLET U.S.S.

Series I, vol. 10, p. 343

Inlet to Cape Fear River, North Carolina
Off Western Bar

3 1/4 fathoms last cast—grounded—forward of stem 7'—swung around hanging amidships—tide set her on shoal in 6'—destroyed with slow match to magazine containing 200# powder.

1 - 12# thrown overboard.
1 - 12# left on forecastle spiked with rat-tail file.
1 - 24# directly over magazine aft. when exploded thrown into the sea.

VIOLET U.S.S. • Tug, Screw Steamer, Wood

August 8, 1864

Series I, vol. 9, p. 367
Series II, vol. 1
Series I, vol. 10

Western Bar Inlet
Cape Fear River, North Carolina
Wreck and lost on August 8, 1864.

Tonnage: 166

Length: 85'   Beam: 19' 9''   Depth: 11'

Battery:
1 - heavy 12#
1 - 12# rifle
1 - 24#

In attempting to pull off Antonica, December 20, 1863, got aground on Frying Pan Shoals and threw her guns overboard but were buoyed and will probably be recovered.

VIRGINIA C.S. (*MERRIMACK*)

May 11, 1862

Series I, vol. 7, p. 337

Craney Isl., Virginia

Put on shore as near the mainland in the vicinity of Craney Isl. as possible and the crew landed—fired and blew up.

We marched for Suffolk, 22 miles, and reached it that evening.

VIRGINIA C.S.

April 19, 1862

Series I, vol. 5, p. 37

Fredericksburg, Virginia

Burned at evacuation.

Also, *St. Nicholas* and 40 schooners.

VIRGINIA II C.S.S. • Ironclad

April 4, 1865

Series II, vol. 1, p. 271

Richmond, Virginia

Draft about 13'

Battery: 4 gun
1 - 11'' Pivot Aft.
1 - 8'' Brooke Rifle Frwd.
1 - 6.4'' Brooke Rifle in each broadside

Blown up by Confederates.

W

W.B. TERRY U.S. • Transport

August 31, 1862

Series I, vol. 23, p. 332

Tennessee River

Arrived at foot of Duck River Sucks. Couldn't get over with load of coal for gunboats in Tennessee River—started down about sundown for Paducah hoping to reach safe anchorage before dark—missed narrow channel and ran onto lower ledge of rocks under Bluff High bank with her steam 20' from shore with less than 2' of water from boat to shore—captured by Rebels—they used her that evening to ferry troops across and next morn stripped and burned her.

W.L. BARTLETT U.S.S. • Schooner, Stone Fleet

Series II, vol. 1, p. 234

Acquired August 13, 1861, at Baltimore, Maryland.

W.W. BURNS U.S.S. • Schooner, Stone Fleet

Series II, vol.1, p. 234

Acquired August 13, 1861, at Baltimore, Maryland.

WANDOO • Schooner

February 14, 1862

Series I, vol. 12, pp. 547–50

Off Bull's Bay, South Carolina

1,800 bushels of rice—sunk.

Lying at anchor inside the shoals.

Also, *Edisto, Elizabeth, Theodore Stoney.*

WARNER U.S. • Army Transport, Steamer

May 5, 1864

Series I, vol. 26, pp. 113, 117

Below Alexandria
Dunn's Bayou Red River
(on river, going down)

Downstream until short point where she drifted on bank with a broken rudder.

Surrendered to battery 100 yards distant opposite bank of battery.

WATER WITCH C.S. • Prize

December 19, 1864

Series I, vol. 16, p. 484

Savannah, Georgia

U.S. Naval Register (378 ton)

WATER WITCH C.S.S. • Side Wheel Steamer

December 19, 1865

Series I, vol. 16, pp. 64, 484, 556
Series II, vol. 1, p. 271

Savannah River, Georgia

Burned December 19, 1865.

Gun salvaged.

Machinery and battery have been removed.

December 19, 1864, at Savannah.

Tonnage: 378

Draft: 10'

Battery:
1 - 32# rifle
1 - 12# rifle
2 - 12# Howitzers

WEBB C.S. • Steamer, Wood, Ram

April 24, 1865

Series I, vol. 24

Sinking of U.S.S. *Indianola*, February 24, 1863.

Series II, vol. 1, p. 271

Tonnage: 656

Length: 195' Beam: 31 1/2' Depth: 12 1/2' Draft: 9 1/2'

Battery:
1 - rifled and banded 32#
2 - Brass 6#

Burned by Confederate at close of war.

Series I, vol. 22, pp. 147, 155, 168

Lieut. C.W. Read, Commanding *W.H. Webb*

1 - 30# Parrott Bow Pivot
2 - iron 12#

Escape out of the Red River to sea.

About 24–25 miles below New Orleans, headed into left bank and fired.

Cargo: Cotton, rosin, turpentine

Armament: 3 guns

At a place called McCall's Point.

Painted white, one smoke stack, two upright engines, one small foremast.

April 26, 1865—The engines of the *Webb*, as well as chains, anchors, battery, etc., will be saved in good order—Act. R. Adm. Thatcher

April 26, 1865—Contracted with Mr. Spencer, Field of Diving Bell Boat Col, of New Orleans, for wrecking *W.H. Webb* on 50-50 expenses paid by latter—H. K. Thatcher, R.A.

Harper's Weekly
August 16, 1862, p. 523

Red River, Louisiana
Mouth of Red River

Stationed to keep cattle and supplies from being ferried across.

*Military & Naval History
of the Rebellion*, p. 708

The Steamer *Webb*, which had been used as a Ram by the enemy on the Red River throughout the war ran the blockade on that river and passed down the Mississippi about April 24, 1865, making an attempt to escape to the West Indies. Being pursued after passing New Orleans and discovering the Steamer *Richmond* coming up the river, her Commander Edward G. Reed, run her ashore and setting her afire, escaped with nearly all the crew into the swamps. The vessel was consumed.

Series I, vol. 27, p. 158

25 miles below New Orleans—broadside fired into her by U.S.S. *Holly Hock*—run ashore and burned. All escaped but 3.

Webb left Shreveport on 17—took on board 50 cords of pine wood and, at Alexandria, 50 tons pine knots.

WEEHAWKEN U.S.S. • Monitor

December 6, 1863

Series I, vol. 15, pp. 161–62

Morris Isl.

Foundered in heavy weather.

Lies in 30' of water.

Send apparatus to raise her.

Sank at Anchorage.

Lay about east of Beacon House on Morris Isl.

WEEHAWKEN U.S.S. • Screw Steamer

December 6, 1863

Series I, vol. 15, pp. 165, 225

Charleston, South Carolina
Morris Island, South Carolina

About east of Beacon House on Morris Isl.
In the Roads.

Single Turret Monitor, Wood and Iron

Top of smoke stack above water—at low water—a foot of pilot house—rests in soft mud—diver sank into it.

January 7, 1864—Recovery not pursued with vigor.

Floating Cap., 150 ton—25 ton ammo received.

Tonnage: 844

*Military & Naval History
of the Rebellion,* p. 451

Sank at her moorings on morn of December 6, 1863, during a northwest gale.

2 - 15'' Dahlgren

Possibly near the mouth of Wilmington River.

Warsaw Sound took the Atlanta.

(Former British Steamer *Fingal*.)
4 shots
Length: 191' Beam: 40'
2 - 6'' rifled guns
2 - 7'' rifled guns
Iron casemate

Inside the Charleston Bar.

Battery:
1 - XV inch S.B. (Dahlgren)
1 - XI inch Dahlgren S.B.

WESTFIELD U.S.S. • Side Wheel Steamer

January 1, 1863

Series I, vol. 19, pp. 464, 466, 745

Galveston, Texas

Tonnage: 822

Length: 215' Beam: 35' Depth: 13' 6''

Battery:
1 - 100# Parrott rifle
1 - IX inch Dahlgren S.B.
4 - 8 inch 55 cwt.

January 3, 1863—her armament is being brought up uninjured.

January 7, 1863—mounted 8 guns

1 - 50# rifle
2 - IX Marsilly
4 - 32# 57 cwt.

Series I, vol. 24, p. 243

Reference to fight, Wainwright—Renshaw

Five gunboats sunk and dispersed by 2 river steamboats armed with 1 gun which burst at 3rd fire.

*Military & Naval History
of the Rebellion*, p. 744

Commodore William B. Renshaw—During the recapture of Galveston, the *Westfield* got hopelessly aground and having a large supply of ammunition and 2 magazines of powder on board, Com. Renshaw determined to destroy her rather than let her fall into the hands of the enemy. Having made all due arrangements, and secured the safety of his men, he stayed behind to light the train before leaving; but a drunken man had, it is said, prematurely lighted the match, and the Com., together with those in the small boats awaiting him, were involved in the general destruction.

Commodore William B. Renshaw: Native of New York—appointed midshipman December 22, 1831, passed midshipman examining board 1837, Lieutenancy 1841, Commander 1861, 31 years in service.

Series I, vol. 19, pp. 441, 450,
451, 663

Paymaster absent—Act. Assnt. Surgeon E.H. Allis—everything in that department was saved that could be. Saved payroll and such papers as were in safe but many books and several files paper left. There was at that time a large stock of provisions and clothing recently supplied for the *Tennessee* U.S.S.

They took from *Lane* and *Westfield* 1 - X inch, 4 - IX inch, 4 32#s 57 cwt., 1 - 50 rifle, 1 30# rifle, 2 - 24# Howitzer.

WHITEHALL U.S. • Gunboat (Old Ferry Boat)

March 10, 1862
Series I, vol. 7, pp. 10, 73, 82, 86

Newport News, Virginia

Is a total wreck—caught fire and is destroyed.

March 8, 1862—abstract log of U.S. *Roanoke*—stood down river and anchored between Ft. Monroe and Sewels Point.

Cargo: small arms, swords, etc., stored from ships in action

Took fire and blew up.

While lying near the landing at Ft. Monroe, 3 guns went off as she burned—another saved by Harbor crew.

WHITEHALL U.S.S. • Sidewheeled Steamer, Wood

March 10, 1862

Series II, vol. 1
Series I, vol. 1

Old Point, Virginia

December 10, 1862—wreck was lying at Mill Creek, Virginia, entirely torn to pieces.

Tonnage: 326

Length: 126'   Beam: 28' 2''   Depth: 10'   Draft - est. - 8'

Battery:
2 - 30# Parrott rifle
2 - 32#, 33 cwt.

WHITMAN • Army Transport

August 7, 1862

Series I, vol. 19, p. 720

Mississippi River
Above Baton Rouge (?)

Ran into *Oneida* at 30 miles point and sank, taking down 40 wounded.

WILD CAT • Schooner

December 22, 1862

Series I, vol. 13, p. 486

Ashepoo River, South Carolina

Ashore.

WILD DAYRELL • Blockade Runner

February 2, 1864

Series I, vol. 9, p. 437

Stump Inlet

Tonnage: 440

Accidentally ashore at mouth of Liverpool.

Fired after unsuccessful recovery.

Cargo nearly discharged—rest destroyed (shoes, blankets and provisions).

Inward bound 2 days from Nassau.

Threw overboard 20 tons coal.

Shoal to Leeward—wind S. and W.

U.S.S. *Sassacus* lost anchor and cable.

Anchored in 2 3/4 fathoms.

Not half cargo thrown overboard deemed valuable, rest consumed with vessel.

WILD PIGEON • British Schooner

March 21, 1864

Series I, vol. 17, p. 670

Sunk by U.S.S. *Hendrick Hudson*—Lieut. Commander McDougal, U.S.N.

37 ton from Havanah.

Run into amidships while overtaking by U.S.S. *Hendrick Hudson*.

Money taken from crew: $726 Confederate, 4 Doubloons, 1/2, 1/4 and 1/8 Doubloon and 3.18 in silver—out of Havanah.

WILL-O-THE-WISP • Large Iron Screw Steamer

February 9, 1865

Series I, vol. 22, pp. 32–36

Galveston, Texas

Riddled by shot.

Partly under water a few miles south of Galveston, Texas.

Landed part of cargo, provisions and small arms, before discovery.

Landed some heavy guns before discovered.

Vessel a complete wreck.

So near the beach it required but a plank to board.

Water barely over 12', 1,000 yards from wreck.

September 20, 1864—Agents: Power, Low & Co.

WILLIAM L. JONES U.S.S. • Schooner, Stone Fleet

Series II, vol. 1, p. 241

Acquired August 13, 1861, at Baltimore, Maryland.

WILLIAM LEE U.S.S. • Ship, Stone Fleet

Series II, vol. 1, p. 241

Acquired November 19, 1861, at Newport, Rhode Island.

Tonnage: 311

WILLIAM SELDON

Series I, vol. 8, p. 35

Norfolk, Virginia

Seized by Rebels and burned when Norfolk was evacuated.

WINCHESTER C.S. • Steamboat

March 16, 1862

Series I, vol. 22, p. 749

Isl. #10, Mississippi River

Map of Defenses of #10 showing location of scuttled boat.

April 3, 1862—Boarded and burned to water's edge by Union Mortar Fleet Recon.

WINSLOW C.S.S.

November 7, 1861

Series I, vol. 6, p. 785

Ocracokie Inlet

A hole had been knocked in her bottom by the lightboat which the Yankees had sunk and burned in September—we put the boats and crews to bringing off such things as we could save. She was then fired.

WINSLOW C.S.S. • Sidewheel River Steamer

Series II, vol. 1, p. 272

Hatteras Inlet, North Carolina

Battery:
1 - 32#
1 - small brass rifled 6#

Wrecked on Sunken Hull outside Hatteras Inlet, while going to assistance of French vessel, which was ashore near there—Former J.E. Coffee

WOODFORD U.S. • Hospital Boat, Marine Brigade

Report of the Sect. of War
V. II, p. 1287

Louisiana

The Hospital Boat *Woodford* had been wrecked on the rapids in attempting the passage up.

The forces under Gen. Franklin, arriving on the 25th and 26th of March, but as the stage of water in Red River was too low to admit the passage of the gunboats or transports over the falls, the troops encamped near Alexandria. Gen. Smith and his command moving forward 21 miles to Bayou Rapides, above Alexandria. There was but 6' water in the channel while 7 1/2' was necessary for 2nd class and 10' for 1st class gunboats.

Y

YADKIN C.S.S. • Wood Steam Gunboat

1865

Series II, vol. 1, p. 272

Wilmington, Delaware

1 gun

Burned by Confederates at fall of Wilmington.

YORK • British Ship, Blockade Runner

January 16, 1862

Series I, vol. 6, pp. 520, 521, 690

Bogue Inlet, North Carolina
N.E. Wilmington

800 ton burden

York of Dublin—run on shore near Bogue Inlet. The anchor dropped 150 yards from shore and vessel hauled to steep beach broadside on. Boarded and burned.

Many tons of wrought iron on board, C.S. Rpt.
(Nothing but 1 flat boat of rigging removed.) but now will be hard to save, if at all.

To the east of Bogue Inlet.

YORK C.S. • **Privateer**

August 9, 1861

Series I, vol. 6, p. 795

New Inlet

Beached, set fire to, abandoned near—pressed by U.S.S. *Monticello* (Union)

YORK C.S. • **Privateer Schooner**

August 9, 1861

Series I, vol. 1, pp. 60, 61, 818
Series I, vol. 6
Series II, vol. 3

New Inlet, North Carolina

Master John Geoffrey—Comm., July 9, 1861

68 Ton

Driven ashore and destroyed by U.S.S. *Union Commander*, J.R. Goldsborough, U.S.N.

Fitted out Norfolk, Virginia.

Also known as *Florida.*
Schooner 65–70 ton.

Painted lead color.

1 gun amidships.

She attempted to go into New Inlet but that, fortunately, I could prevent. He then tacked and stood direct in for the land, ran his vessel on shore, and set fire and threw the gun overboard.

Sighted—Cape Hatteras Light House in sight. Bearing W. by S., distant 12 miles.

Series II, vol. 1, p. 272

Battery: 1 rifled 18# on pivot amidships. Overboard and burned to prevent capture by the U.S.S. *Union.*

YORKTOWN • **Confederate Steamer**

August 25, 1862

Series I, vol. 19, p. 238

At Sea
Gulf of Mexico

Cargo of cotton for Havana out of Mobile.

Crew picked up 72 miles from Ship Isl., bearing N.W.

YSABEL • Steamer

Captured May 28, and sunk June 2, 1864

Series I, vol. 27, p. 667

Mississippi River
Off Quarantine Station

Cargo: Arms and Ammunitio—partially thrown overboard during chase.

From Havana to Galveston.

Slipped her cable and hauled her aground.

YOUNG RACER • British Sloop

January 14, 1864

Series I, vol. 17, p. 633

Jupiter Inlet, Florida

Cargo: Salt

Run ashore and destroyed 15 miles N. Jupiter Inlet.

Z

ZOUAVE • Army Gunboat

January 14, 1862

Series I, vol. 6, p. 582

Hatteras Inlet, North Carolina

Afoul her anchor and sunk.

A

Alabama
  Blakely River
    Althea U.S.S., 12
    Osage U.S.S., 191
    Rudolph U.S.S., 221
  Dauphin Island
    Pink U.S.S., 202
  Florence
    Dunbar C.S., 74
    Kobb C.S., 143
    Orr C.S., 190
  Mobile, Alabama
    Gains, 93
    Glaucus U.S.S., 103
    Josephine, 136
    Milwaukee U.S., 174
    Morgan C.S.S., 179
    Nashville, 183
    Nathaniel Taylor U.S.S., 183
    Osage, 191
    Phoenix C.S.S., 199
    Tuscaloosa C.S.S., 254
  Mobile Bay
    Ida U.S.S., 121
    Narcissus U.S.S., 181
    Rudolph, 221
    Selma C.S.S., 231
    Tecumseh U.S.S., 248
  Mobile Entrance
    Isabel, 127
  Mussel Shoals
    Alabama (State), 7
  Petit Bois Channel
    Advocate U.S.S., 4
    Daylight U.S.S., 68
  Tennessee River
    Dunbar, 73
  Tennessee River (Florence)
    Julius, 138
    Sam Kirkman, 225
    Time C.S., 251
  Tennessee River (Fort Mussel Shoals)
    Alabama (State), Barges and Steamers, 8

Arkansas
    Pontchartrain, 203
  Clarendon
    Queen City U.S.S., 206

Gaines Landing
    Clara Ames, 50
    Lebanon, 147
Island #82, Mississippi River
    Sallie Wood U.S.S., 224
Plum Point
    Cincinnati, 48
    Erebus U.S., 83
St. Francis River
    Mariner, 163
Walnut Bend
    Dry Dock, 73
    Paw Paw, 195
White River
    Diurnal, 71
    Eliza G., 77
    Mary Patterson, 168
    Maurepas C.S.S., 170

C

Connecticut
  Mystic
    Meteor U.S.S., 173
    Robin Hood U.S.S., 218
  New London
    Lewis U.S.S., 148
    Montezuma U.S.S., 179
    Peter Demill U.S.S., 196
    Phoenix U.S.S., 199
    Tenedos U.S.S., 249

D

Delaware
  New Inlet
    Modern Greece, 177
  Wilmington
    Artic C.S., 27
    Union U.S., 258
    Yadkin C.S.S., 271

F

Florida
    Fortunate, 90
    Orate, 190
  Apalachicola
    Finland, 86
    Mary Olivia, 168
  Apalachicola River
    Cygnet, 65

G

P

R

S

T

V